HOUSE AND STREET

HOUSE AND STREET

THE DOMESTIC WORLD OF SERVANTS AND MASTERS IN NINETEENTH-CENTURY RIO DE JANEIRO

SANDRA LAUDERDALE GRAHAM

University of Texas Press

Austin

♾ The paper used in this publication meets the minimum requirements of
American National Standard for Information Sciences—Permanence of Paper for
Printed Library Materials, ANSI Z39.48-1984.

Library of Congress Cataloging-in-Publication Data

Lauderdale Graham, Sandra, date
    House and street : the domestic world of servants and masters in nineteenth-
century Rio de Janeiro / Sandra Lauderdale Graham. — 1st University of Texas
Press ed.
        p. cm.
    Includes bibliographical references (p.   ) and index.
    ISBN 0-292-72757-7 (alk. paper)
    1. Domestics—Brazil—Rio de Janeiro—History—19th century. 2. Master
and servant—Brazil—Rio de Janeiro—History—19th century. 3. Women
domestics—Brazil—Rio de Janeiro—History—19th century. 4. Poor
women—Brazil—Rio de Janeiro—History—19th century. I. Title.
HD8039.D52B64 1992
331.4'8164046'098153—dc20   92-26226

Contents

Tables

Illustrations

Maps

Note on Brazilian currency

During the nineteenth and into the twentieth century, the Brazilian unit of currency was the *mil-réis* or one thousand *réis*, written 1$000. A larger unit was the *conto*, equal to one thousand mil-réis and written 1:000$000. During the period from 1860 to 1910, the value of the mil-réis ranged from a high of US$0.55 in 1863 and 1875 to a low of US$0.15 in 1898 and 1899; by 1910 the mil-réis was worth US$0.33.

Acknowledgments

Aside from all the other things that a book is and does, it celebrates those who participated in its making. First among those are the friends and colleagues who, by their passion to understand and to penetrate the understandings of others, tested, sustained, and encouraged my efforts. I might never have set out on this project had Amelia Humphries nòt shown me, long ago, the pleasures and vexations of reading, really reading, the text. More recently, conversations, frequently brief or casual or seemingly about other matters with fellow historians at Mount Holyoke College made teaching and writing history an even more exciting – and risky – enterprise. I think of Eugenia Herbert, William McFeely, and Harold Garrett-Goodyear, each of whom read and commented on earlier versions. Through Daphne Patai's timely and perceptive criticisms, I learned and benefited much. Over many years, Inga Clendinnen has responded to each phase of this book with rare generosity and insight. Her influence is woven through these pages.

No aspect of the historian's craft gives deeper pleasure, for me, than the research, attempting to cull the pieces of a past world from fragile, incomplete, but astonishingly rich and absorbing records. The staffs of the archives and libraries of Rio de Janeiro have repeatedly assisted in making those records available. At the Arquivo Nacional, I relied on Eliseu de Araújo Lima for his knowledge of the organization and contents of the archive and on Rogério Másala Araújo for his patience and persistence in locating judicial material. At the Instituto Brasileiro de Geografia e Estatística, Ada Maria Coarcy and Hespéria Zuma de Rosso made available for microfilming the 1870 manuscript census lists for the parish of São Cristovão. Robert Slenes kindly gave time from his own research to produce the microfilm of those records. The Arquivo Geral da Cidade do Rio de Janeiro with its extensive manuscript and iconography collections proved invaluable. Librarians at the Instituto Histórico e Geográfico

xi

Brasileiro each time replied cordially and helpfully to my requests. Not by special favors but simply in the course of doing their work, Brazilian librarians and archivists have made mine productive and enjoyable.

Gilberto Ferrez knows my delight in the hours spent poring over the exquisite photographs of his collection and for the talk about the city of Rio de Janeiro that we each seek, in our different ways, to reveal. The images gleaned from those photographs remain vivid and helped to make concrete the city of a hundred years ago. To José Sebastião Witter, former Director of the Arquivo do Estado de São Paulo, I offer warm thanks for making accessible essential editions of legal codes. Fellow researchers Joseph Sweigart and Roderick Barman, bent on their own pursuits, nevertheless remembered to pass on choice discoveries pertinent to my concerns. And for the one private diary I was able to use, I thank Guilherme P. Neves.

A Fulbright-Hays Fellowship from the U.S. Office of Education and a fellowship from the Organization of American States funded research in Brazil. The University of Texas provided support for computer processing. A Faculty Research Grant from Mount Holyoke College enabled me to complete the final manuscript using a word processor.

Finally, and most especially, this book celebrates work shared with Richard Graham.

Austin, Texas 1987

SANDRA LAUDERDALE GRAHAM

PART I

Setting and origins

Introduction

This book is not only about the slave and free women who labored as domestic servants in Rio de Janeiro in the years between 1860 and 1910. Because my concern is to recover the experiences of servant women as they conducted working and private lives, and to see them as they were seen and reacted to by those who owned or hired them, the actions expressed in their lives and the meanings those actions can be made to disclose—the "webs of significance" in Clifford Geertz's phrase—led quickly to the multiple contexts in which servants located their lives.[1] So besides examining the work and the places of work, and servants' connections to masters, this book is also about the working poor and slum life, street celebrations and families, the city as a social landscape, alterations in urban domestic life, contemporary notions of contagion, and the abolition of slavery. Above all, because being a servant meant living in relation to a *patrão* or master, understanding servants' lives requires consideration of the cultural assumptions that made daily domestic life manageable. Servant women met demands for labor and obedience in exchange for protection. For their part, patrões provided servants with daily necessities, care during illness, and the myriad arbitrary favors that made concrete their role as patrons.

The power exercised over dependents within the domain of family and household by masters was private and personal. No public institutions could be appealed to by dependents that might, on their behalf, counter the weight of private power or temper the personal actions of masters. On the contrary, masters drew support for the exercise of their individual power from the traditions of Portuguese and ecclesiastical law reinforced by the local practices of slavery. In the nineteenth century no institution replaced a private, domestic patron with a public, religious or civil one: there was, for example, no Brazilian equivalent of the parish-administered English poor laws. The church might offer charity or sanctuary but only to the specified few—those with permission to beg alms, for example—never reliably or extensively to the many with need. In Brazil no slave code regulated, even in principle, the relations between master and slave. Law and custom, the formally stated and the informally understood, intermeshed to elevate the will of the master as the paramount authority within the basic Brazilian social unit of the household. We would be mistaken to believe that, for nineteenth-century Brazil, benevolence and punishment could be separated or that physical force was the deterioration of a more kindly paternalism. My sense is that paternalism always had its harsh and ugly side: the right to punish with rage, the careless—or calculated—withholding of care, or the more obviously brutal or vicious forms of physical abuse. The power that required as justification the display of concern by masters was the same power that permitted and relied upon coercion.[2]

Despite their firmly fixed inequalities, a shared domesticity imposed its inevitable intimacies. Servants and masters had to live in one another's constant presence, repeating in daily routine the countless and complex exchanges that connected them. Masters could scarcely prevent servants from witnessing at close range the otherwise private habits and events of family life. Nor could servants long conceal from masters their idiosyncrasies or preoccupations. Familiarity and its necessary accommodations threatened to erode the carefully defined differences of their relationship. It is their interactions and the unceasing processes of adjustment in domestic relations that I seek to explore.

A word about the title. Threaded through all the concerns of domestic living were the contrasting images of *casa e rua,* or house and street, by which contemporaries located, and, by locating, interpreted everyday actions and encounters. House signified a secure and stable domain. To house belonged the enduring relationships of family or blood kin. To street belonged uncertain or temporary alliances in which identity could not be assumed but had to be established. Street was suspect, unpredictable, a dirty or dangerous place. Although recognizable categories to both master and servant, the conventional meanings could become reversed or made ambiguous: for servant women house could be a place of harm, punishment, or excessive work, and street sought as a place of greater freedom, while masters faced the inescapable risks of taking disorderly servants into the orderly spaces of house.

My exclusion of male servants from this study derives in part from pragmatism, but also from considerations of the nature of domestic life. Of all servants in Rio de Janeiro in 1872, men made up nearly one quarter, and men who worked as domestics comprised about 15 percent of all working men and about 8 percent of free working men. By 1906 they accounted for 6 percent of all men who were employed.[3] Nevertheless, I have not included them. I chose, instead, female servants who illustrate with special clarity a second side of the dilemma that confronted householders. Although dependent on servants, householders viewed them with the same suspicion with which they regarded the poor and blacks generally. To take "strangers" into their households implied risk. And among house servants women presented the greater risk for they customarily performed the most personal of domestic work. Wet-nurses to whom householders entrusted the lives and well-being of their infants were thought capable of infecting them with appalling diseases. Wet-nurses came to be seen as the alarming exemplars of the dilemma all servants represented. Because of their intimate and therefore incongruous place in the life of the household, women servants—and how they were perceived and reacted to—reveal and accentuate the patterns of culture that shaped domestic life. Their efforts to sustain some measure of an independent, private life, beyond the master's control or cognizance, although reconstructed from fragmentary evidence, allow us to trace those patterns more precisely. Being female placed on women domestics special opportunities, burdens, restrictions, and suspicions that males did not bear. For those reasons the women are the subject of this book.

Most women worked, not only slaves but also free women. In 1870, a census considered 63 percent of free women as engaged in some gainful occupation, as well as 88 percent of slave women (Table 1), suggesting the sheer abundance of female labor available in the city.[4] By 1906, nearly half of all working age women declared themselves employed.

Overwhelmingly their occupations were lowly. The few women in 1872 with "professional" jobs included midwives, nuns, teachers, or those with a craft. Law, medicine, and the public service were closed to women. A scattering of women engaged in commerce, probably as market or street vendors, since men or young boys were preferred as shop clerks and cashiers, although a few foreign women owned dressmaking shops. Somewhat more commonly, women worked in the manufacture of textiles and clothing, some in the tanning and hat industries or in boot and shoe factories.[5] But most women who worked, worked as domestics. During the 1870s, between 61 and 65 percent of free working women were counted as servants, and, together with between 87 and 90 percent of slave women, servants comprised 71 percent of all working women (Table 2). In 1870 and 1872, servant women represented about 15 percent of the total population in the city's urban parishes. By 1906 their proportion in the population had declined slightly to about 13 percent but, as 76 percent of all women who worked, they still represented the largest single occupational group. We can think, then, of Rio de Janeiro as a city where in 1870 as many as 34,000 slave and free women labored as domestics, and where by 1906 more than 77,000 women found work as servants.[6] The presence of servant women in the daily life of the city remained pervasive.

The range of labor that I call domestic includes at one extreme the *mucamas* or personal or chambermaids and the *amas de leite* or wet-nurses, and at the other end casual water carriers, laundresses, and seamstresses. Even women who sold fruits and vegetables or sweets on the street, usually slaves, frequently doubled as house servants for part of the day. In between, belong the cooks, pantry maids, and house servants. What distinguished among them was not only the perceived value of their work to the well-being of the family, reflected in the daily contact each had with family members, but also the degree of supervision. A personal maid or wet-nurse who entered into the most intimate quarters of family life to attend a mistress or to nurse an infant was the most closely supervised among servants. Because cooking and general housework occupied the entire day, those servants also witnessed the goings-on of the household while a mistress routinely oversaw their work. By contrast, hauling water or washing at the fountain meant that some servants labored away from the house and a watchful mistress. Laundresses and, even more commonly, seamstresses might work for several families on a daily basis while living independently in their own households.

I take servants as an occupational group in order to dispel emphatically the stereotype that only slaves were servants or that domestic work was exclusively slaves' work. Rather than a hierarchy of kinds of work that divided free from slave women or black from lighter-skinned women, domestic service cut across those differences. Women of both "conditions" might work alongside one another, and all might labor at similar chores. Nor did being slave—having the legal status of slave— determine much more than the outline of a life, rarely the detail or nuance. A slave might live outside her owner's jurisdiction, hiring out her own labor, returning a fixed sum to her owner, and keeping whatever was left to buy food and pay the rent for a room. Or a slave woman, long the servant to a single family, might be treated with affection or regard, rewarded with her freedom, while a free woman with the right to leave whenever she chose could be viewed with suspicion and given little care. To the extent that servants worked and lived under similar conditions, there might be little by which to distinguish free women from slaves: any servant might experience long hours of exhausting labor, damp quarters, inadequate diet, or the illnesses that generally characterized the life of the working poor. The study of Brazilian women demonstrates that the situations of particular women confound the simple categories of slave or free.[7]

In seeking to recover the lives of servant women, I have not assembled the biography of an allegedly typical servant from the individual qualities of myriad women. Instead, I want to identify particular women, to give them name whenever possible, and to draw from the detail of lived experience. My approach is to discover the range of possible experiences that could characterize their lives. In the glimpses of their actions and reactions, and in those of others, we can begin to know what was for them unusual or commonplace, probable or merely possible, tolerable or clearly insupportable. I attempt to map the territory of their lives in order to discover their expectations and what alternatives were available to them, trying to discern where the boundaries of recognizable experience lay. The challenge for the historian is to trace both the cultural patterns that made dominance possible and pervasive and the ways by which servant women achieved some independence despite that dominance.

The city of Rio de Janeiro furnishes an especially suitable setting for the study of domestic servants. As capital of the empire and later of the republic and as Brazil's principal port and financial center, the city's prominence during the nineteenth and early twentieth century remained uncontested. Emperors and presidents resided there. Members of parliament, cabinet ministers, councilors of state, higher court judges, together with fiscal officers and minor bureaucrats conducted the routine business of government. The great coffee barons and their factors funneled coffee through the city's export firms and warehouses to supply the rich Atlantic trade in exchange for slaves and for the European luxury goods that entered Brazil to satisfy the expensive tastes of a local elite. There the wealthy resided, either permanently in splendid mansions or intermittently in town houses, overseeing their economic and political interests. That elite set the standard for the conduct of domestic life as well, a standard imitated on a lesser scale by those of modest means who nonetheless sought to project an air of gentility. It was a lifestyle that in all its variations relied on servants not only to supply the necessities of daily existence, but also to display the right degree of privilege. At the same time, however, Rio de Janeiro presented a shabbier aspect as a filthy, disease-ridden place of narrow, smelly streets ever more tightly packed with tenements. It was a city of slaves, poor blacks, and poor European immigrants. Domestic servants connected those two dissimilar and juxtaposed worlds.

Because the lives of servant women were so profoundly linked to the changes in urban life, dates that appropriately frame a history of the women also refer to a period of major reform that altered the city's physical and social landscape between 1860 and 1910. Transformations visible by the 1860s had origins in the previous decade. In 1850 and 1855 the first waves of epidemic disease took hold of the city. The significances attached to the stubborn presence of disease would reverberate through all aspects of urban life for the rest of the century and into the next, in time identifying servants as the dreadful carriers of disease. The initial response, however, was to create a Central Board of Public Hygiene, lay the plumbing necessary for piped water, and begin construction of an underground sewage system that would reach eventually to most parts of the city. By the 1860s the first trams enabled the city to spread into new residential suburbs. Those early changes would culminate in a dramatic remaking of the central city between 1902 and 1910 as slums were demolished, streets widened to permit light and air to penetrate, and contagious disease at last contained. Such changes impinged directly upon servants. By seeing those events from their perspective, we understand them differently. Indoor plumbing altered permanently the kinds and places of work familiar to servant women. Demolition of slums designed to enhance the city in imitation of European capitals meant for servant women the loss of familiar neighborhoods or places shared with others of the city's working poor. Thus the city serves not only as setting but forms an integral part of the history of servants.

A second reason compels the choice of those five decades. Conventionally historians of modern Brazil begin or end with the years 1888 or 1889, the years in which slavery was finally abolished and a federal republic replaced the empire.[8] I set those events somewhere near the middle of the period I have chosen in order to detect not only the ruptures but also the continuities that persisted at their own rhythm in everyday lives. From the 1860s domestic work became less and less the province of slaves. Free Brazilian and immigrant women and former slaves combined with the remaining slaves to supply the demand for servants, so that already by 1872 free women accounted for nearly two-thirds of female domestics in Rio de Janeiro (Tables 3 and 4). Through the lives of servant women, we understand the abolition of slavery not as it is customarily understood, the concern of planters about to lose the slaves whose labor produced agricultural products for export,[9] but as a distinctly urban phenomenon where householders worried more about the disquieting erosion of personal authority, focused and intensified by the presence of death-dealing disease and the perception of domestics as the carriers of contagion. By viewing seemingly familiar political and economic events from the perspective of domestic life, I give them a different significance.[10]

Having first considered the city as a socially inscribed landscape, I conceive the ordering of the chapters that follow as concentric circles, with the figure of the servant woman at the center, extending from her immediate experiences to reach finally to the images of servant and wet-nurse as constructed by those who hired, owned, or otherwise governed them and who thus attempted to determine how servants would be publicly regulated. Thus I begin with their work, not as merely harsh or tedious or long—those being our externally imposed assessments—but as the pattern of experiences to which they assigned their own meanings. So a trip to market, certainly heavy work on the return, could also present the opportunity to transact some personal errand or chat with a friend.

At the next remove and permeated by the demands and locations of work, I examine the lives servants managed to conduct privately as lovers, wives, mothers, and as the dwellers of slums that they knew as neighborhoods. Here I consider the street life that expressed the ties and the conflicts of neighborhood. And especially I interpret *carnaval* as not merely the inversion of role or power (the conventional rendering by historians and anthropologists), but as an extension and exaggeration of the usual street life of the poor, whether free or slave. In all this I seek to reveal the situations and extent to which servant women, as members of the working poor, could claim a measure of agency in the conduct of their own lives.

Against that angle of vision, the last section explores the perceptions and responses of masters to the women on whom they so constantly relied and whom they so deeply mistrusted. First I address the masters' understandings of the relationship, its reciprocal obligations and possible violations. The final chapter moves furthest out to examine the ways by which, as disease repeatedly swept the city and the abolition of slavery became fact, masters came to regard female domestics as the dreaded carriers of contagion and disorder and thus sought to regulate them. In these ways masters set limits—no less real for often being ambivalent—on the latitude servants could achieve.

The tensions between house and street, expressed in the negotiated relations of servant and master, and exposed in the routines and crises of daily living, changing through time, are the themes of this book.

1

The social landscape of house and street

In 1835 the French painter and guest of the Brazilian court Jean Baptiste Debret presented his sketch of a respectable Rio de Janeiro family and their servants parading to church.[1] The head of the family led the carefully arranged procession followed by his two young daughters, close to his protection, his wife, and then the servants (all slaves) according to their rank: chamber maid, wet-nurse carrying the infant she suckled, female house slave, principal male servant, and finally, two boys. All appeared in finery appropriate to the occasion: the head of the family wore the official uniform of his bureaucratic post complete with boots, frock coat, and hat; daughters and wife were richly dressed. The servants' clothes, although European in style were plainer and less fine in cut and fabric than their masters', and nicely calculated to display the gradations within their category. Shoes distinguished the chamber maid as the favored servant from the others – each without shoes. A coat and small handbag declared she owned clothes reserved just for street wear. She appeared with a flower in her hair, while the barefoot wet-nurse wore a pendant. Their adornments, in turn, set them further apart from the young girl in only an ordinary print dress. The robust male slave, in long pants and carrying the umbrella, was also dressed for the street with hat and coat, but no shoes. The boys completed the ranking: one wore long pants, while the other used the clothes common for work, loose-fitting shirt and short pants of rough cotton.

Debret had painted not a family, but the key unit in Brazilian social life: the household. As a set of relationships that contained both family and servants – persons occupying widely unequal positions – household existed within a historic culture that invested the male head with authority and responsibility over all members, including servants. It remained for each to return obedience appropriate to their place either as wife and children, or as *agregados* and slaves. As

Plate 1 A family and servants parading to church, 1820s

understood in nineteenth-century Rio de Janeiro, the ideal of household derived from ancient Portuguese tradition which had long established the husband and father as the undisputed head of family or *cabeça de casal*. By that power he legally administered family property, both that of his wife and of any minors still unmarried, and he granted or withheld permission for minors or even a widowed daughter to marry. Nor could he refuse to exercise the powers that custom and law decreed for him, for only with his death could such authority rightfully pass to his wife, or, with regard to underage children, to a guardian.[2]

Male authority did not end with the circle of immediate family but extended to the full membership of the household. The head of household had by Portuguese law the right to castigate physically his "servant, follower, wife, child, or slave."[3] At the same time he was expected to guard the honor of the women of his household, including the honor of servant women. Any man who attempted to sleep with or to marry a servant without permission from her master had once risked banishment or death. Significantly the law stated the more severe penalty if she served "within doors," the lesser if she served "outside the house,"[4] a distinction that remained, although the penalty had long since lapsed if it had ever actually been applied.

With regard to slaves, the exercise of power by masters stood formally unregulated in the absence of a code of slave law.[5] A servant woman, whether free or slave, lived not as an independent person, but as a member of the household, subject to its authority and the recipient of its implied protections.

That servants were unequal members of a household was further demonstrated in Brazilian electoral law. The law denied to all dependents – those who did not form a "separate economy" – the right to vote. Even though male servants might earn a salary that met the minimal income requirement, because it was not income from owned property they did not qualify to vote.[6] The assumption was that as dependents they would vote with the head of household, unfairly duplicating his vote. One vote per household became the explicitly recognized formula.[7] Besides granting the household a political status, the law canceled any possibility of a separate civil identity for servants.

If Brazilians used interchangeably the words "family," "dwelling," or "hearth" to indicate household, its essential referent was the grouping of mutually dependent and co-resident persons. As described by contemporaries, a household was "all those persons who habitually occupy a dwelling, both those who properly constitute a family as well as the agregados and slaves," or "a certain number of persons who, by reason of kinship relations, subordination, or simply dependence live in a dwelling or part of a dwelling, under the power, direction, or protection of a *chefe* . . . and with a common economy."[8] A household might inhabit a room, part or all of a house, or move between mansions, as when a planter family and their domestic dependents moved between *fazenda* and townhouse.[9] Household persisted as the chosen social context in which individuals located their lives. When in 1906 census takers attempted, for the first time, to count individuals rather than households, they met resistance. Eventually they conceded that counting households was "preferable in the current conditions of our milieu [and] accepted with less reluctance by the population."[10] It was as members of a given household that persons knew themselves and wished to be known.

Although the culturally preferred image of household called for numerous servants, in fact only the elite of Rio de Janeiro families fared so well. Most families survived without any servants. Too poor to maintain dependents, they furnished their own domestic labor, while numerous others kept a single servant woman for "all domestic service" or to "wash, iron, cook."[11] Families could also hire for daily or temporary work domestics who did not figure as true household members, such as the cook who "arrived in the morning and left at night," or the laundresses who took wash from various families.[12] Few households could claim a range of servants, while many – modest but genteel – managed with only one or two. Dona Joaquina Roza de Souza, who owned three slaves in 1870, hired out Joaquim for a daily wage as well as Cypriana, and kept at home as her only servant Cypriana's 18-year-old daughter Helena. In the same year a lawyer rented out to other families all five of his female slaves, perhaps as domestics, leaving him without any servants in the running of his own house.[13] Judge Anphilophio Botelho Freire de Carvalho in 1885 explained that he had been detained in taking up a new appointment in another province because his cook, and only servant, had fallen ill and could not travel.[14]

But a substantial household maintained a staff of servants. Advice offered to young *donas da casa* made clear that servants came second only to house, furniture, or food.[15] Foreign visitors who described life in early nineteenth-century Brazil passed on their casually formed impressions that a "decent house" commonly counted six or even ten or twelve servants.[16] As late as 1881, one French resident insisted that a family required at least five slaves: cook, pantry and chamber maid, laundress, and two women to care for the children. Dona Isabel Maria d'Almeida, a widowed property owner and head of an extensive and prosperous family, kept 12 house servants – three free women, the rest slaves. Another household that in 1882 would establish itself in a single sweep advertised for an entire complement of servants: chamber maid, two pantry servants and a young black.[17] By 1877, Dona Leonor Loureiro oversaw a household with eight female servants. Besides a cook and a woman who did ironing, she engaged the others simply in unspecified domestic service. Although one widow and property owner lived without family on the Travessa de São Luiz, she nevertheless kept two servants, a free woman and the free woman's slave, Felicidade.[18]

As a significant expense in a family's budget, the cost of servants influenced the number a family could afford to maintain. By one accounting five hired slave servants could cost a family in 1881 as much as $35 a month. Another estimate was more modest. A family who lived comfortably with two servants in 1893 included them among their household "items of the first necessity," spending 10 percent of their monthly household expenditure, or about $7, while rent took 23 percent and food for their household of seven persons another 37 percent.[19] Cost varied within predictable limits according to the work servants performed. A young girl might earn the equivalent of $4 per month to take care of children, while in one household a young woman of "good comportment" would earn as much as $7.50 to help care for a two month old child. As late as 1905 or 1909, a "colored girl" aged 10 or 12 years still earned about $4 to take care of an infant. A cook earned substantially more, but that too varied. One "poor lady" asked $12.50 to cook for one or two people, while another woman was offered $18.40 per month. A live-in seamstress also expected to earn about $18 for hand and machine sewing, while a Portuguese laundress asked nearly $14 for her services. A house servant, as well as a woman who "washed, carried water, and sold sweets" on the street, earned between $8 and $9. To nurse their infants, householders paid wet-nurses the highest wages of all: as much as $20 per month and room and board.[20] As free labor became increasingly available, householders could expect to pay in wages about what they had paid in hire rates for slaves for similar work: $13 monthly for a chamber maid, $16 for a wet-nurse, and $12 for general housework by 1862 prices.[21]

Exactly how many households in Rio de Janeiro sustained servants is not easy to discover. The only household lists extant from the 1870 city census are those for São Cristovão parish. Despite the presence of two factories and the activities of fishermen along its bay side, by 1870 São Cristovão had become somewhat more residential in character than the older central parishes where the city's commercial firms clustered. That only 249 families or 18 percent of all 1,404 households in São Cristovão identified themselves as having live-in servants in 1870 seems suspiciously few. Those domestics, male and female, slave and free, numbered 673 persons, or only about 8 percent of a total population for the parish of 8,566. Certainly the census undercounted the true number of house servants who lived in the parish. At least 392 households named agregados or slaves whose occupations they failed to record. And some 323 working age slave women appear for whom no one bothered to specify the work each did.[22] In a city where domestic service was the most plausible labor for slaves and the free poor, at least a portion must have worked as servants in their masters' homes. Slave women with young babies were present in three São Cristovão households where infants could also be found among the head of household's own family, suggesting that the women were wet-nurses. Yet on the manuscript lists none of the three probable wet-nurses was assigned an occupation, so their true roles remain uncertain.[23] If each of the 392 households with dependents of unknown occupations had used only one for domestic service, the percentage of those with servants would more than double to about 45 percent. Households that specified servants had on average three each. Two thirds of families with servants kept one or two, and nearly a fifth enjoyed the services of as many as three, four, or five servants. Only two families maintained elaborate households with staffs of 12 or 13 servants (see Table 5).

Fundamental to the order and meaning of daily, domestic life were the categories of *casa* and *rua*, house and street.[24] House represented private and protected spaces that contrasted with the public and unpleasant, possibly dangerous places of the street. The known and trusted ties of blood kinship belonged to house, while less lasting or temporary relations, ones that involved choice and hence risk were associated with street. House distinguished family from the anonymous or coarse and disorderly society that was seen to belong to public squares, shops, and streets. House and street thus set the coordinates of the cultural map by which ordinary and repeated experiences could be perceived, understood, and responded to. What first appear as simply the background structures of household and physical setting become inscribed with more nuanced meanings.

In practice, the boundary between street and house as represented in domestic architecture assumed any of several forms. In newer and thus more spacious parts of town a walled garden with its trees and fragrant flowers, glowing with the "scarlet leaves of the poinsettia or . . . blue and yellow begonias,"[25] gracefully set a villa apart from the noise or dirt that was perceived to wait outside. In other more thickly settled sections of the city, a single building combined both commercial and private living space. A merchant and his family customarily inhabited the one or two floors above their ground level shop or warehouse. Entrance to the upper floors might open from the street as one of the several doors of the shop, or, where storage space for supplies or a coach occupied the ground floor, a stairway at the back might lead to the family's household quarters.[26] Either way a horizontal boundary separated what was below and public from what was above and private.

Internal boundaries reiterated the oppositions of house and street where mansions further separated their many parlors, lunch and dining rooms from the out-buildings that housed chickens, cattle, laundry, and slave or servant quarters. For convenience and supervision in cooking and serving, the kitchen remained structurally part of the main house, while all other dependencies occupied the far side of a patio or grounds well behind the garden.[27] In smaller houses the same pattern repeated itself on a lesser scale. The ground floor of two-story houses did not end with the kitchen, rather kitchen and servants' rooms faced onto a patio with its "chickens, cats, caged birds, ducks," or toward a small stable if the family kept a coach and horse. In houses where stable and storage space took up the ground floor, the kitchen and pantry were located at the rear of the second floor separated from the dining room by an atrium. On the far side of patio or atrium, beside the kitchen and removed from the family's rooms was the one room or perhaps two kept for servants. At least a pantry divided living quarters from kitchen and wash areas, and attached to the kitchen at the back came the servant's room.[28]

Not all residents could afford houses that so thoroughly insured privacy. Those who lived modestly lived in one-story, narrow-fronted houses where a parlor faced directly onto the street without even a veranda to set it off, or perhaps a gate led to a stoop and side entrance. Callers announced themselves either by drawing a cane over the wooden slats of the door or by clapping their hands. Where a window or door stood open, a visitor might call out, "hello, in the house," and expect the reply, "hello, out there." In finer houses glass covered windows, sometimes handsome lead-light ones, muted street noise or a neighbor's piano playing, although more commonly wooden shutters that made rooms private, quiet, or dry also closed out light and air.[29] Even worse off, the poor who lodged in the *cortiços*, or tenement houses, had few resources to shut out the crowding that invaded their living space. An entire family might cram themselves into a single room, perhaps with their own cooking place, but more often sharing one with other tenants. Privacy in any ordinary sense did not exist: at best 50 or 60 tenants negotiated the use of the single toilet. The poor bathed publicly in rivers, in the sea, or at the fountains.[30] As the slum population increased, families nevertheless claimed their own space, dividing and subdividing existing rooms in order to insure that at least a "thin partition separated rooms . . . one from the others."[31] Although the marking of the boundary between house and street became less elaborate as wealth decreased, even when scarcely visible it was no less real or acknowledged.

Fear of the unsupervised street generated regulations that imposed other, temporal boundaries. The commerce of the street was a daytime matter when all classes of persons might legitimately transact business, earn their livelihood, enjoy the company of their fellows, or merely come and go. After dark, however, street life officially ceased and persons were expected to be at home. To mark that hour the bells of São Francisco church and São Bento monastery tolled the Ave Maria—at ten o'clock in summer, nine in winter—for half an hour "in order to call home the citizens." After that time, those "on the street without clear reason, or at taverns, bars, or gambling houses" were subject to jail or fines. Slaves passed through the streets only with express permission from their masters, and cortiços locked their gates against runaway slaves, unruly intruders, and perhaps to keep their own tenants in. During the "hours of silence," even singing 'to facilitate work" was supposed to stop. Artisans or laborers might carry tools on the street during the day, but "after the Ave Maria," tools were considered arms and were forbidden. At least that was how it was until 1878 when the chief of police decided Rio de Janeiro had become too cosmopolitan and the custom of the nightly ringing of the bells lapsed, although ten o'clock remained the enforced curfew. Bars that remained open until 1:30 in the morning in flagrant violation of the curfew suggest that not all citizens heeded the curfew even when still rung.[32]

A conviction that street and house were vastly different social spheres required from women appropriate public behavior. According to one historian, Brazilian men might enjoy "the easy fellowship of the street and plaza . . . where they discussed politics . . . and transacted business," but women of good social position who went out onto the street, even during the daytime, went accompanied by maids who by their presence brought the protecting mantle of the household to the world outside. As late as mid-century some women retained the double security of a curtained sedan chair and a black maid who walked alongside. From the 1860s on women frequently strolled in the Passeio Publico in the cool late afternoon with their children and servant women.[33] One family advertised for a black woman who besides doing light housework would take their two daughters to secondary school. A young widow, in 1886, could not take the sea baths prescribed by her doctor because, as she explained, she "had no person of trust to accompany her. . . ."[34] A sensible woman took her maid along if she rode a tram. Dona Carmen's family acknowledged that she had "encouraged" the theft of her jewelry case when she and her children had ridden alone. Evidently the show of protection mattered more than the fact, for one matron contented herself with a girl of seven or nine years to accompany her.[35] The image of women shielded from the vulgarities or dangers of the street was valued precisely because it distinguished women of some position from those with lesser means who faced the risks of the street alone.

This correspondence between women escorted and women alone with the notions of house and street not only identified women of widely different social classes, it further distinguished among servants of varying rank. Certain maids "knew the streets," but others were engaged on the stated condition that they would "not go out on the street." As companions or as servants who shopped for food or did errands some servant women took street life for granted. Others, like the black cook and house servant for hire in 1855 or the young black girl available in 1872, would be permitted to work only "within doors." The Bernardo José Fernandes household in 1870 kept three female slaves occupied with the "service of the house," while they sent their one male slave out to perform the "service of the street." If masters confined some servants to interior work because the world outside would either harm or tempt them, not all servants needed or warranted such trouble. Older or more experienced women were assumed able to cope with the street, and for younger but less valued women the risks hardly mattered. Thus Brazilian households, following older Portuguese tradition, continued to distinguish those who "served behind doors" from those who "served outside the house."[36] And by that difference a household portioned out the protections that defined it.

To reduce the unavoidable risks of having servants, who as a class belonged to the world of the street, some families preferred to keep their slave servants as household members. "Slaves of the house" – those born and raised within the household – gained trust and were valued as no others, so that parents or grandparents might make gifts of slaves to young family members to assure them of known and trusted servants when they later established households of their own. In 1867 one woman gave her granddaughter a 21-year-old female house servant, a mulatto named Placida. A young man received from his grandfather, Dr. José Joaquin Guimarães, besides cash and furniture, three slaves: Bruna, an African-born pantry maid, Saturina, a 28-year-old chambermaid, and Gregorio a creole cook.[37] Dona Leonor Loureiro could count herself fortunate as mistress of a household in which she and her sister had kept four generations of slave servants. Where mother and grandmother had served before, Serafina and her 10-year-old daugher, along with other servants, continued to live and work in 1875.[38]

Few households were able to preserve such reassuring continuity, so that routinely even slave servants were hired directly from other householders. Through personal communication families of similar status could speak reliably – either favorably or disparagingly – about known servants to one another. Although their transactions went largely unrecorded, occasionally an agreement was noted, suggesting details of how others occurred. One lady of "noble family," described by English travelers in 1857, with nine servants and too little work to keep them "out of idleness and mischief," inquired among her acquaintances for anyone who might give out washing for them to do.[39]

By the 1870s when free women predominated among servants (Tables 3 and 4), employers sought servants who could provide letters giving "good references of her behavior" or "assurance or information from reliable persons," especially from employers who had left the city or gone abroad, no longer present to supply verbal recommendations. Echoing the slave owner in 1851 who, when he advertised his slave wet-nurse, knew to allay fears with the comment that he would "answer for her conduct," later employers required that free servants "name someone to guarantee their conduct."[40] Families who located servants through newspaper advertisements might emphasize that it was "useless for anyone to present herself who could not give good references."[41] One foreign resident nevertheless insisted that competent servants could only be found through Portuguese or Brazilian friends and not by advertising in the *Jornal do Commercio* or going to agencies.[42]

According to some residents hiring servants through agencies only compounded the dangers. Although the city council required all such businesses to be licensed,[43] many agreed that they failed to conduct themselves decently or deal in reliable servants. One family in 1877 who wanted a woman to cook and do laundry refused to accept anyone sent from an agency. Speaking for its readers, the journal *A Mãe de Família* regarded agencies as a last resort that "necessity of the moment obliges us to turn to." A common allegation charged that an agent would conspire with a slave to flee an employer and return to the commission house to be hired out again while the agent pocketed yet another placement fee. As if in reply, the Agencia Portuguesa advertised itself in 1900 as an "old and well known" firm, where families paid a commission only after being "well served," while the newer Agencia Francesa had prudently advertised in 1877 as being "well known already for dealing fairly" with the public, "not taking a cent in commission if the servant did not stay."[44]

In 1879 an official reported that in his parish of Santo Antonio several firms sold or hired out slaves, a "repugnant" business, he said, that only two dared conduct openly. The one belonging to Antonio Gonçales Peieira Guimarães was by far the biggest and the best run in the official's view, but nevertheless "left a great deal to be desired." Allegedly, Guimarães kept some 30 slaves crowded into a small area, he whipped them, and the slaves were sick.[45] Another agent, acting as intermediary in the internal slave trade in the 1870s, received slaves from northern suppliers, selling some in the city. Fonseca of Duarte, Fonseca and Company, claimed that once in Rio the slaves assigned to him from Pará, Bahia, Pernambuco, Ceará, or Espírito Santo were "dressed, fed, lodged and treated in the best possible manner, not less so than in some firms and certainly better than in others." Although ". . . sick slaves [are] sent to the best hospitals that exist here, . . ." out of the 38 sent from Fortaleza in 1879, 22 had died. "With respect to those who died," Fonseca wrote his associate, "we feel the loss as much as those who consign them to us, not out of humanity, but because we recognize the importance of avoiding losses to our friends." Fonseca's records showed that among the 22 sick slaves who died, 12 were women, and of those at least four were domestics.[46] Other companies, especially those "maintained by Portuguese," notoriously sent free servants who were "indolent, immoral, and full of vices and who knows what crimes."[47]

Despite the generally low reputation of agencies, householders did resort to them. In 1856 the Minister of Justice, José Thomas Nabuco de Araújo, rented "the black woman Tertuliana" on a monthly basis and the agent collected the customary 10 percent commission.[48] By 1860 six agencies concerned themselves with renting slaves, some as domestics; ten years later three new agencies specialized in free and immigrant labor, hiring out mainly domestics. The Agencia Portuguesa and the Agencia Central de Emigração placed free women: German or French cooks, Portuguese wet-nurses, a colored seamstress, house servants, or laundresses. By the 1870s even young girls could be obtained through agencies: The Agencia Portuguesa had for hire a 13-year-old Portuguese girl, "just arrived," to care for children or do light housework.[49]

The enduring careers of agents who at first had traded in slave domestics and eventually switched to free women suggest that they flourished and that the abolition of slavery in 1888 made little difference to the mechanisms through which householders arranged for servants. In 1900 one firm had enough women registered to supply "qualified servants for all manner of domestic service: wet-nurses, nursemaids, pantry maids, house servants, laundresses, women who starched and ironed, cooks. . . ."[50] The adaptable Guimarães who had operated on the rua Lavradio in 1879, continued to hire out servants from the same location in 1890. By then he faced competition from the recently established Companhia Locadora Providencia Domestica which claimed to "provide servants either Brazilian or foreign of both sexes for all types of domestic service." Guimarães apparently prospered despite competition, for by 1895 he had expanded to a second location. Still in business in 1910, he moved to the expensive rua Sete de Setembro.[51]

All servants were decidedly not equal, and not just any would do. Where families entrusted their well-being to servants, the acquiring of domestics required finer considerations than cost or availability. Householders based their preferences first on condition – whether a woman were slave or free – and color.[52] Contemporaries used the terms white, *parda*, literally grey and meaning mulatto, or black to distinguish a woman's color. A black or mulatto woman might be described simply as a "woman of color." Sometimes color and status were taken as coincident: "*preta*," or black, by itself was used almost exclusively to indicate slave; while the phrase "senhora of color" distinguished a black or mulatto woman as free, although she might once have been a slave; but white, when clearly not all free women were white, implied the woman had never been and could never have been a slave. In response to the nuances of status and color, employers shared a stated preference for white servants, an ambivalence toward free women of color whom they could neither trust as white nor own as slaves, and often a reliance on slaves. In his medical guide of 1843, Dr. João Baptista Imbert recognized "that white wet-nurses would be in all respects preferable," but, he pointed out, they did not thrive in the hot climate nearly as well as Africans. Better to choose a "young, robust black," he concluded. The fascination for fair-skinned Europeans lingered, so that in 1896 the female novelist, Júlia Lopes de Almeida, writing advice to brides, offered the wholly romanticized description of the perfect house servant: a Swiss lass with "cheeks the color of cream and hair the color of ripe corn."[53] The Agencia Central especially needed foreign women to fill positions as cook, nursemaid, or, if she spoke Portuguese, as chambermaid. So in demand were "free poor women" by the early 1870s that they could "choose their own employers," claimed another agency, serving in homes of "noble families . . . guaranteed good wages paid in advance."[54]

Employers distinguished reliable and experienced older women from younger, less capable, but also less expensive and ultimately more trainable girls. Slave-owning families had long been accustomed to having young slaves whom they raised and trained. One mistress counted four girls aged from 8 to 12 years among her female slaves, and regarded all four as engaged in domestic service. In 1870 the São Cristovão household of Dona Olympia Amalia Monteiro included among their dependents an eight-year-old girl "apprenticed in domestic work." Even after the abolition of slavery employers actively sought girls as young as ten or twelve years because they were cheaper – the mistress might provide clothing or teach her to sew in lieu of wages. On the other hand, women "older than 40 years" or women of "middle age" could be expected to possess all the qualities of reliability and competence that their age supposedly signalled.[55] Employers found those somewhat older women less trouble because they were less likely to become pregnant or to have young children in tow.

Beneath the surface of an expressed preference for free or white – especially European – women and for mature women, ran a countering apprehension. Whereas slavery had permitted at least the illusion that masters retained the power to bestow favor or punishment on slaves who had scarcely any choice but to obey, by the late 1870s doubt marred that once comforting, not wholly inaccurate view. Free women, increasingly present, could not be subject to the same controls. Colored women, more closely associated with the image of slave, even if not actually slaves, and young girls who lived more firmly within their masters' supervision appeared to pose less threat to that order. What counted most was obedience – euphemistically phrased as "good conduct" or having "good habits." Thus as late as 1905 a family might stately "prefer a colored servant."[56]

If Rio de Janeiro's arresting beauty, on the edge of Guanabara Bay where jagged mountains point skyward, exposing expanses of smooth granite or the lush tangle of rain forest before plunging to meet the sea, enchanted nineteenth-century travelers, its location proved vexing, and eventually treacherous for residents. The knobby hills near the sea cropped out of marshy land or mangrove swamps. Although the dangers of mangroves as breeding grounds for deadly mosquitoes would not be recognized for more than three hundred years, it was immediately evident to the first sixteenth-century colonists that the marsh and swamp lands covering the area between the open waters of the bay and the escarpment to the west impeded convenient access to the fresh water streams that cut down through the mountains. One costly well chiseled into the granite surface of Castello supplied water, and that, brackish and scant, for the first small cadre of settlers.[57] In order to use the harbor's natural advantage and to expand, settlement required a more accessible and level site. The port city thus extended north along the existing narrow strip of shore. At the Praça do Carmo where arriving ships docked, a small commercial center grew up. Soon a chapel and Carmelite convent on the square represented the sacred authority of the Church, followed in 1699 by the king's warehouses and a mint. From 1647 a stone *pelourinho*, or whipping-post, stood in the praça, marking the place where the public punishment of slaves and criminals was performed, and thus adding civil, municipal authority to that of church and crown. Short and narrow streets ran inland from the praça where the first business houses were located, while residential streets curved around the north shore of Castello hill. South from this center a road ran along the shore toward Botafogo, skirting the mangroves which screened dry land from the deep waters of the bay.[58]

A watery terrain severely delimited the paths of subsequent expansion. The level area between the hills of Castello, São Bento, and Santo Antonio was nearly all marsh or swamp land. A chain of shallow lagoons separated Castello and Santo Antonio hills, while scattered lagoons divided Santo Antonio from Santa Tereza and São Bento from Conceição. To the west, a lagoon reached into what would become the Campo de Sant'Anna where it connected to an inlet from the bay, the Saco de São Diogo, later drained and named the Mangue Canal.[59] Settlement, then, moved in the only other direction it could: inland toward the Campo de Sant'Anna on the southern edge of the swamps, and west from the chain of lagoons until blocked by the inlet. Despite the scarcity of landfill and difficulties in moving it, colonists gradually transformed the lagoons into firm land, creating new streets "foot by foot." The court's arrival from Portugal in 1808 gave renewed impetus to drain swamps and clear away mangrove. The area thus acquired around the Campo de Sant'Anna allowed new residences to be built in what was called the Cidade Nova or New City as well as construction of a road that joined the older city to São Cristovão, where the royal family would reside.[60]

In Rio de Janeiro, built on landfill that in turn rested on rock strata above a normally high water table where sea water permeated, fresh water wells for domestic use could not be dug. Well water was reserved for irrigation or street cleaning, and only occasionally a well dug on the "slope of a mountain" above the level of salty water provided water for drinking, cooking, or bathing.[61] Instead, fresh water from mountain rivers channeled by means of an aqueduct and wooden pipes to public fountains supplied the city's needs. The first and largest of those fountains, the Carioca, named for the river that fed it, was begun in 1744 with construction of the aqueduct and completed by 1750. An underground limestone canal carried water the last distance to a second fountain inaugurated by the king in 1819 in the Campo de Sant'Anna, a welcome source of water to that new and growing part of town.[62]

The Rio de Janeiro of 1808 with four parishes and at most 50,000 or 60,000 souls to welcome their king had become by 1838 a place of nearly 100,000 persons living in eight parishes. That initial and spectacular growth following the arrival of the court kept pace: 228,743 persons by 1872 became nearly 423,000 in 1890 and reached 620,000 persons and 13 parishes by 1906. In a century the city had grown tenfold. Africans – as many as 59,000 in 1849 a few years before the slave trade ceased – together with the Portuguese, Italians, and Spaniards, especially visible by the 1870s, most poor and seeking work, crowded into the city. They were joined by free blacks and mulattos or by white Brazilians from other provinces and by smaller numbers of profit-minded foreigners with money or talent to invest.[63]

Not all who came stayed, of course, yet their presence combined with a largely imported technology to transform permanently urban topography and urban habits. By mid-century a few public fountains were no longer adequate to provide a dramatically increased population with sufficient water. The 1860s saw efforts to channel additional water from some ten or twelve mountain streams, using reservoirs for storage for the first time. Somewhat earlier, in 1857, the city had contracted with the English-owned City Improvements Company to lay plumbing throughout the city. Owing to more water and English pipes, water became available from street-corner spigots, some 670 of them, and to 2,000 private homes by 1860.[64] A new means of public transport expanded the city when trams or *bondes*, the mule-drawn streetcars that traveled on steel tracks and were named for the English bonds that first financed them, began regular service in 1868. Spurred by great success, the Botanical Gardens Railway Company hurriedly laid miles of additional track. Other companies, some Brazilian, requested and got concessions to establish supplementary lines, so that by 1875 streetcars moved back and forth across the

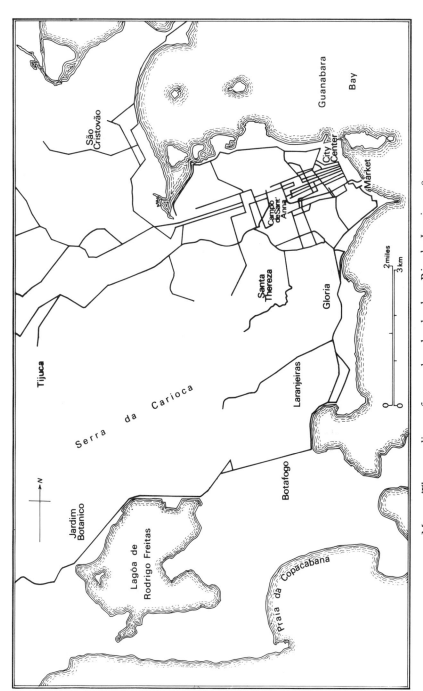

Map 1 The tramlines of central and suburban Rio de Janeiro, 1877

central city, while others leaving from the Largo do São Francisco radiated to the outskirts.[65] Within a few years trams had replaced earlier forms of collective transportation, the over-sized coaches known as *diligencias, onibus,* and *gôndolas,* and even the popular ferries that had brought passengers on the bay from Botafogo or São Cristovão to the center.[66]

Following the tram lines the exclusive residential parts of the city spread up past the convent into the steep hillsides of Santa Thereza, and out beyond the established suburbs of Botafogo and Laranjeiras to the more recent Jardim Botanico, as well as to cool and tranquil Tijuca on the edge of the rain forest from which the area took its name. At the same time, the city center grew in upon itself as the slums, tellingly nicknamed cortiços or beehives, multiplied in the ever more congested older sections that became home to arriving immigrants, free blacks, and to the slaves who hired out their own labor. The 114 cortiços with their 4,003 inhabitants counted by police in 1856 mushroomed into 502 cortiços with 15,054 inhabitants in 1867, and by 1888 the dwellers of the 1,331 slums numbered 46,680.[67] Not only did the number of tenements swell, but they remained concentrated in the older residential parishes of the central city. Santo Antonio, Sant'Anna, Santa Rita, Gloria – parishes with the largest number of cortiços in 1856 continued to receive those who came in search of cheap housing. While outlying suburbs became fashionable for those with means, the poor steadily took over the central parishes, intensifying the crowding that had worried police as early as 1856 for reasons of health and public order.[68] Extension of the outer zones of the city accentuated the increasing congestion of the inner city, a double process whereby rich and poor districts were ever more removed from one another as the century passed.

In that diverse and dense place that was the central city, rich and poor were indiscriminately juxtaposed. If luxuriously appointed carriages attended by liveried footmen, closed and elegant two-horse coupés, or the hired two-wheeled cabs called tilburies still conveyed fine ladies and important gentlemen at high speeds, trams conducted everybody including the poor. Unlike the ferries, trams offered no standard half-fare for the barefoot poor, although occasionally those "without shoes" could ride cheaply in the closed baggage car. In open cars of six benches passengers rode seated shoulder to shoulder four to a bench, while several male passengers might stand precariously on the running boards.[69] Even members of the elite sometimes took trams to the center to shop or do business, as Dona Carmen, a member of Baron Cotegipe's family, did in 1882.[70] Differences of color and rank met briefly in the brothels. One old man recalled the Hotel Ravot with its women "in peignoirs seated in the windows or leaning on the sills beckoning the passersby." There were women for "every purse," cheaper around the cortiços, more costly near the stately mansions in the Catete section of Botafogo.[71] Common eating houses and cafés crowded in alongside fine shops. There were workshops next to the fancy confectionery store with its ice cream parlor upstairs and its own clientele.[72] The juxtapositions were seldom more than superficial and brief, however, for usually the thinnest and most ineradicable of barriers – speech and gesture – kept those "more favored by fortune" distant from the rest.

Although householders strove energetically to maintain the boundaries that secured domestic space, the forces of the street seemed always to encroach. Householders faced the dilemma that, in order to constitute their households, they had to bring servants who belonged to the disorderly outside world into the intimate confines of their homes. Being neither family nor wholly unknown, servants occupied an ambiguous and suspicious place between the two. And so the essential paradox formed: for house to function, it had to render itself chronically vulnerable to the dangers of the street.

PART II

Servants' world

2

The work

The variety in kind and place of domestic work derived from the fact that households, in order to function, required services that only later came to be supplied by urban service companies. By as late as 1860, Rio de Janeiro homes were not equipped with either piped water or a sewerage system. As city dwellers they did not produce the bulk of the food they consumed, and, in the tropics, without iceboxes, they could not store foodstuffs in any quantity or variety. Residents instead relied on servants to carry water, launder at public fountains, and shop daily. Masters distinguished between work that went on inside the house and work done outdoors at public fountains or markets. Servants sent out to the streets and praças, exposed to the rougher public places were assumed to be older, tougher, more experienced, and especially sexually experienced and hence less vulnerable, while those kept "within-doors" were the favored and hence the protected among servants. For servants, however, work and the places of work could assume contrary meanings, ones that reversed or blurred the conventional designations of safe and dangerous, clean or dirty, valued or demeaning. Even the changes in technology and transportation that eventually altered the nature of domestic labor held ambivalent significance for servants. The places of work mapped an ambiguously defined world.

Indoors, work centered in the kitchen. From there cooks sent to the family table dishes that included as standard fare black beans cooked with dried meat (the favorite accompaniment to any meal), frequently fish and especially cod, rice, occasionally vegetables, or beef slowly simmered on top of the stove or roasted, or chicken stewed with potatoes. Eggs, cold meat, wine, or bread might also accompany a meal. Indispensable on all Brazilian tables, high or low, was the manioc meal, served as a side dish to be sprinkled over the beans. A servant prepared the coffee that Brazilians customarily took on rising and set out the bread and fruit that followed at mid-morning.[1] Lengthy preparations produced the afternoon meal that opened with a "piping hot soup tureen placed in front of the dona da casa." It finished with the familiar sweets that foreign visitors found so exotic: *goiabada* – a paste made from guavas and sugar – glazed fruits, usually pineapple or cherries, or the tiny confections daintily spun from egg yolks, egg whites, and sugar according to Portuguese recipes and finally, strong, sweetened coffee sipped quickly from small cups. In the evening she served a final tea or light supper.[2] There were favorite dishes prepared weekly in some households: on Thursdays *feijoada*, the black beans soaked overnight and cooked slowly for hours with fatty pork parts; or, on Fridays, cod that had soaked for 14 to 20 hours in periodically changed water to rinse away the heavy salt and was then baked.[3]

In households that could afford luxuries, cooks served, with considerably less effort on their part, imported or prepared foods from cans or packets: English biscuits, beer, butter, or French pâté, truffles or champignons. From southern Brazil came prepared meats – ox tongue, stewed kidneys, spiced beef, or potted tongue "put up in small tins."[4] On grand occasions Brazilians celebrated with truly sumptuous feasts. At the wedding dinner given in April 1889 for the outspoken and successful abolitionist Joaquim Nabuco and his bride Evelina Torres Soares Ribeiro, seventy guests dined on a rich menu of soups, shellfish, fish, veal, chicken, and salads. Besides champagne, guests chose from among ten wines and enjoyed assorted luscious desserts.[5] Preparations lasting days undoubtedly tested the talents of even the most skilled servants.

Servants who cooked demonstrated wide-ranging competence not only in the dishes they prepared but also in the equipment they used. Since all cooking required either stove or oven, a cook's skill could be judged by whether she merely cooked on top of the stove or could successfully operate an oven as well. Wood- or charcoal-burning stoves with metal cooking surfaces on which pots sat over openings and brick ovens had given way by the 1880s to iron stoves. In either case a cook's success in baking or roasting depended on her ability to gauge and control the oven temperature. She might simply hold her hand in the oven and count: if she could get only to three, the oven was hot, while 20 meant a cool oven. By another method she placed a small piece of paper in the oven for 4 or 5 minutes. If by then it had darkened, she could be sure of a hot oven suitable for pastry or bread. Hence prized cooks earned the title "cooks of oven and stove," while those who cooked only with pans on top of the stove came to be called "cooks of the ordinary." Talented women knew the pride of thinking themselves "accomplished in their art."[6] Everyone readily agreed that the gas stoves that began to replace wood-burning ones in the early 1890s – some 490 families purchased them in the first year they were introduced – were both "more convenient and more hygienic."[7] Even ordinary cooks made a better showing after that time.

Besides the special talents necessary to manage oven and stove, servants also wielded with varied success an assortment of smaller utensils. Even for a small family menus could become refined enough to require a cook to juggle some "eight pans for greasy foods; including one for soup, another for eggs; one for milk, another for sweets, one for chocolate, . . ." enamel-coated and specially shaped.[8] An oblong table of strong, thick wood with a drawer below and shelves above supplied basic work and storage space. To those might be added in fancier kitchens, cupboards, a sink instead of the usual basin, or a copper milk can too dear to be found in every kitchen. Other standard equipment required as much strength as skill. On a marble slab a cook or house servant rolled pastry or kneaded bread; through metal grinders she ground meat or nuts. For the heavy grinding of corn or coffee she worked at the *pilão*, a solid wooden mortar and pestle, the bottom standing three feet, the pestle four feet high or better.[9] No kitchen functioned without a stock of clay water jars. Made of light porous clay, fired but unglazed to allow evaporation, they ranged in size from the stationary, wide-mouthed *talha* that held ten to fifteen gallons to the one and a half or two and a half gallon *moringues*, some with double spouts, to ones of two or three pints that held drinking water.[10] Servants knew even the smaller ones were heavy to lift when filled, brittle and easily broken when empty.

Besides the many necessary kitchen jobs assigned domestics in the running of most homes, a minority of Rio de Janeiro families could afford to assign the serving and the care of silver, china, and crystal to a *copeira* or pantry maid. By mid-nineteenth century the times had well passed among cultured people when husband, wife, children, and dependents ate from the same plate using their fingers, or when a family served meat with only two or three knives shared around the table to each guest in turn.[11] Instead, huge sideboards, some with glass-paneled doors, held stacks of plates, rows of tureens and serving dishes. Before her death in 1873, the widow Anna Angelica do Sacramento Bastos had kept for her table white porcelain for dinner and luncheon together with crystal goblets, glasses, and compote bowls. As well as a chest of matched silver, the inventory of her property listed an assorted two dozen silver soup and teaspoons, knives and forks, serving pieces for fish and rice, carving sets, a silver shell for sugar, and numerous silver trays and candlesticks.[12] Besides the routine washing and drying of china and glassware, silver tarnished quickly in the humid, salty air and thus required from servants repeated polishing and careful storing to keep it from deteriorating.

Family living spaces – parlor, bedrooms, study – generated additional tasks. Rich families cluttered their rooms with a profusion of furniture that required dusting, polishing, or airing. Chairs and sofas, often from fine dark mahogany or rosewood, dining furniture that accommodated 12 or 16, pianos, and china closets filled sitting and dining rooms. Deep and solid chests of drawers, graceful dressing tables, wardrobes, tall mirrors, and washstands with their porcelain basins and pitchers fitted out the bedrooms. Footstools, writing desks, couches, end tables, porcelain or silver cuspidors took up the remaining spaces.[13] Despite warnings to choose furnishings suitable to the damp climate – omitting, for example, heavy velvet drapes that both kept out light and air and became musty – fashion dictated carpets, lace curtains and draperies decorated with thick braid, upholstered furniture, papered walls, and floor length cloths on library tables. All required repeated airings on dry sunny days. Cane-bottomed chairs, sofas, and beds if slightly less luxurious proved cooler in the tropical heat.[14] The same salty air that tarnished silver and threatened fabrics and upholstered furniture with mildew, caused a film to settle on windows. Window cleaning thus figured as a regular chore for domestics, especially in the latter years of the century when glass doors and windows, skylights, and tiles began to replace open windows once covered only with wooden lattices. In well-run households, the presence of servants insured that "carpets should be beaten, furniture oiled, painted walls dusted . . . drapes shaken every few weeks."[15]

Lighting for city houses presented its own set of chores. Until 1854 when gas lighting first became available on a few principal streets, families relied on fish or whale oil lamps with their unpleasant smell and carbon residue or they simply used candles. Servants trimmed wicks, cleaned globes – sometimes tall graceful ones of etched glass that required extreme care in handling – and dipped candles.[16] From the early 1860s, wealthier families requested gas connections for their homes so that by 1874 as many as 10,000 private houses were provided with gas lighting "throughout the house," and even "in all the bedrooms." Although public buildings such as the National Library were lighted electrically beginning in 1885, not until the early years of the twentieth century did electricity furnish light to Rio de Janeiro's private homes.[17] Gas lighting meant that servants in most houses were still called upon to clean blackened globes or remove sooty smoke marks from walls.

Indoor servants answered to yet other domestic preoccupations. Wet-nurse, mucama or chamber maid, and seamstress rendered personal services to members of the patrão's family. When possible a family preferred to select from amongst their house servants a slave who had recently given birth to nurse their own newborn child or to hire a wet-nurse to live as part of their household. In the least satisfactory circumstances, they turned their children over to the "strange hands of hired amas," whom they deprecatingly called mercenaries. Accounts from all sides create the impression that amas of one sort or another nursed all the "more advantaged" born in the last decades of the nineteenth century. In a speech before parliament, one deputy eulogized the black race whose women "protected all of us during childhood . . . served as ama, perhaps to a majority of the honorable deputies." The modernist painter Emiliano di Cavalcanti, born in 1897, recalled that after "seven white wet-nurses, I became accustomed to the breasts of Cristiana, a spirited mulatto daughter of a family slave." And in 1895 a medical student could claim that, "We all still retain the vivid memory of the figure, genuinely Brazilian, of the wet-nurse. In her plump arms a good part of the present generation uttered their first sounds."[18]

To mucamas or chamber maids fell the tasks that closely associated them with their mistresses. A black mucama might accompany her mistress on outings or act as trusted escort while her mistress bathed in the sea. She might even enter the water herself. Maids engaged as companions to old women helped them get about or, perhaps more importantly, patiently heard their reminiscences. Others ran errands to deliver a message, buy a pair of earrings or bring home a bolt of fabric.[19] The mucama Felizarda attended to her mistress's clothes and jewelry. She perhaps helped to fasten the clasps of Dona Anna Angelica's gold brooches or set out her diamond earrings or gold chains, or wound the small gold pocket watch or replaced the silver perfume stopper. She knew the scent of almond soap, or herself used the delicate gold and ivory sewing kit to catch up a hem or secure a button. Service, properly that of a mucama, included doing her mistress' hair, washing and ironing her finer clothes, or doing fancy French pleating called *tuyanté*. Felizarda or mucamas like her picked lice from their mistresses' heads or massaged their scalps, a pleasurable distraction called *cafuné* that sent a pampered mistress to sleep. During lunch a maid frequently "waved . . . large banana leaves to keep away the flies and mosquitoes."[20]

Like chamber maids, seamstresses worked closely with the dona da casa. Wealthy women who did not actually buy their clothes in Europe relied on local dressmakers to imitate styles from abroad. Fashion magazines with color plates pictured the season's latest designs or sketched out pattern pieces; a dressmaker might work from a printed tissue-paper pattern or from a form molded to the dona's measurements. Besides the ornate fashions copied from France for an elegant dona da casa, seamstresses cut and fitted more ordinary clothing for entire families. When sewing machines became common in Rio de Janeiro from the 1870s, fewer households employed a full-time seamstress. Instead, a seamstress sewed for several families, one at a time in "their homes." She might work for one "a few days per week" or for a span of "days or months" once or twice a year. Some households, however, continued to want a servant whose main work was sewing, such as the one that would train a young "apprentice seamstress," so that even at the end of the century, some women could expect to do both hand and machine sewing or dressmaking as live-in seamstresses.[21]

Cooks, wet-nurses, mucamas, seamstresses – all belonged to the domain of indoor work, work that made them witnesses to and, to an extent, participants in the everyday life of the master and mistress. In contrast to those who remained "behind doors", masters with a number of slave or hired servants reserved a second category of work for domestics who "went out on the street." They included laundresses, water-carriers, and those who shopped at the market or bought from local vendors. Three principal sites – the Fountain of the Laundresses in the Campo de Sant'Anna, the fountain in the Largo de Carioca, and the city market – became familiar and accessible places to street servants. Forming a wide-based triangle, the three sites fixed the outer borders of the most densely settled city center (See Map 2). The Fountain of the Laundresses afforded both a public washing establishment and spigots from which servants drew water to carry home. The fountain occupied a far corner of the extensive field where few trees concealed its heavy lines. Slightly south and east, squatted

Plate 2 The fountain of the laundresses in the Campo de Sant'Anna,
1835

Plate 3 The market, *c.* 1880

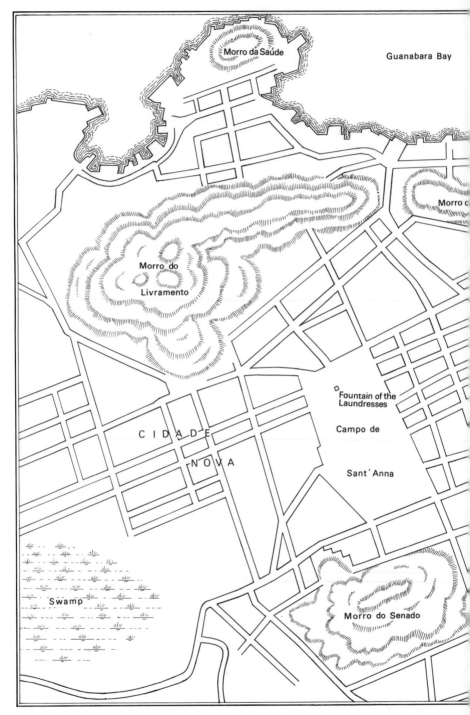

Map 2 The central city of Rio de Janeiro, 1858

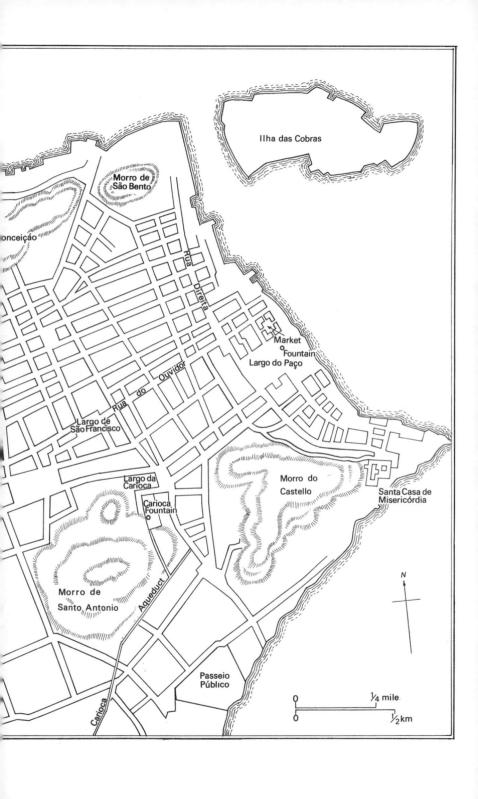

Ilha das Cobras

Morro de
São Bento

onceição

Rua Direita

Rua do Ouvidor

Market
Fountain
Largo do Paço

Largo de
São Francisco

Largo da
Carioca

Carioca
Fountain

Morro do
Castello

Santa Casa de
Misericórdia

Morro de
Santo Antonio

Aqueduct

N

Carioca

Passeio
Público

0   ¼ mile.

0   ½ km

the massive Carioca fountain at the foot of Santo Antonio hill where it received its waters from the towering aqueduct. Water-carriers and laundresses shared its granite washing troughs and water spigots. At a distance of nearly a mile from the Campo de Sant'Anna through the full stretch of city streets, the market, earlier called simply the fish market, was located at the bay's edge where boats delivered stocks of foodstuffs and housewares. Shoppers approached the market through the wide, adjoining square, the Largo do Paço.[22] Although the population grew and the city expanded, no central hub developed to supply all the services of water, public laundry, and market. Outdoor servants thus crossed back and forth the full physical span of the city.

The laundry counted as a major preoccupation in the running of any household. Wealthy families liberally used all manner of linen: plain and embroidered pillow slips, hand towels, linen napkins, kitchen towels, towels for polishing china, others for cups and glassware. Those who advised on such matters recommended house linen sufficient to meet the unexpected – illness or times of rain when "laundresses failed." Dinner and lunch each required fresh linen and for tea a gaily colored cloth. A proper table was always set with the "white linen damask cloth" that required "special work from the laundresses."[23] Washing, bleaching, drying, pressing consumed the major share of many domestics' working hours.

For many servants, laundry work meant washing at public fountains. Houses generally lacked any direct source of water – either wells or piped water – until the 1870s and 1880s and for many homes much later. In the early decades of the century, away from the more settled parts of town, laundresses washed in the streams – the Catete, for instance, where it wound splashing down from Laranjeiras and flowed under the bridge. Knee-deep in water they beat clothes on the flat boulders of the stream bed. Carrying "huge bundles of soiled linen on their heads," they went from the city in the early morning and returned only at nightfall. Slave women principally, they delivered the clothes well ironed, "perfumed with the scent of rose, jasmine, sweet acacias," if we can believe one account.[24]

By mid-century, however, women commonly laundered at public fountains. There the slap, slap of cloth being beaten clean was heard the whole day long. At the Campo de Sant'Anna scores of laundresses – 200 by one count – washed clothes and linen using big wooden bowls as wash tubs. Across the stunted grass, on bushes or on lines stretched between trees, women spread clothes to bleach and dry in the sun.[25] City mansions or villas with spacious grounds occasionally enjoyed the luxury of a fresh water stream or a rare well. With water and space for stone washtubs outdoors, such houses provided servants with a private place to wash.[26]

By necessity, much of domestic life had been organized around the daily procurement of potable water. From fountain or street corner tap, water was transported by all manner of means: by the "spare and feeble old woman, creeping along the pavement with a pail of water on her head" observed by a foreign visitor in the late 1850s, or delivered for a fee in huge wooden barrels mounted on ox carts, or sold by the bucket or even by the glass in public squares. Sometimes a single servant, besides her other chores, carried all the water for a small household. Once home, water stored in clay jugs sparingly supplied a household's needs. From the clay jugs came the water not only for kitchen work – cooking and cleaning up – but also for a family's personal use. Servants filled the enamel basins used for shaving and washing or the big wooden tubs used for bathing, carrying pitcher after pitcher of water.[27]

The times had passed by 1860 when male slaves balanced on their heads the famous *tigres* or barrels of waste in nightly or daily treks for dumping into the sea or into cesspools – marked by a black flag when they became full, indicating another should be used – at the Campo de Sant'Anna. Even before underground sewerage existed or when it served only a few families, householders could contract with private companies to empty every few days the fecal matter or kitchen garbage that accumulated in backyard barrels, so that paid collectors and specially designed wagons replaced slaves.[28] House servants, though, still included among their chores the emptying and cleaning of chamber pots or keeping to a minimum the filth and stench, especially on sultry summer days, from waste not removed daily. From disgust or indifference and despite a long-standing city ordinance that no one will "throw on the street liquids or solid matter," servant women no doubt contributed to the persistent practice, reported by a local official in 1893, of emptying out the window onto the street at "seven or eight o'clock in the morning . . . every filth possible to imagine."[29]

Another set of chores meant more carrying and walking for servants. In order to supply perishable foodstuffs to houses without cool cellars or iceboxes for storage, servants set out each morning to do the shopping. The principal market, purveyor to the entire city, stood facing the bay at the water's edge, a "great square building," each wall with a gate, together with smaller buildings and a courtyard. A fountain occupied the center courtyard, not as decoration but as a source of water for scrubbing down the place at the close of each day's selling. Around the fountain were arranged rows of stalls shaded by umbrellas or awnings. Along the inner rows servants could buy fish, vegetables, fruit, and flowers; from outer stalls they bought live fowls, roasting pigs, caged birds, even monkeys, or kitchen wares and locally made pottery.[30]

Between house and street, at the margins where the two zones overlapped, existed the neighborhood where a household's particular reputation remained known, but where the diversity and commerce of the street also flourished. Certain provisions could be bought only locally: meat, bread, and milk. Householders in 1881 could send their servants to buy from one of the 160 butcher shops around the city. Located at "well-known spots they sold meat at any time of day, whatever cut or quality desired, and, according to the hour, at prices more or less low." In competition with the butcher shops, peddlers sold door to door fresh meat and giblets from "trays or wooden tubs" or hawked chickens or calves' feet. House servants received bread delivered from the bakeries or bought bread and biscuits from slaves who sold on the streets in defiance of city regulations. Early each morning servants bought the day's milk at the door from a vendor who led his cow through the streets. A house servant provided a pan and the cow would be milked on the spot.[31] Up and down the streets vendors carrying baskets or tin or glass boxes hawked sweets, ice cream, cigarettes and matches, or fancy yard goods. Commonly they sold fruits and vegetables or *quitanda*. Some offered roasted or ground coffee or even ice, while others specialized in selling newspapers, empty bottles, or onions.[32] House servants heard them approach, as vendors "shouted out their stocks in lusty voices," chanted rhymes, or banged wooden clappers,[33] so that they shopped from doorways or through unshuttered windows. Corner stores or groceries stocked with "heaps of jerked beef, cod, bags of beans and rice, . . . cheese from Minas," manioc flour, red Lisbon wine, or small bunches of split fire wood also competed with the market. Such familiar and frequented places, where in the early 1870s even a slave could buy on her mistress's credit, supplied last-minute items or the regular provisions for households that bought in quantities too small to warrant market buying.[34]

The standard view of city life held that streets and public praças were hazardous places where the hazards could be either physical and therefore tangible and "real" or social and therefore perceived or

Plate 4 A cow being milked at the door, *c.* 1860

"fictive." Certainly a trip across town caused servants to pick their way through tortuously narrow streets, exposed to dirt, traffic, and the weather that were real enough. In the oldest settled areas, wrested from marshland, an economy of effort had dictated narrow streets in order to open several frontages in a small but eventually congested space. Typically the distance between shop fronts on opposite sides of rua Rosario or rua da Alfândega measured twelve feet, the carriageway only six. Adequate when slaves on foot had supplied nearly all transport, such streets later barely admitted carriages to pass one another, and then only by sweeping close to house or shop fronts. After 1860 wheeled vehicles – commercial wagons or carts added to the congestion, substituting the heavy labor of male slaves who had borne 132 pound sacks of coffee from warehouse to ship. By the 1870s when mule-drawn trams provided the principal public transportation, a pedestrian might find it necessary to duck into a shop or squeeze against a house to avoid being hit as a tram passed. The crowd of shoppers on the fashionable rua do Ouvidor prompted the municipal council by 1891 to ban carriages from early morning to late at night. Only the broad rua Direita comfortably gave way to carriages, hacks, and tilburies,[35] although their presence, especially at the Largo do Paço, added confusion and risk for heavily burdened servants who crossed on foot to and from the adjacent market.

In a city without sewers or garbage removal, streets collected refuse and generally presented an "aspect of decay." Animal carcasses left in the street gave off a foul stench believed to transmit disease. So many dead animals accumulated that the editor of one scientific journal in 1881 suggested collecting them for fertilizer, thereby additionally providing a "small industry" for the poor who would do the collecting.[36] To deal with the mess of rubbish, putrid animals, dirty water and human waste, the better constructed streets sloped toward a center gutter that supposedly drained away both refuse and rain water, except that during a downpour the overflow became a "regular stream," and in dry weather the beating tropical sun only aggravated the rotting and the smell. If in later years nightly work teams cleaned the streets "whether it rained or not,"[37] as officials claimed, then everybody including servants got about more easily.

Through congested, "irregular and miserably paved" streets, filthy and reeking, trudged servant women.[38] And they went in all weather skimpily clad. At best shod in rough wooden sandals called *tamancos*, they more often went like the rest of the poor, barefoot. If servants felt cooler in summer in their thin clothes, even without a parasol for shade, than ladies corseted into layers of fitted European-style dresses, they also shivered unprotected against the heavy chill that could settle over the city in dank winter.[39]

Climate imposed other worries on outdoor servants. In high summer the heat could be intense. Locals recognized one o'clock as consistently the warmest time of day, and knew the heat would lessen by about four. Shopping was best done in the early morning, for after midday the street sale of fresh meat and fish was prohibited and produce would have been kept overlong in the wilting sun. With good cause public health officials sought to speed up the transporting of meat from the abattoir that too often sat spoiling in railway cars in the oppressive heat before reaching city butcher shops and their domestic customers. In the months of worst heat, October through March, garbage was collected before 11 in the morning, by midday in the cooler season,[40] just as servant women made their way to and from market. Dry weather exposed servants to dusty streets, fearsome because the dust reputedly carried yellow fever infection, while on rainy days water shot down on passersby from copper spouts that jutted out from beneath roofs or balconies.[41] For laundresses the rainy season meant that laundry already burdensome to carry, had to be held away from splashing, mud-spattering coaches and wagons. One hundred rainy days per year, on the average, hampered their efforts to wash and dry clothes on time. Some years were worse. The 235 days of rain in 1890 rendered clothes-drying a near hopeless enterprise and must have caused the entire city to go about in damp or dirty clothes. Washing outdoors when the winter temperature dipped to fifty degrees was rough work.[42]

All servants who left the house bore their share of strenuous labor. Hauling water, washing at public fountains, or delivering laundry from cortiços meant that laundresses balanced heavy and bulky loads on their heads as they wove their way across town. Except for families who happened to live close by, daily shopping also meant for a servant a long trek to the market located as it was on the "far edge of settlement." The return could be especially taxing if she carried filled baskets and a live chicken tied by the feet.[43]

Besides requiring of servants the burdensome work associated with risky and dirty places, masters exposed some servants to the threats that made public places into socially dangerous ones. Street arguments could escalate into fighting, with fists, broom handles, or even knives as weapons. More often the injuries were verbal. Coarse words hissed or shouted at women, and frequently by women, were intended to give insult. The language of the street was provocatively sexual and racial. Instead of the usual "whore and cow," the mulatto slave woman Lucrecia Esmeria do Sacramento heard herself jeered at scatologically as the "Viscountess Wood-pecker." In a loud voice, allegedly heard by the entire block, one woman vented her anger on the male owner of a slave laundress whom she accused of stealing a blouse: "Thief, swindler who sleeps with slaves . . . son of a whore, common pederast."[44] The stream of complaints and arrests that portray street life thick with drunkards, inebriated women and men, the disorderly, and vagabonds were not all exaggeration or allegations produced to justify police harassment.[45] Not only the language, but the behavior of the street, by numerous accounts, was crude or suggestive. In 1870 a slave boy was accused of "committing an indecent act," and in 1895 the "skinny black woman" Olinda Maria da Conceição was charged with "practicing immoral acts in the street."[46] Although city residents repeatedly refused to pass a law against prostitution, they nevertheless found repugnant the prostitutes who walked the "central streets" or who brazenly showed themselves at doorways or windows "half-naked."[47] Servant women on the street for domestic chores found themselves readily mistaken for "women of the street." We can surmise that at least some of the women who identified themselves, when interrogated, as cooks or general domestics were servants wrongly charged as "public women," while others worked at both professions, and most probably hoped to pass themselves off as suitably employed servants.[48] Simply being on the street unescorted was sufficient to raise questions about a woman's purpose and morals.

That servants routinely witnessed or even became victims of the offenses of the street, masters took for granted. They further assumed that servants once outside the direct domination of paternal authority would likely fall into bad habits. One master in 1872 candidly disclaimed responsibility for his slave: he could not answer for her conduct when she went out to do shopping or sell vegetables.[49] The well-off avoided the scenes they found distasteful outside their houses by sending their servants instead. And they preferred to send some rather than others.

When patrões reserved indoor work for selected servants, they not only shielded them from the heavy jobs and rough encounters, as they understood them, but they also bestowed favor. Because those with authority recognized in indoor work a requirement for finer abilities and sensibilities, servants could find satisfaction in valued work done well. A meal meant a performance in which the serving maid presented unobtrusively both to family and to their guests her talents at waiting at table. On such an occasion she became a representative of the household. Serving assumed supreme confidence on the part of the copeira who, before the audience of diners, first placed a steaming hot soup tureen, then received used plates and distributed clean ones, while not forgetting to place the head of the fish in one direction or the leg of lamb in another. After several courses and the carrying of weighty glass compote dishes together with other desserts, she offered coffee from a tray balanced gingerly on one arm while she poured, not overfilling the cups and adding just the right amount of sugar. If that smooth routine often broke into a noisy confusion of passing plates, waving flies away, supplying suddenly called for serving spoons, or ducking hot-tempered remonstrations, house servants nevertheless moved the meal through to completion.[50] For cook or table servant the production of a meal involved a display of talent in which she could find a measure of pride in her success and affirmation from others.

Personal servants – chambermaids and wet-nurses – could hope to be rewarded with affection or trust. In the course of their duties such servants routinely crossed into those spaces of the house set aside for family members, and were engaged in daily contact with them. Through the myriad attentions that they furnished, they witnessed at close range the leisure and wealth that casually belonged to a class from whom they, as servants and poor women, despite routine contact, remained utterly and permanently remote. Yet they reasonably identified with the families to whom they belonged. Being a mucama or ama brought tangible rewards – ones understood as such by both sides – in return for valued service: finery or styles that were a sign of special status like a silken scarf to tie up her hair or a pair of slippers; an outing or occasionally a long journey as when Dona Alice Neves de Moura sailed for Montevideo in January 1891 with her 2-month-old son, the wet-nurse and her son; or perhaps marriage with the owner's esteemed male slave. As the privileged among house servants, a mucama, although a slave, could perhaps hope to be freed.[51] As slaves became fewer and went unreplaced in Rio de Janeiro homes, so the personal maids of a lifetime, tightly bound by loyalty and privilege, gradually disappeared. Favored servants nevertheless remained in slightly altered guises. The free woman, nurse to a family's several children, might keep a place in the household long after the children had grown, a retired and ancient figure who merited care and affection.

Servants easily grasped the significances of being assigned one kind of work rather than another and of the privileges conferred or withheld or the risks imposed. Just as often, they probably accepted the differences without reflection as part of the work, part of what they coped with every day. At the same time, however, we have glimpses of servants' conduct or demeanor that suggest that work and the places of work assumed meanings other than those masters intended or took for granted, and to that extent their world became distinct.

Kitchen work was hot, messy, and tiring, even if indoors. The most ordinary dishes still required bloody and laborsome preparations. With a small, precise cut in the neck vein, a cook killed and quickly bled a chicken, singed and plucked its feathers, then dressed it for cooking. Or on a wooden chopping block she cut and separated from the bones slabs of meat for roasts. For hours she slowly boiled raw sugar in a wide, shallow copper basin, stirring and testing until with further cooking the sticky brown mass finally became dry, white sugar. Painstakingly she cleaned rice, picking out bits of dirt, washing it again and again, and with a bottle she pressed the hard chunky salt fine, or beat beans free of their wispy dry husks.[52] Conditions where she worked rarely met the recommended standards. Few kitchens boasted a dispensary, "well ventilated, with a cement floor." Instead of a larder suspended from the ceiling, at least minimal protection against ants, roaches, and flies, or hooks from which to hang dried meat and bacon, servants struggled against soured, rancid, or molding foodstuffs. As often as house servants worked in kitchens where the walls were ". . . lined with tiles, the floor paved," where a window gave out onto a "fine and large garden," many more found familiar kitchens "without ceiling or floor," or ones where refuse heaped high in the patio produced dangerous "miasmas." They struggled with the "pure black mud" of a beaten-earth patio that did not drain properly or they worked not far from the kitchen's "open sewer, clogged with filth."[53]

A servant's long and strictly regulated day began before dawn when in winter the sun would show only after six o'clock. From the arrival of the milk cow in early morning until the supper at nine or ten o'clock in the evening that ended the daily round of meals, a cook alternated between periods of hectic preparations and slacker times when she might tackle the other tasks. So frequently did dinner include last-minute guests that outwardly their presence was treated casually. In 1873, Senator João Maurício Wanderley had been asked by a colleague at the last minute to "take a spoonful of soup, without the least ceremony . . . today." With equal informality, the same senator, then a member of the cabinet, invited former minister João Alfredo Correia de Oliveira "to share our dinner," at home today, if "you have no plans."[54] Although the endless stream of social calls stretching through teatime betrayed no sense of being occasions, they necessarily meant added and hurried work for servants. Only when the eating had finished and the cleaning up was done, did a cook or kitchen servant end her day, a short five or six hours before the next one began.

House servants could expect to work to strict schedules, especially in comfortable households managed by confident mistresses. Because Rio de Janeiro was the imperial capital, domestic schedules and official meeting times were made to conform. Parliament sat from midday to four or exceptionally until five o'clock, while the High Court convened from ten until two, so that maids served dinner as early as two o'clock but more commonly in late afternoon. Whatever the agreed upon time, one woman of a prestigious family recalled that with them mealtimes were always punctually observed, and other activities gave no excuse for tardiness – not for family and certainly not for servants.[55] A mistress might require that her cook, with menus already assigned for the week, divide over several days the additional jobs of scrubbing the kitchen floor and polishing the stove and faucets; pantry work that included cleaning boots and shoes every day still left time for cleaning lamps and wardrobes or for polishing furniture. An upstairs maid who daily cleaned the bedrooms and went out with the children in the afternoon might also wash children's clothes on Mondays and Tuesdays, mend linen on Wednesdays, take the children for outings all day Thursday, and finally iron laundry on Fridays and Saturdays.[56] Probably few households ran so mechanically, while many servants no doubt found ways to resist the imposition of so rigid a schedule, but such could be the demands.

Withindoors where masters located their sense of security, servant women had reason to feel confined or vulnerable. A house servant knew to keep to the service areas of pantry, kitchen, and patio while the comfortable rooms – parlors, dining room, verandas – were forbidden unless work or a hurried errand justified her intrusion. Never could she betray familiarity or claim a right to those rooms however minutely she knew the contents of every cupboard or drawer. So conscious was the distinction between kitchen and parlor that the novelist Bernardo Guimarães could credibly have house servants describe themselves as belonging to the kitchen and not to the parlor.[57] On the other hand, those parts of the house designated for work never belonged exclusively to servants, and a dona da casa or the children of the family came and went casually. Her work ever supervised, her demeanor noted, a chamber maid or a wet-nurse seldom escaped the watchful presence of her patrões. She knew to be alert, careful to avoid reprimand or stinging punishment. Precisely because work indoors brought proximity among those more powerful where she held no right to object, she could fall victim to a mistress's rage or to sexual abuse from master or master's son. She could always be accused of stealing ". . . napkins, small spoons, knives, small pieces of china, children's clothes, adult's clothes, or jewelry."[58] Instead of protection, the seclusion of the house could conceal the isolation or injury of servant women. In that domain of privately exercised authority, a house servant could find herself bewildered or helpless.

If servant women all too often discovered their masters' houses to be offensive or harmful places, thus reversing the usually understood connotation of house as safe, the meanings of street could similarly be turned around. The city provided a contrasting setting apart from the one imposed by patrões indoors. For servants who went out, the public places beyond the houses – streets and praças – came to be mapped in terms of their experiences, broken down into a known landscape of familiar sounds, smells, and images. Individually, servant women could establish a favorite way through streets where recognized landmarks gave orientation or marked the distance from place to place. They could invest particular places with private significance. Congested and dirty streets where all manner of shops, private residences, warehouses, and public buildings crowded together became ordered by the particular meanings a servant woman assigned them. In that world, temporarily away from a watchful mistress, she possessed both the local knowledge and the opportunity necessary to attend to her own concerns. If seriously worried about an overdue menstrual period, she could seek out the herb seller near the church for a "remedy." She knew where to buy amulets and where, in truly desperate straits, to find the *feiticeiro*, or sorcerer, who could summon the forces of white or black magic on her behalf. If it was the action and risk of the street she sought, she could bet, as the laundress Carolina Alves did in 1906, on the illegal numbers game with the postcard vendor who operated from the doorway of the barber shop. In the early 1870s whenever an errand took the slave servant Belmira to the rua Carioca she would pause at her friend's house to chat through the open window.[59]

Servants shared among themselves and with all those whose labor similarly took them out on the streets the life that went on there. Street life allowed a more genuinely intimate social world to form among those who counted one another as equals. Away from the surveillance that went with indoor work, a woman might expect to meet up with other servants embarked on their chores, or on her way to do errands to meet briefly at some prearranged time and place with friends or a lover. The streets thus became a meeting ground for a wide and diverse segment of the city's poor.

Household shopping brought repeated contact with vendors or tradesmen who themselves were slaves or who belonged among the lower ranks of the free. Women bought both from men and from other women. At least a few of the licensed slaves sent out on the streets, to sell notions or knick-knacks were women. In 1861, for instance, the license for the black woman belonging to Felix Martins Corrêa was renewed so that she could continue selling "small wares

Plate 5 A street vendor of small wares, *c.* 1895

and trinkets." Two years later another slave woman was licensed by her owner, Rosalina Soares who lived on the rua Paulo Mattos, to sell "trifles" on the street.[60] Somewhat more commonly, servants bought from female renters of market stalls, such as Maria Luiza da Conceição who in 1879 sold fruits and vegetables.[61] From the many women who hawked quitanda or produce from the baskets they skillfully balanced on their heads, house servants purchased peaches, pineapples, onions, or greens. Another woman, photographed at the turn of the century, her hands strong and rough from work, sold giblets from a case she carried strapped around her neck.[62] For the most part, though, servants traded with men who filled the cadres of vendors.

Even among neighborhood shops and familiar street-sellers,

Plate 6 *Quitandeiras, c.* 1895

servant women traded in fairly aggressive situations. Marketing
demanded a certain strategy or plain hard bargaining if she expected
to meet a dona da casa's demands or to save small change for herself.[63]
Similar social or racial backgrounds hardly insured against shady
dealings from vendors who would sell dear if not out-and-out cheat
the unwary. Servants chanced buying meat or bread weighed on false
scales, and when the price of meat suddenly doubled in the ten years
between 1890 and 1900 and for a briefer period almost tripled, true
weight and a fair price mattered.[64] Alert servants watched for
merchants who knowingly sold watered milk, bread baked from
putrid flour, or decomposing meat,[65] and searched out reliable sellers
who knew they meant business. If quick to discern quality and
assertive, she could then deal confidently in that predominantly male
world. With assertiveness went both risk and satisfaction.

Washing at a crowded fountain or cortiço laundry tanks or
queuing up to fill water jugs brought their own social pleasures.
Clothes drying or bleaching in the sun spelled a long wait for
laundresses, time enough to wash their own clothes or tend their own
children, brought along to the washing place or left to run about in a
courtyard. Washing afforded the chance for camaraderie. For a span
of hours or even a full day, women were freed from the need to

Plate 7 Laundresses and water carriers at the Fountain of the Largo da Carioca, 1844

behave deferentially, to move silently about. Instead the fountain site rang with their talk and their labors. Water carriers who waited at the fountain or street corner spigot could enjoy having the time to chat or flirt.[66] Save for encounters with the men who might also come to get water, trips to the fountain or neighborhood tap, unlike shopping, involved women in a largely female world. Street life engaged servants in a community larger than household or neighborhood. Streets and public praças could offer a setting far more egalitarian than masters' houses. There individual identity could form and find expression; bonds with others were established, tested, enjoyed. Servants thus assigned to the outdoor places of work their own meanings.

Experience did not always reverse so neatly the definitions of house and street, of safe and dangerous places. Frequently servants found themselves in highly uncertain situations where inventiveness or sheer will was the only way out. If some women found the street a lusty place, and if others grew restive or daring under the restricting protection of the house, all paid for their freedoms.

Servants never fully escaped the watchfulness of the household. The street-world was a crowded, closely observed place where no secrets could long be kept. A family's passing neighbor or relative might glimpse a servant's unseemly behavior and later report on her. The woman who dallied at the water spigot, drawing out her task in order to savor the company of others gathered there, risked being kept home by a mistress wise to her ploy while men were paid to deliver the water instead.[67] The street imposed its own rules and its own surveillance, at least intermittently. One summer evening in 1855 the slave woman Benedicta found herself arrested for "being encountered after hours" outside the house of her master, General Autero. Throughout the city local inspectors were posted to each quarter to keep track of residents, investigate complaints, enforce city ordinances, and report "all extraordinary happenings."[68] The freedoms of the street were circumscribed.

For Belmira, the young domestic slave who in 1872 belonged to Francisco da Veiga Abreu, resident in Santa Thereza, the freedom of the street carried clear and socially degrading assumptions. Although owned originally by Abreu's parents and thus with the family for many years and strictly as a house servant, she was no longer so protected. By Abreu's account Belmira regularly when out to do shopping and occasionally she hawked fruit and vegetables. A neighbor recalled seeing Belmira accompany the daughter of the family on strolls and excursions away from home. A Portuguese goldsmith remembered that Belmira once came to his shop, sent by her owner to fetch a pair of earrings for his daughter. Later, in his testimony before the court, the jeweler added that he "supposes that Belmira is not a virgin; . . . it is enough for her to go out on the street to presume this."[69] Merely because a servant was sent out to do errands, it could be assumed she was not a virgin. Such a woman, the assumption implied, neither deserved nor required protection. But paradoxically, the non-virgin servant woman, by her protecting presence, nevertheless conveyed to the virgin daughter the purity and security of the household. For Belmira the right to come and go with some independence came at a price. Whether the jeweler's casually formed but unchallenged assumption was accurate or mattered deeply to Belmira we do not know, but she could not have ignored wholly what was said about her.

For their part, indoor servants had their own ways to avoid what they might regard as excessive demands. Although the lofty councilors of state might comment that, "No one denies that in the governing of a house, the patron frequently has need to demand of his servants small services of a transitory nature," it was also the case that a servant might refuse to go beyond her specialty. According to a Frenchman long resident in Rio, slave servants never resisted openly or disputed an unreasonable order, but resorted to other evasions.[70] Mistresses know well, he continued, that they cannot ask a cook to touch housework and that the slaves employed with the linen or with the children will never consent to wash a parquet floor. Or they will do it "very badly, dirtying everything, walls and drapes." They were always ready with the reply: it is not our service. The single servant who performed every service was denied such a convenient excuse, of course, but she could still work slowly or badly. In the matter of passive resistance, slaves ironically had the edge over free domestics who could be fired, while slaves, went his argument, who have little incentive to work well will nevertheless be fed, housed, and clothed for, after all, they represented an investment.

In 1859 one slave wet-nurse escaped the isolation of her master's household by taking as her lover the slave Bonifacio, rented out by her master to a nearby family.[71] Bonifacio came to her nightly, slipping through neighboring back gardens after curfew, to sleep with her in the same bed she already shared with the nursing infant. She paid dearly for her illicit pleasures when her owner discovered her "already filled up" and his daughter ill from her changed milk. He appeared to be as offended (but not surprised) by the fact of her behavior as by her deception, for the other slaves of his house "all knew before me or my wife" of her affair. As punishment and to "give example to the other slaves," he sent the wet-nurse away and planned to sell her lover.

Beyond the particular households in which servants worked, they could draw from their neighborhoods to construct a larger social world. And neighborhood implied the presence of other servants. If other city parishes approximated the residence patterns of São Cristovão, then no quarter lacked servant women altogether and no household was visibly isolated from all others.[72] Servants from neighboring houses could thus maintain on-going contact with one another, or at least meet in passing. Even a woman who worked as the only servant for a family, or one who generally remained indoors, could know the presence of fellow servants nearby.

The absence of basic urban services had combined with the attributions of household work to pattern it into recognizable and predictable routines. Yet transformations in daily life accumulated, as technology or newly established city services became widespread. Piped water and an underground sewerage system, in turn made possible by an increased and more reliable water supply, together with a network of public transportation gradually altered the nature of housework and hence the labor required from servants. Improved urban services appeared haltingly over the span of several decades. Wealthier families or those in spacious, more recently settled suburbs enjoyed them first, others only later, and some never. Nevertheless a spirit of change and renovation can be said to have characterized Rio de Janeiro from the 1860s and especially the 1870s. By the 1880s, substantial changes were widely visible. Houses with "inside water and gas" or with a spacious backyard and a "washtub with an abundance of piped water" could be had as early as 1875, while ten years later in some houses even the servants could expect a toilet for their use alone.[73] Innovations that translated into altered domestic arrangements had for servants, although again for some sooner than others, the consequence of modifying the places and social contexts of work.

Piped water fundamentally reformed domestic life. City works that sent water into individual homes or equipped them with drains and sewerage changed the work servants did. Although the piles of dirty clothes and house linen did not diminish, fewer servant women trudged across town bearing weighty bundles of laundry for, instead, some had the convenience of washing at home. Piped water also lessened or altered the labor spent keeping city families bathed. By the 1880s those who could afford them had complete and elegantly appointed bathrooms with porcelain bathtubs.[74] But the benefits were equivocal. While servants no longer endlessly carried pitchers of water to fill basins, they now scrubbed porous and easily stained sinks and tubs, mindful not to chip their brittle surfaces, and they mopped up afterwards as they always had. In houses with plumbing, domestics coped with frequent sewer backups, and water shortages persisted, serious enough to force city officials to urge that water be used "only for essentials," prompting complaints to become more bitter. The parching effects of drought in October of 1878 caused "hundreds of persons [to gather] every night and morning round the taps in the Largo da Carioca," and water was rationed.[75] Poorly installed plumbing, uncovered reservoirs with high bacteria counts, the shutting off of water during the day, "exactly when domestic service most needs water," or the lack of water to entire sections of the city because pipes had not yet been laid meant that not all servants had an equal chance at the supposed improvements.[76] Chamber pots and privately contracted waste removal continued well into the twentieth century.

Plate 8 The fountain of the Largo da Carioca, *c*. 1890. The square
became a turn-around for trams and the laundresses were gone

Calculated against their social consequences, the advantages of the
new technology became even less certain. For many servant women,
changes in work meant a concomitantly narrowed social world. As
trips to fountain or corner water taps became unnecessary, they found
fewer reasons to escape the confines of house for the more open life of
the street. Servant women lost permanently the fountains as favorite
places where they had not only worked but conducted important
moments in their personal lives. The stone washing basins at the
Largo da Carioca ceased to be a gathering place and became instead
merely background to the bustling traffic that streamed past. By
about 1890 not a single laundress could be sighted.[77] Earlier the
"fountain of the laundresses" in the Campo de Sant'Anna had been
removed altogether. In 1870 a formally arranged garden with a small,
ornamental fountain locked away at night behind a wrought iron
fence replaced the busy, boisterous, colorful washing place.[78] On a
lesser scale, collective laundering went on in cortiços but without the
same triumphant sense with which public fountains and squares had
been boldly claimed by servants as theirs. Instead, servants worked
more hours indoors, in backyards or in walled off patios with their
ambivalent offer of protection that also admitted the obtrusive or
censoring presence of a dona da casa.

If, through the 1870s and 1880s, some work sites gradually ceased to be the busy and frequented places of recent times, the city itself expanded. Tramlines criss-crossed older city sections or joined them to still thinly settled districts. Trams brought once distant suburbs, especially those unreachable by ferry such as Jardim Botanico or Tijuca, closer to the center, stimulating further residential settlement. In spacious suburbs families took roomier houses where larger grounds allowed for a garden or back lawn in contrast with the living quarters above a shop that had typified the cramped older parts. More families thus sought servants who would work and live far from familiar lower class areas in the city center – far from the very places to which by poverty, race, or family ties servant women claimed allegiance. From where Antonia Mendez worked as a maid in Tijuca in 1899, she had to go by tram a long way to an older part of town near the Campo de Sant'Anna to meet her lover.[79] For those same women the public market also became more distant, requiring longer trips and more time taken up with buying fresh produce. True, they gained time out on their own, but once home, they still had to cram the usual work into what was left of the day. In the absence of local street markets, domestics continued "to come from the suburbs to shop daily."[80] While the poor, and among them servants, could not afford the 200 *réis* or 10 cent tram fare as a matter of course, they could pay it occasionally. Apparently laundresses, like the one photographed on the rua Camerino in 1890 resting her load while she waited, came to rely on streetcars. In 1913 their presence as passengers provoked an ordinance forbidding the transport of "soiled clothes" in passenger cars, a rule which conductors and the public largely ignored.[81] Although travel on tracks gave a smoother ride, nothing prevented a mule from taking fright and plunging headlong into a corner kiosk. On the whole, though, trams proved safer than the earlier collective coaches. Accidents like the one in 1868 that injured several passengers, including the pregnant slave laundress Anna, on her way from Laranjeiras to the city, were unusual.[82] If safer and less effort than walking, riding a tram kept a woman from spontaneously calling in at a grocery to chat, and the immediate, peopled landscape encountered on foot became distanced, less animated from a tram. It is easy to overstate the changes that occurred, and therefore necessary to bear in mind that urban life was altered slowly and unevenly. No part of the city nor even any household changed overnight, so that late in the century many servants continued to labor in the old ways.

3

Private lives in public places

Salvador Barbará, a 36-year-old Spanish immigrant to Rio de Janeiro, one day in May 1899 found himself accused of breaking into a tenement room on the Campo de Sant'Anna. An employee at the tenement saw Salvador enter room four with a key "identical to that belonging to the woman who rented the room." Without first finding "his patrão" the employee went for the police. Both the employee and the landlord who let the rooms thought Salvador's presence suspicious, for they knew the room belonged to the absent Antonia Mendez. According to the landlord, Salvador fed their suspicions by appearing at first "flustered" and then by insisting that "he owed no explanations." Landlord and employee persuaded the police to jail Salvador. Salvador gave the incident an utterly different coloring. He claimed the room as his residence. Having "made up" with his "mistress" Antonia Mendez and "in order to save money" between them, Antonia had given him the key to the room she rented and sent him there to sleep. He had gone there for the last four days, but when he arrived that afternoon to change clothes and rest, police arrested him. He urged police to check with Antonia, who would back him up. Not knowing the exact place where she worked, Salvador asked that the police look for her.

Evidently they did not try or tried unsuccessfully, for only three days later did Antonia arrive at the police station, and on her own initiative. How she knew to look there for Salvador, she did not report, but at once she acknowledged Salvador as her lover, and that she had given him the key, authorizing him to leave his things there. By her telling, Salvador, far from breaking into her room, did her a favor. Employed as a domestic in distant Tijuca, a considerable tram trip from the Campo de Sant'Anna, Antonia could go to her room only every now and then – "she only comes every eight days," the rooming house employee had said – so it fell to Salvador to look after

the possessions she kept there. Convinced by Antonia's corrobor-
ation, police freed Salvador. Salvador expressed relief at having "his
good reputation restored," since, he said, he had "always been an
honest man and a worker."[1] In the end, police remained satisfied that
no break-in had occurred. Antonia and Salvador could resume the
usual course of their lives.

The seemingly small matter of Antonia's room can be made to
disclose larger meanings. Above all else, Antonia, a live-in servant,
conducted a private life quite separate from the household of Senhor
Carlos Coutinho where she worked. She did so energetically: she
made the long tram trip from the suburbs to the center where she
knew or discovered that rented rooms could be had around the praça;
she saved money enough to pay the rent, as much as $5 a month from
a wage of probably $8. All that when work left her scant time, once
every eight days at best, to enjoy the independence she so committedly maintained.[2] Apparently Antonia had rented a room of her own
before joining up with Salvador, and not merely because of him.
Later she came to include Salvador as her lover in that precariously
autonomous life she had established.

Both Antonia and Salvador, despite their poor circumstances,
successfully claimed respectability. Until the incident over the room,
neither had thought it necessary to explain to the landlord their
relationship nor the fact that they would share the room. Both
understood, however, that to acknowledge their relationship gave
identity and legitimacy to each: Salvador could rightfully use the
room; Antonia would not be taken for a prostitute. Certainly, the
investigating police concluded, "in this capacity . . . [as] Salvador's
lover," Antonia had appropriately given him her key.[3] Although
together only a short time, their efforts to "economize" and their
mutual care of one another's possessions – the fact that each owned
some goods or furniture – underscored personal respectability and
indicated their sense of future plans and an intention to remain
together. Theirs was not to be thought a casual or transient union.
Work bestowed an even more secure measure of respectability. We
know that Salvador thought himself an honest man who worked for a
living, a reputation he valued. Like Salvador, Antonia set herself
apart from the "vagabonds" and the beggars for she too held a job
with an employer whose name and address she could provide.
Employment enabled her to rent the room, and no one had voiced any
complaint against her. Moreover, like Salvador and unlike the
arresting policeman, she could read and, somewhat shakily, write her

name.[4] Thus confident of her position and her ability to make herself heard, she presented herself to the police on Salvador's behalf.

However particular the details, in a larger social context Antonia and Salvador's life, as conveyed in this brief event, did not appear odd or unrecognizable. Antonia is more than a plausible figure, for while her energy and assertive manner perhaps distinguished her, she also exemplified other servant women. Even before the abolition of slavery, live-in domestics managed to arrange times and spaces in which they could conduct private lives away from their work. They did so in numbers sufficient to prompt lawyers and laymen in the 1880s and 1890s who drafted work agreements aimed at regulating domestic service specifically to forbid a servant who "sleeps at the place of employment" from "renting a room in any other dwelling," and, before 1888, to forbid a slave domestic "even with her owner's authorization" to "establish her own residence."[5] Although the councilors of state eventually ruled against many such suggested regulations on legal grounds, they agreed – and by their agreement attested to the usualness of the practice – that provision should be taken against the "frequent abuse" and neglect of their duties by servants who "went out to enjoy themselves or on some private matter principally at night, without their employers' permission."[6] It is impossible to know how many servants, like Antonia, kept double residences. Those who did, combined with those who snatched time now and again for themselves, numbered enough to prompt concern and action from employers.

Along with those whose closely supervised and demanding work routines required that they maintain private lives clandestinely, belong the rest who as a matter of course lived apart from their patrões, openly managing their own lives. Scores of women, attached to particular households, returned late to their own places once the work finished. They were the ones who slept out. Others got only, but all of, one night a week away, usually Sunday night. Still others – nearly half the servant women identified in São Cristovão in 1870 – lived independently,[7] working on a daily basis for various families or taking laundry or sewing. Even slave women occasionally lived on their own, such as the three counted in the São Cristovão census in 1870, or the slave Rita who in the 1880s lived alone and "hired herself out on her own account."[8] Slaves who earned a daily wage beyond the amount owed the master could rent rooms directly or sublet from free persons, a situation common enough in the view of police to warrant a city ordinance against such practices. In this way, a scattering of slave laundresses or wet-nurses lived, as a nineteenth-century jurist put it, "almost exempt from a master's subjugation, almost free."[9]

Whatever separateness and respectability servants like Antonia Mendez could claim, they also came up against stubborn restraints. Taken as a group servants belonged to the class of urban, working poor, along with the porters or street peddlers or market vendors, all those who hired out their labor on a casual basis. On the other hand, the working poor distinguished themselves and were seen by others as distinguishable from the beggars, vagabonds, prostitutes, the sick and broken people. The fact of working accorded an identifiable and respectable place in society, however lowly. It was a place attained precisely because those who worked were linked as dependents to an employer or patrão, connections that conferred social identity denied the poor who, without work, remained anonymous. Thus, the working poor, and especially house servants who so visibly belonged to a particular master, remained firmly linked to those for whom they worked. Nevertheless, for servants who evaded at least partially the impositions of paternal authority, their measured, "sideways" independence opened up the possibilities for conducting private lives.

If as workers in other peoples' houses servants are set against a background of comfortable living, we must seek them in the context of the urban poor to whom by birth or kin or economic means they belonged if we are to recover anything of their personal lives. However particular the life style of the poor, it was never, of course, elected. The poor did not choose the features of their existence: poverty imposed or exaggerated the problems with which they coped. But in their manner of coping, they built up their own store of meanings and ways of acting that oftentimes differed from those of the better-off. Servant women shared with the rest of the poor their necessities and their solutions. Like all those who relied on a patrão for security, servants knew their position to be precarious, while the maintenance of alliances among their own kind served as a precaution. Thus their fragile independence, with its elements of assertiveness and adaptation, was insurance against vulnerability. It matters, then, to discover the way of life of the poor with its elements of street life, distinct dress, in *carnaval* at one extreme, and in the routines of family life at the other. Antonia and her room provide a point of departure.

Contrasted with the well-off of the city, screened from view in their closed-in carriages, behind their walled mansions, or inside fine churches, the separate lives of the working poor belonged more to the world of the street. There they found entertainment, arranged encounters, or met by chance in the familiar and accessible settings of the city's squares, parks, and markets. More appealing than the damp, dark, airless rooms of the cortiços or shabby row houses, the open courtyards or street-corner gathering spots drew them. The poor shared such places not merely with kin, but with neighbors and equals or with those who simply lived, homeless, on the streets. The dominant social places for the poor, then, where they forged the relationships and engaged in the activities that connected them to one another were the public places of the street, places doubly familiar for the women who went out in the regular course of their work as servants.

On a day-to-day basis the places most frequented were the tavern or corner store. Both served equally well as casual gathering points where people went for talk and drink, as well as to buy groceries. Each sold foodstuffs and supplies, reputedly "at exaggerated prices," as well as rough liquor by the drink. Taverns, often situated handily at the entrance to a cortiço, such as the one on the rua do Rezende in 1879, offered tenants credit as a way of encouraging – or obliging – them to remain at a given cortiço rather than moving on to another. Most frequently men met there. Fewer women did so, although buying some needed household item could become a welcome pretext to linger. One old servant woman who nightly balanced an enormous tub of swill on her head for emptying at the beach had the "habit of visiting vendas" for a nightly drink. We know from a case heard in 1870 that a young black woman used the store run by a Portuguese on the Campo de Sant'Anna as her rendezvous. There she could leave her water can, to be filled later at the nearby spigot, free then to walk for a while with her soldier.[10] After work men drank cheap brandy at open air taverns, while women and children could chat at open windows or meet outside for talk until it was time to go to bed.[11]

Time spent at the tavern set locals at odds with neighborhood inspectors and police, heightening their sense of fellowship. Not only did taverns not close by ten or eleven o'clock as licensing rules required, but they drew attention by their sometimes boisterous goings-on. Customers – according to police – "provoked disorder with their rowdiness and obscene words called out in loud voices." "People of all social positions," "of doubtful morality," "even slaves and suspect persons," gathered inside, spilling out onto the street.[12] One store owner, who sold "odds and ends," cleverly attracted crowds by having musicians play in his store, although, he assured the local inspector, never beyond nine at night. Sometimes a cortiço sheltered within its gates a tavern that thus succeeded in remaining open "day and night," such as the one in the "great cortiço" on the rua General Caldwell in 1876.[13] One public health official alleged in 1882 that, on any given day, of a population of 300,000 some 60,000 persons drank "cheap alcohol" at one or another of the city's 2,812 taverns.[14] Whether the mood of the drinking often became mean or vicious or remained merely noisy, we do not know. For the official, the bare fact of so many persons in taverns apparently made the drinking seem excessive and thus unwholesome, while the tavern could be, at least for some, a local meeting place.

And there were other settings. Cortiços supplied services that strengthened the poor's self-reliance or enabled larger cortiços to function as nearly self-contained entities. At the back could be found an array of workshops: "tailors, shoemakers, cabinet makers, carpenters, painters, tinsmiths, as well as an eating house."[15] Skilled tenants thus had cheap quarters in which to work their trade, perhaps avoiding the obligatory city licenses, while other tenants could call on someone they knew for needed repairs. On a smaller scale, the kiosks or circular stands that sold matches, coffee, or, allegedly, cheap alcohol at busy street corners and on city squares provided casual spots where a working man on his way home might stop, perhaps to meet briefly with a servant out on errands.[16]

The church – or better, the open place in front of and around the church – rivaled the tavern or corner store as a second meeting place. Unlike the tavern, though, the space near the church was dominated by the presence of women. Young women held rendezvous here with their lovers. The herb seller, consulted about illness, prescribed the necessary ingredients for cure or to induce abortion.[17] Here at the "market of amulets" women bought all manner of wax or wooden figures and saints' images, as well as amulets. Manuela, vividly sketched in the account of the French resident Charles Expilly in 1863 as the slave woman too spirited to be kept as a chambermaid and sent instead to sell fruit on the street, went to the market to buy new charms. Replacing the old ones, which with time had lost their powers, and pausing to enter the church where she lit three candles and dipped the charms in holy water, Manuela could then believe she had repelled the malevolent influences that would interfere with her intention to find again the attractive foreigner to whom she hoped to sell the luscious peaches she had carefully saved just for him. Most numerous at the market were the wet-nurses who could buy amulets for themselves or for the babies they nursed against the recognized dangers of illness.[18]

Throughout the year and mostly at night, in streets and praças accessible to those who boarded in the center, countless stalls offered their entertainments: penny betting on little wooden horses that moved mechanically around a circle, a game "similar to roulette" with its "hope of riches," or an acrobatic performance, or a balloon ride. City authorities had once attempted to ban the "circulos" on grounds that they corrupted the morals of children, "as well as taking up the time of slaves who, leaving the houses of their masters, pass hours there in harm to themselves."[19] But the gambling proved too persistently popular and the police gave up. Besides diversion, these stalls offered occasion and venue for meetings, spontaneous or anticipated.

Friendship and support, loyalty, or affability found expression in more privately conducted relationships. When in 1906 Dona Maria Coelho announced to her servant that she must go some place else to deliver her child, Etelvina promptly collected the wages owing her and left. Rather than staying alone in the room she rented, however, she went a few days later to the shack belonging to a friend on whom she could rely. This was Pedro, a factory worker and poor himself, who provided her with companionship and a place to stay. What she insisted was a miscarriage, others accused, but never proved, as infanticide. Pedro saw her through the ordeal, saying that she had arrived at his place with a "stomach ache," for which he had gone in search of medicine. When he returned, she was sitting up in bed and showed him a "cloth with a little dried blood" – proof of miscarriage, he said. The story that she had aborted or even committed infanticide, he later testified, was a lie "spread by someone wanting vengeance against her."[20] Friendship also made the difference for the slave woman Honorata, forced in the 1860s and early 1870s to divide her time between domestic work and prostitution, who did not always succeed in earning as much as her owner demanded. The coachman who often took her to and from her "encounters," and who had witnessed the reprimands she got for being late or for bringing back too little money, helped her avoid those scenes by loaning her money to make up her *jornal*, the earnings she owed her mistress. Another man who slept with Honorata and knew that she was virtually forced to turn over all she earned, kept back some money until they were alone, intending it, he said, just for her. A regular relationship developed with another client who followed her from place to place "finding her wherever she worked," except at one house where, he said, "because of my color," he could not go.[21] Some women kept a more solitary existence. For her part, the free woman Maria Francisca da Conceição felt none of the gestures of friendship that sustained Honorata. As a seamstress in 1876, Maria Francisca worked first in one place, then another with the result that no tie of affection or reasons for friendship linked her to a neighborhood. In fact, while at one job, she could say she actively "did not get on with the neighbors."[22] Antonia Mendez and Salvador Barbará perhaps found added solidarity in the fact that both had migrated from Spain. Support among recent immigrants showed plainly enough, causing Brazilians to refer contemptuously to the "commendable effort with which the Portuguese [immigrants] among us mutually protect themselves."[23]

Against a background of familiar places and in the company of equals, women chanced more audacious projections of personality than their work as servants allowed. A prized gold chain, a long bright-colored shawl, or a pair of fine slippers conveyed a poor woman's sense of glamour or herself as a sexual person. A turban of soft white muslin or splendorous red silk owed its inspiration to Africa.[24] If the elite's standard for feminine beauty consisted of "three white things: skin, teeth, and hands," and of "three black things: hair, eyelashes, and eyebrows," the often dark-skinned poor understood differently. In the course of testifying for the "divorce" that the former slaves Rufino Baleta and Henriqueta Maria da Conceição sought in 1857, Rufino declared that he thought his wife a "pretty black and of elegant stature."[25]

Yet no other expression of street life or collective identity rivaled the pre-Lenten celebration of carnaval, for no other engaged energies and imaginations as intensely as it did or revealed popular awareness so vividly. Beginning as scattered local actions then spreading to involve the entire city in revelries, carnaval burst the bounds of neighborhood to become a truly popular demonstration. Rather than bonds of kin or ties between friends or neighbors that belonged with the cortiço, tavern, or parish churchyard, carnaval affirmed a looser but more encompassing unity among the city's poor. By jest directed at their social betters, the poor set themselves apart.

Early in the century, carnaval had consisted of the *entrudo*, literally meaning to mock or poke fun at. Through the streets ran persons gaily throwing wax balls filled with perfume, water or vinegar; they hurled flour from paper cones or sloshed water from wooden bowls.

Plate 9 The *entrudo* at Carnaval, 1820s

Revelers made light of the socially expected sober and respectable demeanor with their masquerades as clowns or fools or dancers.[26] The entrudo exempted no one from its pranks, so that the usually aloof respectables could expect to be surprised with a sprinkling of flour or a spray of perfumed water. Nor did it exclude anyone from being prankster. All could join – blacks, whites, slaves, free, women, men – this rowdy display that made rude fun of public order and proper conduct.

Out of the play and license came colorful inversions of rank, race, gender, and respectability. Masks or disguises were first introduced into Rio de Janeiro carnaval from France in 1834. "Grave or jovial, made of fine wax or cardboard," they depicted animals – a cat or pig face, a parrot's beak – or false noses. Soon people appeared in *fantasias* or fancy dress, imaginative and often outrageous, a playing out of fantasy more than an accurate imitation. Traditional carnaval personalities included the devil, the harlot, clowns or knaves, a marquis or feudal lord. The poor, and blacks among them, masqueraded as colonial aristocrats got up in garish satin and

powdered wigs. Prominently by the century's end, men, freed briefly
from the onerous burden of their own authority, could parade as
women, typically harlots or brides. They could even buy false "ladies'
breasts in order to dress up as women." By 1911, poking fun at
religious orders was taken seriously enough so that to dress as a priest
was prohibited.[27] The lavish clothes made of "wool and fine silk
muslin" with "flowers in her hair and gloves," clearly in violation of
appropriate servant dress, could plausibly, according to opposing
witnesses, indicate that Honorata was either a prostitute or dressed in
a carnaval fantasia.[28] In the ambiguity that was carnaval, women
could appear in bold dress and provocative disguise without seriously
compromising modesty or respectability. Disguise made mockery of
hierarchical order by rendering the usual guides for identifying and
responding to others – demeanor, skin color, and dress – hopelessly
ambiguous.[29]

Carnaval filled the three days before Lent, and for those three days,
carnaval particularly meant no work. Such a holiday profoundly
reversed the poor's customary long labors. Slave masters could
impose constant work to maintain order even when the rhythm of
work might have permitted a break. And because of the free poor's
acute need to work in order to earn barely enough to live, they
labored long days on end. A saint's day now and then or a few hours
respite on Sunday was as much as most usually could hope for.
Certainly for servants Sundays and holidays often gave more work
than rest. But during carnaval, the usual routines of housework,
cooking, or caring for children turned into confusion as servants
joined the revelers. Even servants usually restricted to the house were
permitted or contrived some time out on the street. Three whole days
without work, three whole days of open disorder struck at the center
of a world that took the relation between master and slave and,
therefore, of labor as its paradigm for social order.

During carnaval, the poor declared the street to be *their* territory,
publicly and triumphantly displacing the conventional distinctions of
house and street. For the poor and the servants for whom the patterns
of work and daily life routinely belonged to the street, carnaval did
not invert the ordinary but rather celebrated and exaggerated it. By
their celebrations, common people bestowed on their way of life a
legitimacy usually denied it. They converted familiar streets into
festive and glittering places by decorating them with tree branches,
flags, and lanterns suspended from posts. The entrudo ridiculed
ordinarily perceived street dangers with the play of water syringes

and flour bombs. People jammed into the city's commercial center or gathered for fireworks in the Largo da Constituição, or cheered the acrobat who "went through the streets performing true feats." Brass bands, individuals in fancy dress, or full scale processions heightened with more movement, more color, and more sound the usual commotion of the street.[30] Not in the street to toil in the service of others, for three days the poor ruled by their brazen, gaudy presence. For common people, then, the street remained street, only more so – exaggeratedly, excessively so.

For their betters also, carnaval did not disrupt but rather affirmed the established understandings of house. Wealthier persons "more secluded" – the phrase indicated privilege – retained their suspicions about the polluting street. They watched processions from upstairs windows or vestibules, protected from jarring or unruly crowds. Not only did they not join street festivities, the rich conducted their own celebrations, but indoors. At hotels or at private clubs, "the best families" played hosts to luxurious balls where in sumptuous clothes they masqueraded safely among those they could count as equals or near equals despite their masks. Even a middling class managed a modest ball with supper for "only 90 cents although it included a carafe of wine and as much bread as desired."[31] From behind the wooden lattice-work that covered windows or second-story verandas or from vestibules, from, that is, the safety of the house, some squirted water syringes at unsuspecting passersby. At the borders between house and street, the protected attacked the street.[32]

Rio de Janeiro's elite did more, however, than simply remove themselves from carnaval's outdoor madness. Some sounded a clamor of opposition that rang in yearly counterpoint to popular carryings-on. Their opposition is telling both as a measure of the threat some perceived in carnaval and, because such opposition failed, as a measure of popular determination that disorder should have its day. Opponents disdained carnaval "with all its excesses, noise and vulgar display." It was "the brazen season . . . a waste of time and money," a time of "flimsy costumes and garish processions." Those who would ban it saw participants as "idle vaga-bonds," or worse as the "most wanton and disreputable class of people in the city," who performed "indecencies of dress and conduct."[33] The bishop found grave fault with carnaval's pranksters. The Holy Virgin Mary, "as everyone knows," he preached in 1877, "was ignobly and sacrilegiously desecrated in effigy through the streets and squares of this court city during carnaval. . . ."[34] For a portion of Rio de Janeiro's citizenry carnaval not only did not transform the assumed dangers of the street into harmless gaiety, but rather gave license to the crude, the immoral, the impious, that is, to the anarchic. To them, carnaval's threat seemed clear.[35]

Carnaval jest was deemed threatening enough to elicit action that would punish revelers. Throughout the nineteenth century and into the next, opponents identified the entrudo as the real trouble and attempted to suppress it. City regulations had censured the entrudo since as early as the 1830s. At mid-century police had "employed energy . . . [in] a persistent campaign against the entrudo." In 1853 city authorities banned the entrudo with the penalty that "any person who plays will incur a fine of $2 to $7 or two to eight days in jail." The punishment aimed particularly at slaves who automatically got eight days in jail "in case their masters do not order them punished at the jail with a hundred lashes." Local inspectors received authority to confiscate any wax balls they spotted. The ordinance further prohibited anyone from being on the street between ten o'clock at night and four o'clock in the morning or appearing on the street "with a mask." The chief of police requested an additional one hundred police "for the days of the entrudo."[36] That the ban failed to curb the season's yearly excesses testified to popular strengths. In 1887, authorities again warned that the entrudo, "so prejudicial to public welfare, opposed to civilization and the good habits of the population," must be "extinguished," although in 1893, the newly formed republican government, probably with astute self-interest, by decree approved "in the appropriate season the entertainment called 'carnaval.'" By 1907 police again sent out circulars to prevent appearance of the "pernicious game of entrudo." Year after year city councils issued ordinances until the prohibition itself acquired a carnavelesque quality of self-caricature,[37] while the mischief and masquerade continued. To that extent, common people and street life did have their day.

For all its exuberance, carnaval was not spontaneous. Joking and exaggeration were impossible without awareness and reflection.[38] By their serious jest, working people expressed their keen awareness of being accorded "the least favored" place, and instructed others in how to envisage that lower rank. By their playful turnings of customary order, they potentially disrupted order. By their gleeful breaches of the gestures of deference and obedience, common people revealed that their usual behavior was not, could not have been simply authentic. Carnaval presented – and those who ordinarily exercised authority accurately understood – that popular awareness. In fantasy, allegory, pranks, music, and exaggeration the poor played out the tensions between house and street.

As an antidote to disorder, Ash Wednesday brought carnaval starkly to an end and marked the commencement of the austere Lenten period. The word carnaval, derived from old Italian, meant also "the putting away of flesh," initiation of a fast in anticipation of Easter's feast.[39] The time dedicated to revelry had a fixed end beyond which carnaval's excesses could not continue. So contained, any real threat to order appeared extinguished. Carnaval provided a safe time, without lasting danger for the rich and without true accountability for the poor.

As a time out of time, extraordinary and strictly circumscribed, carnaval was but a brief counterpoint to the persisting concerns of everyday life. Never solely dependents in service to their patrões, servant women shared with the poor not only the festivities of the street, but also the ordinary conduct of family life. They too formed families: took lovers or husbands, experienced pregnancy, and raised children. Occasionally we can glimpse them as daughters or sisters. Although they wished to duplicate the culturally approved arrangements of family life, poverty restricted their ability to do so or tempered their reasons for trying. Instead, they fitted traditional patterns to the circumstances of poverty and domestic service. To bring into relief what was distinctive about the personal lives of servant women, it is necessary to set them against the background of formal definitions and conventional expectations.

The ideal of family presumed a patriarchal, extended family based on legally prescribed marriage. Thus family and marriage served as keystone to the entire social edifice buttressed by the supporting institutions of canon and civil law. Legal (as well as moral) status was accorded exclusively to those marriages celebrated by a Catholic priest and "by words [said] while present at the door of the church," and only when all qualifications to marry had been met.[40] Performed as a holy sacrament according to Church ritual, marriage nevertheless drew much of its meaning from secular law. Above all, because it determined heirs, marriage controlled the division and distribution of family property. Rather than leaving such matters to individual discretion, the state retained authority over conjugal property and inheritance through the law. By refusing full testamentary freedom the law determined that family and property should remain inextricably joined: at death two thirds of a person's property passed first to descendent, then ascendent, or finally to collateral kin. Only the remaining one third could a person dispose of freely.[41] If no written agreement was contracted prior to the marriage (irrevocable once the marriage was consummated) stipulated otherwise, a couple's property was held communally.[42] Only if no prescribed heirs existed, could all property be assigned to the surviving spouse or to any other designated heir. In these ways the law insured that property would be preserved first among blood kin, thereby protecting and perpetuating family position.

Since marriage determined access to inherited property, the rules of marriage had been designed to prevent unions that would produce unsuitable heirs and thus divert family property to a lesser line. Because women can hardly deny maternity as men can deny paternity, marriage rules necessarily and particularly restricted women. Women who conducted socially "inconvenient" affairs risked producing inappropriate heirs. By that calculus, virginity at marriage proved that a woman had not produced and was not then pregnant with an illegitimate or unwanted heir. The same logic protected a woman from unwillingly having to marry an inappropriate seducer. Instead, as compensation against her lost virginity a woman could demand that her seducer endow her, enabling her to arrange a proper match. Since 1603 the law had stipulated that the dowry be "arbitrated by a judge, according to the rank, income, and status of her father," or "double what she merited, according to the rank of her person" if she were a minor seduced by her own guardian.[43] Turned around, the same law protected men against women of lower station from using their sexually compromised state to exploit unduly a socially superior seducer, for a woman could not sue for more than her own familial rank merited. The law also regarded women as sexually responsible persons – not merely seduced, but seducers. If as a minor a woman slept with a man or married without parental permission and thus denied to her parents their rightful authority over property that would pass to any eventual children born from that union, she could be fully disinherited. If, however, she married "better and more honorably" than her parentage warranted, thus improving her family's position, she could lose only a part of her inheritance.[44] Through marriage, social position and property remained securely interlaced. Those at least were the stated presumptions regarding marriage.

In the actual worlds of Rio de Janeiro servant women the prescriptions for marriage and family operated somewhat differently.

Most servant women were not married. In the early 1870s, as many as two thirds to three quarters were single, while roughly only a third to a fifth were married or widowed. There were variations, of course. The overwhelming majority of live-in servants in the parish of São Cristovão – 95 percent – were single, while of those who lived independently only 53 percent were single. While the number of married and widowed women among servants was considerably fewer than for heads of households in that parish, of whom a majority were married, their number did not differ substantially from the general population (Tables 9 and 10).[45]

Reasons that can explain why most of the population failed to marry are easy enough to assemble. Requirements of eligibility conspired to delay if not wholly defeat attempts to marry. Those from distant parishes or from abroad, those without known parents or whose whereabouts were lost, or those of uncertain birthplace or date could barely construct the necessary proofs of eligibility. The burden of proof fell heavily on the poor who were more likely to be illegitimate, who most lacked the literary or social skills to arrange the proper documents, and who could ill afford the fees, official and unofficial, that encouraged authorities to copy out the pages of certificates. Exemptions could be granted, not as a right, but as a favor depending on the individual case.[46] Although the church, in order to encourage the poor to marry was empowered to "dispense freely," freely apparently did not mean without charge, for parish records carefully noted each dispensation together with its fee. The requisite 16 or 17 stamps and fees could cost as much as $35.[47] Anyone who married clandestinely or permitted others to do so risked fines and prison.[48]

Ironically, in this regard African-born slaves found the qualifications for marriage simplified, for the Church threw up its hands trying to imagine how slaves might secure from Africa the papers that so characteristically belonged to Iberian culture and language. An African thought to have married in "his land" according to local rites – rites so dissimilar to Christian practice as not to count – the Church concluded, could receive permission to marry without the usual proofs.[49] Africans, their own religious practices dismissed, could nevertheless marry only in the Catholic Church, and only after first demonstrating rudimentary knowledge of the faith, surely a gesture of compliance more than of changed beliefs.[50] Those who professed a faith other than Catholicism – principally immigrants – faced severe discrimination until 1861 when the state finally agreed to recognize in their civil aspects unions performed in other churches. The requirement that persons younger than 21 years supply notarized permission from parents posed a hardship for the free poor who wanted to marry but could not name or locate parents, while slaves of whatever age could marry only with express permission from their masters.[51] In 1906 proportionately more persons were married or had once been married than in 1872, owing perhaps to changes in the law that permitted civil marriage beginning in 1890.[52] Even so, about half of all persons of marriageable age in Rio de Janeiro were still counted as single (Table 10).

What is most striking is not that so few servant women married, but that, faced with the obstacles, so many did. Seemingly for the poor without substantial property to manage, marriage, entailing its web of legal responsibilities and restrictions, lists of abuses and redresses, or inheritance disputes, would hardly seem worth the bother. On the contrary, it appears that marriage, precisely because it bore implications for both property and respectability, mattered profoundly, as the poor made clear. The former slaves Henriqueta Maria da Conceição and Rufino Maria Baleta keenly understood, and with careful accounting, that property occupied a central and disputed place in their marriage. They even differed over the buying of Rufino's freedom. In order that she and Rufino could be joined "in legitimate marriage," – as well as "obeying the impulse of her heart," she added – Henriqueta claimed she had paid for his manumission from slavery. Rufino insisted that he had purchased his own freedom with money he had saved, although he acknowledged giving the money to Henriqueta because while "still a slave he did not want to keep money with him" whereas she, already freed, could safely present it to Rufino's owner in payment for his freedom. Once married, Rufino regarded that Henriqueta's turning over half of what she earned to him as simply fulfilling her obligation to her husband according to what he termed the "law of the whites" whereby "half of all that a wife had belonged to her husband." Henriqueta did not dispute the point, but required that it apply equally. Rufino should work, she insisted, with half of what he earned going to her "in order that the law of the whites could be justly observed." Despite his talk about "communal property," all their expenses, she charged, came from her half of their earnings. She said he even "poked about in the drawers, keeping what money he found." Together they had nevertheless produced enough property for a legal separation to be necessary, while without considerations of property Henriqueta could simply have left. In 1857 after two years of marriage, Henriqueta was awarded a separation and the "right to half their goods."[53]

Although marriage functioned to regulate inherited property, unmarried parents did not necessarily ignore concerns over inheritance. Such parents could assure illegitimately born children a legal claim to their property by the notarized act of recognition. One poor couple, who continued to live together although they remained unmarried, recognized both their children in 1880. A mother frequently recorded recognition of her children without naming the father, enabling them to inherit only from her, as did Camilla Josefina Voituron in 1864. Less often a father did so. In 1871, four years after his daughter Amelia's birth, Francisco Ferreira da Silva legally recognized her. Francisco thought it necessary to note that the unnamed mother had been a free woman, indicating that Amelia was therefore born free (the child's color must have suggested that her mother could have been a slave) and qualified to inherit property.[54]

By the 1860s and 1870s the traditional meanings of property, virginity, and marriage had altered: marriage now guarded not only property but also virtue. No longer did society treat copulation or seduction principally as a threat to family lineage and property. In a more complex, somewhat more fluid society, seduction violated the woman herself and her well-being. A woman's virginity, having once dispelled apprehensions about inappropriate heirs, by mid-nineteenth century also implied virtue, a moral eligibility to marry. Seduction that robbed a woman of her honor thus required marriage as compensation, and the law excused a man from marrying a woman who was not a virgin when he seduced her. By 1870 the law made no mention of a "suitable" spouse or of proper "quality" or "status," but rather understood marriage as a panacea "capable of remedying all irregularities between a man and a woman. . . ."[55] Failing marriage, a compulsory dowry compensated as it always had. In lieu of either, the law imposed a fine – a gesture as futile in righting traditional concerns over lineage as it was in compensating lost honor. The newly written 1890 criminal code eliminated all compensatory measures and instead punished seduction with prison.[56] The completed shift away from family and property to virtue and punishment left the concerns of both rich and poor women legally unresolved.

Despite the law's changed emphasis, in practice the old ways persisted – or at least poor women could hope they would. Women with few resources, but "honest," bargained hard for marriage either with their virtue or with a meager dowry. Sometimes one purchased the other. In the early 1900s, both Alsira Felisberta da Conceição's and Angelica Barboza Ribeiro's appeals to custom succeeded. At the start things had not gone well for the dark-skinned Alsira. In reply to her mother's warning that Antonio Cespedes Barbosa Sobrinho, a telegrapher, would never marry her, Alsira defended herself and him, saying that "he said he does not distinguish colors." On the matter of race Alsira believed herself safe. She had not counted on Antonio's being already married, however, so that when, her virginity surrendered, her parents insisted on some "way to repair the evil he had done," some solution other than marriage had to be found. Finally Antonio "proposed to endow their daughter." Satisfied, Alsira and her parents accepted.[57] Angelica's case turned out differently. Against her own insistence and the urgings by her father, brother, and "others" that João Cardoso de Albuquerque, a stonecutter, should repair the damage of having deflowered her by marrying her, João countered that she had not been a virgin, and "for this reason he did not want to marry her." He conceded he would marry her if a medical examination showed her recently deflowered. The physician's report (the examination had been performed in the "full light of day") supported Angelica and on 14 September 1910, the wedding hurriedly took place.[58]

Not all women who at the turn of the century pressed their hopes for marriage did so with effect. Although Olympio Gomes da Silva acknowledged deflowering Laura da Cruz Almeida the night they attended a dance together at his sister's house in the spring of 1909, contesting neither her virginity nor his duty to marry her, he would postpone marriage, he said, until he had "money to set them up." Laura's father, a laborer, insisted on an immediate ceremony. Certainly for Laura marriage presented the solution, for neither Olympio nor her father, who lived "in a state of abject poverty," could sponsor the dowry adequate to attract any other husband.[59] Similarly Tiburcia Sebastiana da Conceição's charge of seduction against Manoel Afonso in 1909 came to naught despite a favorable medical examination and her father's urgings. Described as a "person who lives in a state of much poverty," the father could not endow his daughter, and without a dowry the "black and robust" Tiburcia's prospects for marriage dimmed.[60] Although in the end Laura and Tiburcia failed to arrange either marriages or dowries, they had proceeded with the reasonable expectation that custom would serve them and that marriage, never distinct from concerns over property, was the logical goal of decent but poor women.

Besides protecting and distributing property, marriage bestowed family name and signified connection to others – that is, marriage provided a persuasive social identity. Surrounding the unpropertied as well with its aura of stability and respectability, marriage mattered. Again, Rufino Maria Baleta, in 1857, thought himself justified in reprimanding his wife who had jeopardized their appearance as a decent married couple by going out "on the street at night, returning at ten or sometimes eleven o'clock," to attend "dances and diversions" with her friend, behavior he said that was "ugly and inappropriate in a woman as virtuous as she."[61] The image of respectability that Rufino guarded, another used as ammunition: in the hearing of several neighbors one woman in 1870 meant to end a street quarrel with the parting shot, "who are you to argue with me? I am a married woman."[62] Respectability through marriage was a currency worth acquiring. And as Antonia Mendez and others knew, unions that approximated marriage could similarly confer legitimacy.

Although valued and imitated, conventional notions of marriage and family were not the only measure of family life among the poor.[63] In the personal lives that servant women conducted the reality was more varied. Even a partial outline of the kinds of families they maintained is worthwhile, not only for dispelling the supposed isolation of their lives, but in suggesting something of the emotional tenor of their lives, and in recording the adaptations they made.[64]

Servants frequently formed families based on informal unions. The seamstress Rita de Jesus, a former slave born in Mozambique, was described as the *companheira* or common law wife of Antonio do Espirito Santo and listed in the 1870 census as living in the tenement on the Praça de Dom Pedro I. In another family, the unmarried Antonia da Costa lived with Bernardo José da Costa, also single (coincidently each took as surname their African birthplace, the Costa da Mina or Mina Coast) and their son Bernardo. Similarly, Bemvindo and his woman Marcelina Correa Buena, both given as single, and their two children comprised another family in the parish of São Cristovão. Households that included a single man and woman, near in age, and children who seemingly lived as a family but who shared no common name and for whom the census taker mentioned no connecting relationship remain a puzzle.[65] Partnerships not sanctioned by either church or civil law, perhaps not known about even by employers if a woman kept details of her personal life secret, may not have been recorded on household census lists. In São Cristovão in 1870, only two servant women lived in explicitly noted consensual unions, but if we include those who lived in households where probable partners can be identified, then they number as many as 49, or about 5 percent of all servant women in the parish (Table 9).

Sometimes individuals, each unmarried and with children of their own, joined to form one family. In a room at the Mauá tenement in 1870, the laundress Euphrasia Maria da Conceição and her two children lived with a single man and his young son and the two orphaned children the couple had recently taken in. A widow, Libania Maria [Encarnação?] Flores, with three children had combined her family with that of a widower and his two sons.[66] We can plausibly conclude that besides rearing children, such couples joined to meet economic needs or give comfort and companionship. There was probably something of each motive in the union of two former slaves, Felicianna Cathirina Goze and Joze Antonio Pinto da Costa, who in their sixties continued to work, and who by then were too old to beget children.[67]

More commonly servants maintained families as single mothers with their children. In São Cristovão, at least one fifth of all single domestics who lived on their own had children with them (Table 9). That parish registers recorded one third of all babies baptized in 1884 as illegitimate gives a rough indication of how frequently unmarried women in fact bore and reared children. And often more than one. Among the 47 slave and poor women who entered the city's charity maternity ward in 1881 only two had married. Of the rest, 33 had previously borne at least one other child.[68] In 1870 Candida Roza da Silva, a seamstress and 42 years old, headed her own household on the rua do Bomfim with five children all of whom worked, including the daughter who was also a seamstress. Another seamstress, the 30 year-old Guilhermina d'Souza Machado, was mother to her own two sons, whom she managed to send to school, as well as a third child not her own. The domestic and "poor woman" Paula Maria Barreto lived with her four children, as did another single woman, Maria Jacintha de Nazaret, whose youngest child bore a surname distinct from that of the other three, suggesting the child had a different father. The widowed laundress, Engracia Maria da Conceição, who died at the age of 56 just as the census was being conducted, had lived on the rua dos Lazaros with her own 12-year-old daughter, a granddaughter of 14 years, and her 19-year-old nephew.[69]

Within larger households where they worked and lived, servants sometimes had children or grandchildren present with them. Domestic labor, more than field or factory work, enabled women to keep children with them. Children might play at the fountains while their mothers scrubbed and dried laundry, or out on errands a woman, her shawl tied loosely around her hips, gently cradled her baby in its folds as she walked.[70] Four generations of servant women had stayed together in Dona Leonor's household, although by 1874 when Olympia was ten years old her great-grandmother Quitérita had been dead for some time. Even young children could be put to work doing some small bit of housework, so that the African-born Maria, 60 years old and a domestic had kept with her a daughter and an 11-year-old granddaughter who themselves both worked as domestics. Another family preferred that their two servants, cook and house maid, should be mother and daughter, perhaps a way to encourage house servants to remain after abolition. Not all employers saw advantage in their servants' children, so that one slave woman who in 1881 contracted to work off the price of her freedom agreed to work a longer time at a lower salary for the right to keep her "infant on her hip."[71] In 1870 children accompanied at least 7 percent of São Cristovão's live-in servant women (Table 9). The burdens of being a single parent were perhaps eased in the context of a larger household. As parents these women became responsible in their own right toward young who depended on them, who learned from them how to act toward others and how to raise families of their own.

Similarly, even the slave women who lived as domestics in their masters' houses might nevertheless claim family of their own. Carolina, a chambermaid, and her husband David, the cook, were listed in 1870 as a married couple among the domestic slaves at the city mansion of Henrique Mangeon. The hired slave servant Delfina had a husband living apart from her in another household, perhaps separated by the owner's decision and not by choice and perhaps visited whenever possible, but differently important for not being daily present. As a single mother, Marianna had two children with her, each with different surnames. One household recorded their slave Carolina as having with her a daughter "not yet baptized," for whom they gave no name and merely indicated her age as being "younger than seven years." The slave woman Josepha had with her her young daughter Florinda who had been baptized, "as if [born] of a free womb."[72] Because households often neglected to list full information for dependents, particularly slaves, and family relationships were not usually stated but must be inferred, other ties of kinship almost certainly existed that cannot confidently be recovered.

The readily conjured image of servants as wholly isolated in the houses of their patrões requires qualification, for even the women who lived without men or children of their own did not necessarily reside without kin. Occasionally a sister or brother, a parent or grandparent was present. Such was the 16-year-old black Amelia Carolina do Soccorro who in 1870 lived at the Mauá tenement with her three brothers and sisters and their grandmother, a former slave, contributing her labor as a seamstress to their household. Probate records for the estate of Anna Maria da Conceição show that the young slave girl, Julia, separated from her mother and "not knowing how to do a single thing," was for two years unsuccessfully rented from house to house as a domestic. She had nearly used up the time allotted for earning the price of freedom owed to her dead mistress's estate when her father appeared. He "took charge of her," paying the nine months of wages still owing so that in 1859 Julia might be freed.[73] Even where a servant lived without ties to her own kin, she might live among families of her own kind. São Cristovão households included among their dependents some 27 slave and 30 agregado families, and in extensive households sometimes more than one. For the other servants present, family relationships among those their equal could occupy a customary place in their experience. To some extent they could witness or participate in the exchanges that made family life and kinship among them important.[74]

At the same time, however, any rendering of family life must recognize that slaves and the poor were less able to control the circumstances of their lives, enduring more than their share of separations. Despite the felt hardships, we can discern the commitment with which some preserved family ties and something of the deep frustration that poverty or slavery imposed. Florença da Silva dictated to a paid letter writer, barely literate himself to judge by the spelling and grammar, the message she sent her daughter Balbina in April 1862. Both women were slaves when Florença, learning that Balbina belonged to a new master and where she was, sent to reassure her that all her efforts went toward securing Balbina's freedom: ". . . and so I write to you giving you my news and to tell you that I am struggling for your liberty for this I write also to your owner on this occasion." "Everything is on your behalf," Florença pledged. "Nothing more do I have to say, only that I am your mother who cares for you, much, much." Taking for granted their separation, Florença would act instead to overcome the even more stubborn fact of her daughter's bondage. Confident that through their efforts a better future awaited them, she reminded Balbina to treat her master well so that eventually he would agree to her freedom. Tenderly she affirmed a mother's love. At the same time though, Florença chided her daughter for not answering an earlier letter. This time she insisted on a prompt response, "for I am old and I am looking for you and not you for me." Nothing kept Balbina from replying, she assumed, if she just would. Theirs was not, then, a perfect relationship. Florença acknowledged it as such, nonetheless constant in her affections. Besides what the letter described, the act of sending a letter to a daughter announced that Florença was not wholly alone in the world. She claimed a place among kin. Not merely a slave who belonged to a master, she was a mother with reason to send her daughter a letter.[75]

A longer separation had parted the slaves Maria Lourindo da Conceição and her husband Casemiro from their daughter Victoriana when they were sold to new owners in the far south of Brazil. Thirty years later, in 1860, her husband by then dead and she herself freed, Maria Lourindo searched for her daughter. "Possessing a small fortune," she proudly wanted to free her daughter or perhaps her grandchildren – she had no way of knowing what course Victoriana's life had taken.[76] After long years apart, mother and daughter could not be persons known to one another, important or comfortable figures in one another's daily lives, yet freedom and money meant for Maria Lourindo the chance to reestablish family ties, still durable and valued.

Through court records we can trace in greater detail the steps by which the free black Maria Anna de Souza do Bomfim affirmed family ties and acquired freedom for her daughter Felicidade. Mother and daughter were separated in Bahia in 1868 when Maria Anna came south to Rio de Janeiro and her daughter, then 20 years old, was sold separately. Soon after arriving, Maria Anna asked the Portuguese slave dealer Joaquim Antonio da Cunha Guimarães to find out where her daughter had been sold. Upon learning that Felicidade was in the mining town of Ouro Preto in the neighboring province of Minas Gerais, Maria Anna financed Guimarães' trip there to "buy her or by any other transaction secure her release," bring her to Rio, and "as the means became available to her," she would free her. Within a few months Guimarães sold Felicidade to Antonio Viêtas, a businessman with a warehouse in the central city. For nearly a year Felicidade lived with her mother on the rua da Saude, 146, while Maria Anna paid the monthly "rental" of 30 mil-réis, being installments on her daughter's purchase price. When for two months, Maria Anna failed to make the payments, Viêtas called Felicidade "to his power," suspending the permission he had granted for her to live in "company with her mother." At this point Maria Anna took action. Going to the police, she charged that Viêtas had "incarcerated" Felicidade and revoked the freedom already granted her. In the end the parties agreed out of court that the two women would pay the full purchase price, interest due, and expenses with their joint labor as "personal and domestic servants . . . for a period of three years . . . at the rate of 42 mil-réis per month." Viêtas, for his part, formally recognized Felicidade's freedom, not after receiving the full amount owed, but "from now on." Thus, after nearly two and a half years of determined effort, Maria Anna was reunited with her daughter when, on 27 March 1871, the municipal judge declared Felicidade free.[77]

Events that marked out the life cycles of all women, became accentuated for servant women, who like other poor women gave birth, faced illness, cared for children, or witnessed death without the resources available to wealthier women. Instead, they invented their own solutions and thus shaped a way of life. Although we do not know for the nineteenth or early twentieth centuries how many children a Brazilian woman bore, or the number of pregnancies, miscarriages, or still-births she might experience (nor do we possess reliable infant mortality rates), we can follow the experiences of individual women, culled from fragmentary evidence, to discover their troubles and how they coped.

Prominent among their cares were the serious matters of pregnancy and childbirth. While doctors might attend the deliveries at home of rich women, midwives assisted the births of women from all classes. At one time a black cross painted on the portal had indicated the house of a midwife where she could be sought. In nineteenth-century Rio de Janeiro, some like Madame Joanna Beau or Madame Cocural presented themselves as having diplomas in midwifery from Paris or training from the Rio de Janeiro Faculty of Medicine.[78] Unable to afford the expensive French ones, poor women had recourse to the numerous midwives who claimed no special training beyond experience. The several words in Portuguese for these unlicensed midwives – some were slaves – bespoke their common use: *curiosas* or *aparadeiras* and *comadres*. Alternatively women could choose to give birth at a Casa de Maternidade or maternity clinic. Madame Daure received at her maternity, in 1880, any from among the poor, "pensioners as well as slaves or free persons," where in "separate rooms" the women, it was promised, would get good care as long as they could pay the "low price."[79]

All women faced dangers in giving birth, but for poor women, already weakened by impaired health, inadequate diet or heavy work, the dangers of childbirth multiplied and increased the problems with which they were forced to cope. Breech birth, a ruptured uterus, septicemia – all presented grave risk. Infections after pregnancy sometimes produced coma and convulsions, then death. Other women faced the "cruel pain" inflicted by instrument births, 15 percent according to the records of two charitable maternity clinics in Rio in 1881.[80] The slave Euginia was sent in 1861 from domestic work in Rio de Janeiro to the plantation, "tired and needing rest." Despite bottles of cod liver oil and iron-fortified syrup, she died days after her daughter was born, not, it appeared, because of the birth itself but because of an "old illness" and a lingering fever. After five successful deliveries, the poor woman Emiliana, in 1869, lost her sixth child at birth. Still with milk and "being obliged to work in order to have the necessary subsistence," she set out 12 days later in heavy rain for the Santa Casa in search of a child to nurse for a fee. Within two weeks she fell ill. She likely owed her recovery from serious respiratory disease as much to the medicines as to the diet she received in hospital: chicken and eggs, certainly not the nourishment she could provide for herself. The doctor noted her weak constitution.[81] As for others, it was the consequences of poverty that had endangered their lives.

Poor women faced pregnancy and illness lacking hospitals or clinics geared to their needs. Certainly the conventional wisdom offered in ladies' journals did little more than mock their situations. Pregnant women, these writers cautioned, ought principally to eat "good meat, soup, bread, wine," avoiding heavy starches, and they should not sleep in unventilated rooms, especially those in low lying, humid areas. Moderate exercise was a good thing, provided a woman did not travel by tram or go up and down stairs much. Such counsel was useless for working women who relied on cheap and starchy foods, who lived in crowded, dank rooms, and who stood for long hours to cook for others or who carried heavy bundles of laundry for delivery. Almost certainly no servant woman remained in bed for seven days after giving birth as leisured women were encouraged to do.[82] Serious efforts began in the late 1870s to found a maternity hospital that would furnish poor women including slaves with the "indispensable cares and protections that among us are only the privilege of the wealthiest." Compelled to fulfill its traditionally established and generally ignored obligation to provide for the "well-being of the local poor," the Municipal Chamber operated a maternity ward that lasted for two short years from 1881 to 1883. Crowded in between infectious disease wards at the Casa de Saude on a narrow and thus congested and unhealthy street, the hospital allegedly drained public funds without effectively meeting women's needs.[83] Not until 1901 did Dr. Moncorvo Filho, long devoted to public health care, open his Institute of Protection and Infant Welfare with the aim of making basic medical care and advice available to the poor, especially to women and children, including free medical examinations during pregnancy and assistance with home deliveries.[84] Both more ambitious and more successful than their municipally sponsored predecessor, in the period from April 1904 to August 1905 the clinic's doctors saw some 606 patients, including colored and immigrant women, treated 72 women with gynecological problems, and assisted with nearly 300 deliveries.[85]

For women who wanted to terminate their pregnancies, abortion methods were "known and used" as doctors of the medical academy acknowledged in 1885.[86] Maria Roza da Silva, who counseled "home remedies" for "menstrual problems," suggested lavender tea sweetened with honey, or when something stronger was needed, black beans without salt, taken on an empty stomach. In one Rio de Janeiro parish, the local herb seller contributed his own recipe for a "purgative": epsom salts boiled in penna leaves, taken to create friction in the womb at the time of menstruation, or alternatively the citron herb, dried pennyroyal mint and garlic all crushed in sweet almond oil.[87] Presumably, for a price midwives could be persuaded to perform real abortions.

Women without other options who felt forced to decide that they could not care for a newborn child sometimes left it on the "wheel" at the Santa Casa de Misericórdia. Between 1859 and 1908 more than 17,000 Rio de Janeiro children were orphaned in this way. Occasionally a mother returned. After bearing a son, Alfredo, in July 1860, Marianna Vitorina da Vasconcellos became gravely ill and unable either to work to support him or care for him, she left him at the orphanage. When she recovered, however, she went back for her child. Afterwards, in order to "ease her conscience," as she said, she recognized Alfredo as legally her child.[88] Poor women, it was said, having anonymously left infants with the nuns at the Santa Casa, or slave women who were forced to do so by their masters, tried then to hire themselves there as wet-nurses hopeful of nursing their own child.[89]

Plate 10 A woman placing a child on the *Roda*, 1856

Besides confronting the dangers that pregnancy and childbirth occasioned, poor women more frequently than the better-off saw their newborn or young children die. And they died from conditions exacerbated by poverty, conditions poor women were largely helpless to alter.[90] Faulty diet or damp and unsanitary housing made the poor especially vulnerable to tuberculosis and dysentery, common causes of deaths among infants. In the late 1870s, doctors reacted with alarm at what they understood as an extremely high incidence of infant deaths.[91] Blacks and mulattos fell victim to tuberculosis in disproportionately high numbers both as children and as adults. Worsened by conditions that one doctor described as "excessive physical work . . . without necessary rest, without a restoring diet . . . in the fouled atmosphere of unhealthy houses and shops, dark, poorly ventilated . . . saturated with humidity, lacking in oxygen," tuberculosis spread. Parents could pass the disease on to their children. Doctors who assessed higher morbidity rates for slaves attributed them to the fact that slaves "are less well fed, clothed less well, and are treated with less care for their illnesses." One count for the period 1867 to 1871 showed that children, particularly infants several days to a month old, died from poor health or inadequate care more than from specifiable diseases. Out of 859 babies, some 755 died of "congenital weakness" before reaching one month. Tetanus and digestive illnesses caused other deaths, while abandoned infants commonly seemed to die of "aphtha" or thrush.[92] Nor did survival beyond infancy mean that a child possessed good health. A study conducted among children apprentices at the National Press and at the Mint in 1910 showed at least incipient tuberculosis among 70 percent of them.[93] Servant women who raised their own children did so against difficult odds. They could expect to know the pain of watching them die or the struggle of seeing them through illnesses.

When faced with death, the poor buried their own as best they could, and burying, like everything else the poor did was somewhat public. The Santa Casa performed funerals, including death certificate, coffin, and hearse, at a wide range of prices. A "first-class" funeral could be bought for $189, while an "eighth-class" funeral cost a fraction of that. For even less slaves could be buried in rented boxes. Of the city's five cemeteries, two public ones were reserved for slaves and the poor. The true outcasts without kin or neighbors or fellow workers to bury them, their bodies "found on the streets or on the beach," were deposited at the city necropolis.[94]

Grief, the constant presence of disease, or the varying stress of meeting daily problems with few material resources made feelings of insecurity or apprehension inevitable responses among the poor and servant women. Danger or distress required action to restore control or to ward off evil. In order to act, the poor drew from particular cultural constructions. To command the forces that could heal or protect or wreak revenge took initiatives that frequently involved the seeker in a direct relationship with a feiticeiro or practitioner of black magic, with a spiritualist, or in the company of others – with the full assembly of an Afro-Brazilian *candomblé* ceremony where one entered into a trance to receive the summoned spirit. Although the house of a spiritualist or the compound of a candomblé high priestess could not announce itself with visible signs or symbols, it was readily known to those who sought its rituals and the drums could be heard throughout a neighborhood.[95] There the feiticeiro could be found, on "one of those narrow and dirty streets in the Cidade Nova." Others practiced in "dirty rooms, walls painted with elephants and arrows, and herbs and dried alligator piled about" and, throughout, the smell of sweat. To such places, a slave mother and wet-nurse hurriedly went in search of advice or information that could reunite her with her own baby, taken from her lest she refuse milk to her mistress's child. On the street, a troop of women spiritualists conducted their business of offering consultations for a fixed price: Galdinha on the rua da Alfândega, the black Rosalina on the rua da America, or Zizenha Viúva on the rua Senhor de Matazinhos. In the early years of this century, the black Samuel, once a cook, went from house to house to do the "laying on of hands. . . ."[96] In lesser and more individual ways, people sought the forces that would intervene against danger or influence personal relationships in some desired way by wearing amulets. The *figa*, of African origin, promised health or longevity, the pomegranate offered fertility, while a silver cylinder guarded against bad luck or a heart aroused by passion. Amulets roughly fashioned from bits of corn husk, necklaces of shells, animal teeth, cloves of garlic, or olive pits were put on children as protection against illness.[97]

Practices that relied first on personal initiative in order to evoke the forces that could intervene brought at least the semblance of action and control in a world where poverty and dependence rendered stability precarious or at best temporary. Even there the poor found themselves set against the larger culture that expressly viewed belief in the spirit world with distaste or saw it as harmful. In 1876, municipal authorities refused permission to Adela Neval who wanted to give "consultations of magnetism, spiritism and somnambulism" in her house on the rua Gonçalves Dias. "Besides the immorality which presides at these consultations," they ruled, "they are instead of being useful, prejudicial to those who have recourse to them." Yet police, who themselves perhaps believed in the powers of spiritists or at least feared interfering, could be trusted to leave them alone.[98]

It would be a grave misreading of the experiences of servant women to slight the private lives they conducted. Diverting, boisterous times at public praça or local tavern or carnaval's three anarchic days were salient moments in fashioning a self as one among equals away from the watchful and unequal presence of patrões. It was a world shared by slaves and former slaves and free women, some Brazilian and some foreign, a world shared with men and the poor of the street and the slum. Threaded through those moments were the constant concerns of family, so that private and working lives were never wholly separate. Servants carried the preoccupations of pregnancy, birth, illness, children, companions and husbands into the places of work, insistent reminders to patrões that servants were indeed persons with whole lives, lives partly lived outside their domain. Against the shadow cast by patrons' authority and the routines of work, we should recall Antonia's room.

PART III

Masters' world

4

Protection and obedience

The conduct of domestic life was awkwardly personal. Countless daily exchanges between patrões and servants within the narrow confines of city houses accentuated the perceived tensions between family and non-family. Where neither could stay entirely aloof from the other's near-constant presence, their mutual but unequal dependence became compellingly immediate. By relying on women who as outsiders they did not trust for the services that maintained their households and made privilege concrete, patrões rendered themselves continuously vulnerable.[1]

The dona da casa's relationship with her servants exemplified those strains. Custom directed that as wife she oversee the running of the household, including taking charge of servants – although one young wife hired a servant, "a white lady of faithful character and with sufficient intelligence . . ." in order to learn from her how to carry out the duties of mistress. An experienced servant with her own way of doing things might seek to assert her voice in household matters. To make clear her bid for expertise and reinforce her rule over servants and the spaces of the house, a mistress frequently performed some work herself. By tradition Brazilian women prepared the fancy desserts that delighted their guests, or the salad would be "made by the hands of one of the ladies of the house." Others sewed, either machine work, making coarse work clothes for dependents or the fancy handwork of embroidering sets of table and bed linen.[2] She also made manifest the distrust with which she viewed servants. Caution argued that a mistress accompany her servant to supervise the shopping, for she assumed that a cook would "buy the more expensive bird," thus going beyond "stipulated expenses." Yet experience taught that being too "antipathetic and abrasive" caused servants to leave, while too much "good-natured condescension," provoked disrespect.[3] The contemporary playwright José Joaquim

França Junior, writing for a popular section of a daily Rio de Janeiro
newspaper in 1878, offered sketches of domestic life in which he
satirized the opposition between mistress and servant. The otherwise
obvious wit gained its bite from a scene intended to be uncomfortably
familiar to readers in which a dona da casa complained hotly to
another of how her cook, among other faults, had broken such a
quantity of china that she considered selling her as far away as
possible, while the servant who was cook, laundress, and cleaning
woman made known to the neighbor that her master allowed only a
stingy amount for the shopping.[4] As França Junior's humor darkly
portrayed, each had acknowledged resources for retaliation: against
threatened sale, a house servant could resort to gossip by inflicting
harm to public demeanor with the right remark. There was the hint
that the broken china, if not exaggerated in the telling, may have been
subversive carelessness by a resentful slave.

    In the on-going balancing and unbalancing of domestic relations,
patrões and servants were forced to some accommodation that
accepted and mediated their differences. Domestic life turned on a set
of expectations – articulated in action and at times made explicit – that
expressed the distinct obligations of each. Patrões made themselves
accountable for the provision of basic care – food, shelter, some
clothing, medicines when ill. In return for what some described as
their paternal duty to supply a "moral and religious education," they
demanded that dependents offer obedience. In the late 1860s, the
prominent Brazilian jurist Agostinho Marques Perdigão Malheiro
argued, following Roman slave law and describing Brazilian notions
of correct action, that patrões retained the responsibility to act as
"protector, defender, a father [and] the obligation to feed . . ." even
freed slaves. In return, the freed person owed "personal service" and
could be punished if he were "ungrateful" or refused to "fulfill his
obligations."[5] To the extent that patrões met their responsibilities,
they intended to exert authority over those who served them. As
Captain Antonio José Coelho de Albuquerque put it in 1880: ". . . in
order to maintain them in obedience, [I have] to feed them at night."[6]
Put somewhat differently, Dona Felice Augusta Carvalho e Silva
reported to the city census taker in 1870 that the young widow, a free
woman described as an agregada who washed, cooked, ironed, and
sewed for her, and her seven-month-old baby "live by [my] favor
because I took pity when I saw her poverty, but this only as long as
she behaves well and works at something that makes it worth giving
her some salary besides [their] food." According to *A Mãe de Família*,

the goal for donas da casa was to maintain among their servants "discipline and good order."[7] Care traded for service, protection for obedience – those were the expectations in the exchange. For servants care took the form of everyday necessities: a room, some clothing, food. A maid's room seldom if ever met the tidy, blue and white gingham decorated style prescribed as ideal quarters, but a mistress could require that her servant keep it neat because "It is I who provides everything." Far more often, makeshift quarters fell below tolerable levels of health or cleanliness. Contemporaries who disapproved claimed that "We see even in wealthy houses slaves herded together in dirty quarters or in humid rooms, dark and without the least ventilation. Other times . . . sleeping in corridors, exposed to the drafty air. . . ."[8] By the latter decades of the century, domestic architecture more often took account of servants by including rooms for servants, although even large houses usually included only one room. In 1896 a gracious Laranjeiras residence, described in the *Jornal do Commercio*, with three parlors and five bedrooms had but one room for the servants to share. Houses that became equipped with "English" bathroom plumbing for the patrão and his family, might provide an ordinary latrine for the servants. And a domestic could accumulate her own belongings. In 1892 an iron bed, shelves, a table, a lockable trunk, and a velvet-covered box fitted out the room of Eva Pereira de Carvalho, the "black" in Antonia Magalhães' household on the rua Frei Caneca, 94 in the Cidade Nova.[9]

If many among the poor had only rags to wear, provoking the city council by 1870 to order that on the street a person must wear "decent clothes, that is, not letting show any part of the body offensive to public honesty and morals," contemporaries concluded that house servants went about "decently clad, as a general rule."[10] For dresses to replace those that had burned, the house servants Violante and Julia received from their dead mistress's estate in 1858, yards of common cotton and for shifts, a piece of slightly finer "American cotton." One traveler to Brazil found the blacks she saw grotesque, "thrust into the worn-out European clothes of their masters." Cheap or worn, clothes could still be colorful: "a striped skirt and old cotton jacket with short sleeves" or "a purple skirt of cheap cotton . . . and a jacket of navy blue and white polka dots."[11] Although their clothes identified servants with the poor and dependent, special clothing could distinguish valued servants, such as the two slave wet-nurses photographed around 1860 wearing fine European dresses complete with shawl or cape and jewelry, reminiscent of the chamber maid in Debret's painting who wore shoes and a coat. Their more eleborate clothes departed from the formula for servant apparel: "plain but decent, without luxury but clean."[12]

The usual diet of the poor, according to a medical student's thesis written in 1865, consisted principally of black beans cooked with fat, sometimes with a little dried meat, sardines or cod added, and sprinkled with manioc flour. If adequate in quantity, such a diet could be nutritionally adequate. Common vegetables and fruits such as sweet potatoes, yams, squash, collard green, turnips, watercress, okra, or amaranth (also called pigweed), bananas or oranges added to their dinner. Coffee or sweetened hot water and bread made the morning meal and the evening supper. Wine, the preferred drink, was too expensive to give to servants, or if given it was likely diluted with rough alcohol, honey or water.[13] Some contemporaries held that too much meat produced "violent, unloosed passions," or caused people to become "courageous and independent." Hence the recommended diet for slaves: vegetables that would "blunt the prod to their passions," making them "docile and passive" while also generating in them "pusillanimity and servility." Others plainly argued for meat as "the essentially nutritive element . . . the only one that can serve organic renewal."[14] House servants, unlike rural field-workers or city street vendors, enjoyed the chance to nibble or save food for themselves when preparing meals or clearing leftovers. A tight accounting of provisions or a locked pantry made outright stealing of larger amounts difficult, but on a small scale servants could vary what they ate.

Patrões granted that for an infant to be healthy, the nursing ama required food "a little more nutritious." Her diet should not be wholly different from what she customarily ate, though, for a woman used to food "less delicate, should not suddenly eat only chicken." Garlic, raw onion, salty foods, or rich foods such as pork would pass into her milk and cause the suckling child "digestive irritations." Nor should she eat all the fruit she wanted. Her food should be easy to digest: cooked meat and vegetables, thick soups, no alcohol.[15]

Of the fears that gripped nineteenth-century Rio de Janeiro imaginations, fear of illness dominated. Illness often meant deadly epidemics, debilitating respiratory diseases, especially tuberculosis, chronic dysentery, or extreme anemia. Besides these, women suffered the routine dangers of childbirth and subsequent infections. To take seriously the illnesses of dependents, with medicines or doctors, became for patrões a principal responsibility that none could casually ignore. Minimal care hastily dispensed did not fulfill their duty, however. It was the mindful show of concerned attention that counted. Although Francisco Peixoto de Lacerda Werneck, an influential and wealthy landowner, spoke as a planter, he voiced an imperative that applied equally in urban settings and for free dependents as well as for slaves when he instructed his son: "Their illnesses ought to be treated with care and humanity."[16] Plausibly, one householder explained to the city census taker in 1870 that more than three house servants normally resided at his town house, but "the others have gone to the doctor for illnesses and were kept [there] to take medicines."[17] Dependents too ill to be treated at home could be taken to a Casa de Saude or to the charity wards of the Santa Casa da Misericórdia where, for example, some 25,000 slaves were treated during the period from 1852 to 1888, while free poor and slave women shared the charitable facilities of the municipal maternity hospital during its brief tenure.[18] In the late 1850s, Aguida Maria da Conceição had paid the Santa Casa 1$200 per day for 109 days to treat a young slave girl. A few years later, the same hospital provided one day's care for a slave that included the rental for a hammock. Well-connected patrões assisted one another in caring for servants, as when Dona Anna Maria da Conceição's doctor for years treated her house slaves without charge, receiving warm thanks in her will in 1863.[19]

After unsuccessful treatment by one doctor, a slave woman's master in 1868 sent her to the public infirmary of the Faculty of Medicine, by tilbury, for paralysis in her legs prevented her from walking. Some twenty days before, the public carriage on which she was riding had been in an accident, throwing passengers about and bruising them. The next day Anna, then six months pregnant, miscarried. Severe uterine bleeding followed, then anemia until she lost all sensation in her legs and became extremely weak. After two days of a restorative diet of meat at lunch and dinner, along with wine, coffee, and bread, sensation in her legs returned and after four days she walked with assistance; a week later she walked freely, felt strong and in good health.[20]

The same public health doctor who treated Anna also treated other women who lacked reliable masters. What began as gastroenteritis and blotches from hemorrhaging beneath the skin – the result of a two month passage to Brazil from Portugal with little more than biscuits, salted meat, and brackish water for sustenance – became typhoid and acute scurvy with the loss of black blood that failed to coagulate when Delfina Rosa Pereira continued to work as a laundress as she "was accustomed to do." Gradual improvement came with medicines and a diet of meat soups and ample amounts of wine and lemon juice. Meat, cooked eggs, wine, and coffee removed the symptoms that Januaria Amelia Cabral blamed on the fact that as a widow her poverty obliged her to "serve as a maid in a humid, low-lying house where, besides excessive work, she lived in the worst conditions of hygiene."[21] The care that provided poor women with needed protection, also served to reinforce inequalities, perpetuating unbroken the cycle of dependence.

To be persuasive, care for dependents had to be witnessed by all those who took seriously the role of patron. Because also clearly functional, no occasion more accurately represented the pageant of paternalistic relations – ranked order, attention to the ill, the work, and finally the praying that united all to a higher authority – than a plantation slave muster. As scripted by one planter:

A half hour before daybreak, the administrator should call the muster, at which time all slaves should awaken promptly and assemble at a given point for the day's tasks. They should separate themselves by height and sex, the tallest to the right, and the women in front of the men. The foremen take the center. It is up to the foremen to conduct a review to see who is missing whether by illness, in flight, or by omission. He grants leave to those who have recently returned from the hospital, and rounds up those he finds ill. He sees to it that they have the proper tools for the day, which should have been ordered the previous evening. Immediately he will command them to cross themselves and say two or three prayers, and send them on their way, with the foremen in the rear.[22]

In urban Rio de Janeiro, the weekly *benção* or blessing palely imitated the rural ritual. In a two-person drama described to the court in 1871, Maria Elenteria de Albuquerque required that her slave, often rented out, return each Sunday "in order to receive [her] blessing." The slave woman, complained her mistress, "complied very irregularly."[23]

Besides the routine and repeated enactments of care and authority, on special occasions, to mark a birth or baptism, or from a deathbed or at the reading of a will, patrões bestowed grander rewards on servants for devoted service. Slavery, especially, afforded opportunities to reward worthy slave servants with freedom, a promise of freedom, gifts, or life-long care. "In order to show her my recognition and the same sentiment on the part of my wife," Doctor Francisco de Paula Barboza Leite Brandão conceded to the black Clementina "her liberty that she might enjoy it . . . in return for the good services she offered, and especially the care and patience she took with my son Antonio Torquato during the long and dangerous illness that he suffered in his infancy." Clementina's reward came only after long years of service. She guessed her age then to be forty years, almost old for a slave, with not many years left to enjoy her new liberty.[24] Revealing of the bond between master and wet-nurse, a planter born in Rio de Janeiro asked in 1883 that "if the freed black Isabel who nursed me still exists, I leave her the quantity of 200 *mil-réis* [or $88] and I hope that she will continue to live on the fazenda . . . where she resides. . . ." Maria Bernarda Esteves, a nun at the city convent of Ajuda, deposing her will in 1864, modestly fulfilled her duty to several domestic slaves "from here," with "alms" of 20 or 50 mil-réis or about $10 to $27 each.[25] Other owners who conceded freedom to their slaves, did so not so much because it was deserved, they said, but "by reason of generosity." Without stating remembrances, the widow Francisca Joaquina de Souza Ramos in 1881 gave "liberty to be effective immediately upon my death to my old slaves" who numbered ten, some African-born, others Brazilian creoles. She also added funds that five masses could be said for their souls.[26] Another Rio de Janeiro master, apparently without reason to pay tribute, dryly recorded in his diary that on 18 January 1886 he had "delivered to the parda Narcisa a letter of freedom . . . releasing from service as well the two freeborn daughters of the same Narcisa." He duly noted that the letter was registered at the notary and that he was thereby exempt from paying the slave tax.[27]

Patrões might specify elaborate legacies. Besides freedom to his slaves, João Martins Vianna, in 1861, left alms of 200 and 500 mil-réis, or $104 and $260, as well as instructions and money to an executor "to buy a house for [my] slaves to live in and use . . . while they live, the last being able to dispose of it." José Pinto Ferreira left to his maid, whom he referred to as "Albina so-and-so" suggesting he did not remember or did not know whether she had a surname, ". . . in recompense for the good services she offered, his house, . . . all furniture, clothes, silver, as well as all other objects of use. . . ."[28] The very wealthy Lourenço de Souza Meirelles, single and without direct heirs and therefore permitted by law to dispose freely of his property, discovered the tolerated limits of paternal largesse, however, when he bequeathed to the "parda Virgolina," freed by his will dated 1850, "in recognition for the willingness with which she always served him," the "two-story house . . . for her residence" in addition to the income from ten bonds until her death when the property would revert to other, named heirs. He further provided eight houses for all his other slaves, whom he freed. Within a few months of dictating his will, Lorenço qualified the bequests in a codicil, withdrawing all grants of real property to his former slaves, presumably because the other, would-be heirs had protested.[29]

Once slavery became extinct and freedom no longer the prized reward, patrões continued to reward free servants with property or cash. In 1909, Augusta Hansen was allowed to keep the "jewelry, bedroom furniture, clothes, and belongings," that she had used as servant in her employer's household. On the occasion of Severino Antonio Correa's death, his servants each received a small sum of cash, a mere token alongside the monthly income that the former wet-nurse Emilia gained in 1911 from the employer whom she had suckled when he was an infant.[30] Like slaves, free women waited for their rewards, thoroughly instructed in the principle that only life-long service merited exceptional compensation.

Benevolent gestures affirmed – before an audience of family witnesses, legal counsel, and servants themselves – authority coupled with the ability to bestow or deny tangible favors. By their formally phrased and presented acts patrons firmly set the bounds that casual, everyday exchanges might otherwise slowly erode. Carrying the display of care beyond the household to more visible settings, in 1864 the entire city could content itself with an "act of lofty and thus edifying morality" that took place at a church where "a family composed of five persons, father, mother and three children, kneeling at the foot of the altar, received from the priest the letter that freed them from captivity, followed by the nuptial blessing that united the heads of the family."[31] In a single scene, the presence of priest, patrão, dependents, and, within the slave family, parents and children perfectly repeated the correct ordering of authority. In later years also, the well-to-do would demonstrate their concern for the poor in public gatherings. At a benefit in 1903 for a clinic established for the poor, a "committee of benefactresses" sponsored a garden party and concert. They appropriately chose the then lushly landscaped and fenced Praça da Republica (once the Campo de Sant'Anna) as venue: across the street stood the clinic, nearby the city's poorer areas of dingy houses, rented rooms, and cortiços. The poor watched from the street side of a tall wrought iron fence. Those inside represented both houses of parliament, the press, and numerous prestigious associations. Even the President of the Republic appeared. All agreed the ladies had arranged "a charming afternoon, destined to mitigate the suffering of many children."[32] In these ways the wealthy fulfilled their social duties, mirroring authority and charity as much to themselves as to those they would help, while strengthening the ties of duty and gratitude that made daily life manageable for both sides.

There is danger, when trying to recover the assumptions and prescriptions of a culture different in its premises and remote in time, of seeing its participants as cynical or consciously deceptive. Considered that way, domestic relations would have been bad faith. But patrons could understand their actions as appropriately expressing responsibility and, for many, regard or affection toward particular servants. We can assume that contemporaries behaved more or less sincerely, with a measure of calculation permissible on both sides. Accounts by the reputed jurist Malheiro in the 1860s of masters who freed slaves "solely from humanity or in recognition of service," and the "proverbial goodness and charity of Brazilian senhoras" toward slaves they had raised become convincing.[33] And servants took them as convincing. Some asked that the bonds that properly linked patrons and servants be extended to them. Rather than higher wages or fewer hours of work, some asked to be "well-treated" or "esteemed" as "persons of the family." Two white women, orphaned sisters, advertising in the newspaper for work in 1877, asked no "gratification" for sewing and light housework, only to be "treated as persons of the family,"[34] seeking the security that a household could confer.

Yet it was also true that most households could only perform their assumed responsibilities imperfectly. While a household's ability to convey authority and protection rested on an assumption of its being patriarchal and wealthy, in fact most departed from that standard, often appreciably. In São Cristovão in 1870 less than half the households with servants were headed by married couples. In the majority, unmarried women or men acted as head of household, with authority that was perhaps less persuasive than when invested in a couple. Often São Cristovão families were not as large as notions about familial power and prestige implied. Typically they numbered six family members, expanding to households of nine persons when their servants are included. Most families had children, often as many as three and seldom more than six. The great, extended families were few. Such families could, however, find themselves in dispute when authority overlapped. When a man's sister and her husband came to reside bringing their own servants into the household, or when a widow lived with her widowed children, grandchildren, and each with assorted slave and free servants exactly who gave orders, with what priority and in which situations could become confused.[35]

Nor in all households did a dona da casa directly supervise the servants. Men without wives who headed households especially relied on housekeepers. One widower with a sizable household wanted a "capable lady to take charge" of his house, someone who also knew how to sew and to cut men's, children's, and slave's clothes. . . ." Another gentleman would turn over the "entire charge" of his house to a "respectable middle-aged woman who thoroughly understands housekeeping." A family with many servants might hire a woman simply to help with the job of managing an extensive household, while others did so because the mistress was "absent" or ordinarily "out during the day."[36] The presence of a hired housekeeper altered the social dynamics of domestic work, for although she assumed the role of mistress in directing servants' labors, she might also become intermediary between servants and family.

A man who lived without any family created a doubly ambiguous situation for a servant woman. Not infrequently she became companion, hostess, or lover. Such was the "buxom, dark-skinned, 35-year-old" woman who "officiates at table, discharges the other duties of a housekeeper," and substituted as wife for a successful and unmarried Rio de Janeiro merchant, described by an American visitor in 1867. In 1890 one woman knowingly chose to protect herself from the possibility of just such an involvement. A widow herself and "honest," she would work only for a "widower with children" or for a couple.[37] The wealthy Antonio Hernandes, without children or other relatives, had lived with his two slave servants. By his will in 1862 he freed Catherina as well as Felix for "his good services," leaving to each the income from government bonds. Catherina remained uppermost in Antonio's concerns. As tribute to their intimacy, Antonio left her "all the objects of my use in my house . . . except my papers," together with his "handkerchiefs and personal linen," while Felix would receive his freedom only after she had been provided for. When Catherina became "ill from mental alienation," Antonio freed her immediately, taking measures to apply the bonds to her stay in hospital until she improved and could again manage her own affairs.[38] If the ties that Antonio and Catherina formed found little or no social approval, they probably had developed with seeming inevitability from the daily proximity of servant and master, combined with the particular needs, vulnerabilities, and generosities of each.

Not every household possessed the resources that permitted or encouraged appropriate care for dependents. If most who took servants could supply them with the expected standard of food, clothing, and shelter, there were others – clerks, craftsmen, even other laundresses or seamstresses, some who lived in cortiços – with servants in their households who likely found their maintenance an economic burden.[39] Genteel but impoverished masters did not reliably offer security either. The two house servants of Joaquim Maria Machado de Assis, the great mulatto novelist, had not had much of a household to look after. The inventory of Machado's property, following his death in 1908, mentioned some furniture, all of it either old or in bad condition, and an assortment of glasses, cutlery, and serving pieces. Perhaps they dusted the 1,000 or so books in his library. As a fitting epitaph for this master of dry irony, Machado not only omitted any small bequest for the two servant women (what stocks and bonds there were went to his niece's daughter), but he neglected to pay them the $34 owing for their wages for the two months before he died.[40] It was perhaps no coincidence that the mistress accused in 1871 of shuttling her slave between prostitution and domestic service and refusing to treat her respiratory infection described herself as poor and sometimes took in laundry. Without means, she apparently felt no obligation to provide for her slave, while desperately relying on her as her principal source of income.[41]

Arrangements made possible in the city could further dilute the ideal exchange between patron and servants. In the context of a money economy, householders combined remuneration in goods or favors, or both, with cash payment. Whether a woman were slave or free did not by itself determine whether she received a cash wage. While some householders recognized that for first-rate servants they would have to "pay well" or ignore "price as unimportant," others, even beyond the end of slavery, would compensate young girls with "good treatment and clothing." In 1900 one family offered to a "white or colored" girl who would care for two babies, "good food, clothing, and good treatment." These families followed a tradition borrowed from Portugal when a dependent younger than 12 years could not ask wages as long as the patron fed and clothed him.[42]

While free women might forsake wages for personal well-being, slaves might labor for money. Although abolitionists, anxious to discredit slavery's appeal, argued that slaves had no incentive to work since they would continue to be fed, housed, and clothed by the mere fact that they represented an investment, householders understood differently. Wet-nurses, they charged, took knowing advantage of the fact that they were needed to demand high rates. They "want only money," and for that they "abandon their own children" in order to nurse others for a substantial fee.[43] Any particular slave's worth was readily calculated from the rental that her labor could draw. Hence slaves purchased freedom with their own labor according to formally agreed upon rates. In the 1870s, the 24-year-old Fumina could buy her freedom at $18 per month over three years, while the older Eva whose "service would be compatible with her age" of 59 worked off the cost of her freedom at only $9 per month.[44] The slave Maria Joaquina, who lived on her own in a cortiço on the rua São Luiz Gonzaga, worked as a laundress and returned to her owner in cash a portion of what she earned, living on the remainder herself. That she did so with "license from her master," trimmed somewhat her independent state. Similarly good business sense had granted the slave laundress Leocadia, a light-skinned mulatto, permission in 1876 to "reside where it best suits her in the capital," in exchange for the fixed monthly sum of about $18, collected by her owner.[45]

Arrangements such as these implied consequences, however, for a master could refuse responsibility for his slave. "From her I receive a daily sum of money," declared Manoel Jorge Gomes de Mattos in 1865, "and have nothing to do with the clothes she launders." Dissatisfied clients, he indicated, could take up their complaints with the laundress herself. In this regard slave women were not so different from the free laundresses or seamstresses who lived on their own, without sure claim to a patron's protection. An argument with a customer, "who did not want to pay for the delivered clothes," landed the free Amelia Francisca in jail in 1906 after they had an "exchange of words."[46] The other side was that masters forfeited their right to expect loyalty, contributing to the mistrust they already felt.

The traditional protections or payment in goods, combined with wages, provided a continuity that smoothed the formal shift from slave to free labor. Despite an arrangement figured in money terms to which all had agreed, the dona da casa saw those whom she paid as "her *famulos*," that is, dependents in her household and under her care. One year after slavery ended, the councilors of state confidently affirmed that "No human effort" could undo the differences between the master who had the "right to order because he pays" and the servant who had "the duty to obey because he receives."[47]

Servants themselves found ways to bargain against authority that further tilted the precarious balance of domestic relations. A

Portuguese woman who in 1875 wanted work several days a week doing dressmaking and ironing linen stated the limits she set to subordination: "I will comply with my duties, but I wish not to be mistreated." If her terms did not defy established ways, something about the straightforward manner by which she acknowledged the nature of the relationship indicated she meant what she said. Another free woman, seeking a position as nurse maid in 1882, "was willing to be useful," she said, "in anything not menial."[48] The slave mother, Florença da Silva, who considered tactics worthwhile, urged her daughter to "treat your masters very well so they will have pity on you in order to help me in my efforts eventually to buy your freedom." Florença's attempts resulted in her daughter's former owner writing to her new master "to know if you consent to giving her freedom and for how much."[49] Even slave women negotiated by fleeing situations that they found intolerable as Honorata had in the late 1860s when she refused to work for one household where she had been sent by her owner, or Serafina when she was denied the freedom long promised by her mistress and sold instead by her mistress's sister to a slave dealer in 1874.[50] Assertiveness may have caused servants to be even more reliant on subsequent patrões for help or protection, strengthening one set of dependencies because others had frayed.

Above all free women could simply leave. And according to patrões servants regularly did just that. Some said servants stayed no longer than "eight or ten days," others that one month was usual. A ladies' journal in 1881 declared that "changing servants is no longer a notable event . . . hired servants come and go almost daily." Servants who slept out were accused of working only a few days, just long enough to earn a measure of trust, then leaving one night after receiving money for the next day's shopping, never to return. Householders alleged that servants took advantage of competition among them, setting them against each other, and allowing themselves to be "induced by outside suggestions" from another dona da casa to take "a more advantageous position." Instead of receiving deference from servants, patrões could believe that servants "go from shop to shop, door to door in a cortiço spreading bad will, attributing every evil to those who pay them, even saying that they do not get paid." They neither "recognize reason," nor "do they understand loyalty." "When they fight with their lovers, and no other appears, they knock on a family's door and ask if they need a maid."[51] Even the minister of justice's report in 1882 conceded, however, that cases were not uncommon in which "poor treatment or lack of payment of salaries justifies complaints."[52] The admission allowed that agreements were reciprocal and left matters open to negotiation.

Patrons felt themselves challenged, however, when free women pressed their claim for a separate existence by "sleeping out." In 1877 a young free woman, skilled as a cook and at shopping, declared she would accept a position only on condition that she "sleep out." Through the 1880s and 1890s women repeated their insistence. For most that amounted to "work by the day," or, like the expert cook for hire in 1882, to "arriving in the morning and leaving at night," but for others it meant one night a week away from employers, "sleeping out on Sundays."[53] All were new phrases in the language of hiring servants, and employers heard in them a muffling of the authority that relied on the physical aggregation of household. By leaving at night, servants openly eluded their jurisdiction. Sensing the need to bargain, some patrões volunteered to let a servant sleep out, or said it did not matter. Others, resisting the erosion of old ways, pointedly required that a woman "sleep at the house of her patrões," or would permit her to sleep out only on Sundays.[54] The Council of State, the body of cautious and respected men who advised the emperor on all serious matters, in 1889 concurred that a woman who "passed the night out without . . . permission" from employers gave sufficient grounds for being dismissed, even though dismissal was a disruption they did not readily condone.[55] Especially by the turn of the century, employers countered servants' claims by requiring that they "sleep at the place of hire," or stating simply that a woman "may not sleep out."[56] Women who would comply were still to be found, though. One woman in 1909 placed an advertisement for work that captured all that householders might wish for in a servant. She described herself as "carefully trained by a respectable family," able to offer "written references regarding her behavior." She was available as a maid, she said, "for a house of good treatment, for all internal domestic service, not going out on the street, and sleeping in the house of the patrões."[57]

Besides an imperfect carrying out of domestic authority, some masters visibly failed to fulfill the duties to which their position obligated them. As seen by their equals, their violations required redressing. In 1883 the slave woman Deolinda argued before an appellate court that she ought to be a free woman. She rested her case on the accepted principle that an abandoned slave became free by default. For two years, she said, her master had neither treated her illnesses nor provided clothing, and, further, he "left her to live outside subjugation to his authority." On her own she had a hard time supporting herself, for an eye disease kept her from being able to work steadily. Without an identifiable master to assume responsibility, the condition of slave had no meaning. The court declared Deolinda free.[58] In 1872 an appellate court saw fit to summon Maria Elenteria de Albuquerque "for the bad condition of her slave." No law explicitly forbade prostitution or using slaves as prostitutes, yet putting her domestic slave into prostitution was the apparent issue. Her crime was not against her slave or even against public mores, but rather against the standards that defined proper paternal behavior. By abusing her slave, she had transgressed the responsibilities that defined her role. Proceedings focused on the mistress for ". . . loosening the tie of respect and obedience that ought to bind her" and her slave. Accordingly, the mistress did not so much deny charges about the "illicit and immoral" use of her slave as present herself as one who "lived honestly, with modesty, having order, respect, and decency."[59] In the end the court returned her slave but warned that further failure to meet her responsibility would bring censure.

In another situation, a mistress was accused of outright violence. In 1896 the twelve-year-old Alice found herself entangled in an ugly and, to her, inescapable relationship with the two women for whom she worked. In their house she was "nurse maid to a child of seven months, swept the house, washed the child's clothes, served as pantry maid and did shopping on the street, . . ." From them she reportedly suffered severe physical abuse. One of the women, others accused, "barbarously beat" her, threw boiling water on her legs, and fed her inadequately. Despite the telling evidence of "scars, bruises, cuts," fear kept Alice from corroborating the charges made against the mistress by neighbors and shopkeepers. The court, however, with jurisdiction over her as an orphaned minor, intervened to remove her from the household.[60]

Doctor Antonio Alves de Azevedo Nogueira erred in the other direction. For domestic life to remain manageable, masters were expected to maintain a correct and distanced demeanor toward servants. Yet, sexual liaisons between master and servant were easily tolerated as long as notoriety did not impair the ability of masters to command respect, or property was not transferred into unsuitable hands. By openly loving the slave woman Marcellina, Nogueira offended public sensibilities as well as damaging family honor and squandering family property. When he took as his mistress the slave who had served as mucama to his wife, freed her, and set her up, he ignored outrageously the differences that by all understandings did and should irrevocably separate them. As if that were not enough, Nogueira had "unfaithfully dissipated the fortune of the couple," and had "reduced [his wife] from her former opulence almost to poverty" by cheating her of property rightfully hers as a widow who had inherited from her first husband. Everyone (save Antonio perhaps) quickly forgot Marcellina. What remained was for court and colleagues to condemn Antonio for his serious breach of behavior. In 1887 the court embargoed all property, while Antonio's agent returned as indicting evidence the letters Antonio had sent containing tender and longing messages for Marcellina. What began as an indiscretion to be cloaked with male silence had become serious transgressions that even friends refused to ignore any longer, so that in the end associates testified against him. Thoroughly discredited, Antonio left Brazil for Europe.[61]

Nogueira's case was exceptional, but not altogether unique. João Rodrigues Pereira d'Almeida provoked his wife to seek from the Church, in 1872, a permanent separation when his affair with Eduviges became known. Almeida had bought this "good-looking" slave woman, then 23 years old, as a personal maid for his wife. Within two years Eduviges had borne a son by him. He then freed her, rented a house for her, and left his wife and daughter to live with her. Publicly rejected by her husband and without any independent means of support, Anna Figueira d'Almeida alleged that she had no choice but to return to the house of her father, the senator and supreme court judge Jerônimo Martiniano Figueira de Mello. Although Almeida did not challenge her request for the legal separation that involved a division of their communally owned property, he denied that the "mulatta [was] the cause of disharmony between them." By the time the ecclesiastical court granted Dona Anna her petition in 1874, Eduviges and Almeida had parted. According to one witness, when Almeida stopped supporting her, she left him, "shifting her feelings to new loves."[62]

When masters were seen to abuse authority by irresponsible or inappropriate conduct and hence jeopardize the legitimacy of all, the usually sacrosanct domain of household could be intruded upon and the offending master called to heel by others of his class.[63] To that extent authority over dependents was circumscribed. By contrast, no one thought it remiss when in 1906 the dona da casa Maria Coelho, faced with a pregnant servant who would soon give birth and not wanting the trouble of seeing her through delivery, "recommended that she find a room where she could have the child." Although her "recommendation" amounted to a refusal to fulfill her role as protector, she had the power to make it, just as she could later decide to rehire the woman, her delivery over and the child dead.[64]

House servants experienced most sharply the profound tensions that characterized the relationship of master and servant as one personal and proximate, perhaps long-lasting, but never one between trusted equals. The closeness allowed for the tender recollections of wet-nurses, but also for the suspicion or resentment with which patrons viewed servants. For masters the ties with servants were necessarily unstable, because mistrust, even contempt, for those on whom they relied for the maintenance of family and household resonated with ambivalence, requiring repeated confirmations from servants of reliability and loyalty. The bond that linked family and servants surely held a different meaning when servants lived in their own housing or worked for a family only sporadically. A family could not expect the same loyal and devoted service, nor a servant the same favor that a closer relationship or one of longer standing merited. Even the weaker bond, though, required that both patrões and servants meet their reciprocal obligations at least minimally.

5

Contagion and control

Beginning in the 1870s and into the next two decades, the structures of traditional authority were severely tested. The abolition of Brazilian slavery came in May 1888 after long anticipation. That anticipation had had time to penetrate and modify everyday experience. Since as early as 1831 when Brazil grudgingly decreed an end to the African trade in slaves, and, especially from the early 1850s when the decree was finally enforced, slave owners recognized slavery as doomed, since slaves in Brazil died more readily than they reproduced, without fresh imports slavery could not be perpetuated. Brazilians continued to buy and sell slaves, establish plantations that relied on slave labor, push up their price by competitive bidding, acting in ways that seemed to deny that slavery could ever end. But by the early 1870s denial had become resigned acceptance. Parliament prepared for eventual abolition when it planned the first national census to discover how many slave women of child-bearing age would produce new generations of slaves, and more importantly to count the total slave population in order to calculate the cost of indemnification (in the event never paid). In 1871 parliament passed the law that bridged the passage to freedom. The Rio Branco Law, named after its principal sponsor Viscount Rio Branco, or Law of the Free Womb, declared all children subsequently born to slave mothers freed on condition that each serve the mother's master until age 21. Under the master's authority until their majority, they were also his responsibility to raise and educate.[1] An ambiguous slavery persisted.

In Rio de Janeiro slavery dwindled to an end. The city's slave population dropped from an estimated 100,000 in the late 1860s to 30,000 in 1885 and to a mere 7,488 in 1887, whether by flight or death, by sale to lucrative coffee-producing areas, or by freedom granted or purchased.[2] In a city where 90 percent of all working slave women were domestic servants, declining slave numbers would seem likely to disrupt the supply of servants to local households, but in fact they were little affected. Large numbers of free women as early as the 1870s had contributed to the rank of household servants, and freed slave women who remained in Rio de Janeiro almost certainly continued as domestics. The shift from a mixed slave and free labor force to one wholly free came gradually so that, by slavery's official end, the initial groping adaptations to a new regime were well underway in the capital.

The approach of abolition, however, called into question far more than the number of actual slaves. Slavery combined with paternal authority had set the paradigm for all master–servant relations. Masters assumed individual, personal and virtually private authority over and responsibility for slaves and dependents, although as we have seen there were socially enforced limits to private license. One brief incident catches something of the meaning of personal responsibility understood within the terms of slavery. In 1873 authorities had sent the apparently abandoned slave Albano to the public depository for unclaimed property. He became violent, managing to arm himself with "lengths of iron" with which he dangerously attacked other slaves and police employees. In order to restrain him, authorities transferred him to the dungeon of the House of Correction. Belatedly, the owner appeared to claim his slave who was quickly released to him upon payment of a small fine. No one raised the question of whether Albano was still a danger; the slave's demonstrated violence did not fundamentally concern authorities as long as a master took responsibility. More routinely, whether taking a slave into their hire or renting out a wet-nurse, householders asked for someone to "guarantee her behavior" or offered "to answer for her conduct."[3] Assumptions of personal responsibility for slaves' behavior also appeared, at least ideally, in situations where owners authorized their slaves to hire themselves out as casual labor on the street, arranging their own jobs and payment. The Camara Municipal directed that such slaves be licensed. Besides an owner to guarantee the slave's behavior, the slave was to wear "at all times and in a visible place a numbered metal plate," to identify and explain her or his presence on the street. If on the street past seven o'clock in the evening, a slave was expected to carry written permission from the master.[4]

Responsibility implied its corollary: control. Control hinged on the fundamental fact that one person owned – bought and sold – another. A master sought to retain control over the whole life of a slave, directing not only a slave's working life, the tasks, the hours, the punishments or rewards, but all other aspects. Masters left the mark of their power clearly stamped on the biographies of their slaves. One child freed at baptism, for instance, was nevertheless still treated as a slave in 1870 and rented away from the household where his mother and sister remained. Nicolao, a slave who thus could marry only with his owner's permission, and the freed woman Felipa Maria Carneiro in 1876 were denied "nuptial blessings" with the terse explanation, "time inappropriate." Only in 1869 did the law forbid separation of husband from wife or a child from either its father or mother by sale, underscoring what had been a common practice and giving householders reason not to record kinship among slaves in the 1870 and 1872 censuses.[5] Even the emotional and sexual life of a slave belonged within the master's jurisdiction. Those concerned with health in the 1870s and 1880s casually instructed that a wet-nurse's sexual relations ought to be "either prohibited or permitted with great parsimony" on grounds that her milk suffered harmful alterations from "ardent emotions, sorrows, and extreme passions." By default control could extend to a slave's old age. Sick and no longer good for work in 1870, Leonida Rosa do Amor Divino lived as best she could, an indigent who begged alms to pay for a place in the household where she had probably once served.[6]

Slavery's terms permeated, and corroded, all social relations, and extended to free persons. In order to gain the necessary city license, free people who hired themselves out as casual labor supplied a sponsor or guarantor just as slaves did. A comedy of reversed statuses resulted when one freed African readily signed his request for a license while his sponsor barely managed to scratch out his name, and moreover referred to the African respectfully as "senhor." The conviction that slave servants could be taken on safely only when their behavior had been vouched for by someone with authority carried over to free women, so that a foreign cook and a white ama were each expected to provide "good references for their conduct."[7] A patrão's power to decide life events intervened in the existence of the free and persisted beyond the time of general emancipation. The gradual approach of abolition did not therefore presage deep rupture to urban domestic life. The steady and discernible dwindling of slave numbers combined with the anticipated end of slavery did, nevertheless, make real to householders that at least some supports to authority were loosening.

Simultaneously, another issue pressed painfully on the question of public order. Ever since the middle of the nineteenth century a new factor had imposed itself on the experience of local residents so as to remold their judgment of the "less favored" poor. Beginning in 1850 contagious disease spread illness and death in epidemic waves through a vulnerable population. Yellow fever, absent from Brazil since 1686, reappeared in Rio de Janeiro in 1849, swelling into an epidemic a year later. The pattern was set: 4,160 persons died in 1850; the next year only 471; in 1852 the number of deaths reached 1,943. In three years more than 6,500 persons had fallen victim to yellow fever. Yellow fever rooted itself in the city, erratically ravaging the population into the next century. After few or no deaths in the mid-1860s, the death toll mounted again in the 1870s and 1880s. The worst came between 1890 and 1895 when 14,944 died of the disease, so that by 1896 the committee on sanitation recorded with resignation that "yellow fever is now a constant." Between 1850 and 1901 in Rio de Janeiro, a staggering 56,000 persons died of yellow fever alone.[8]

In mid-winter of 1855 the first case of cholera in Rio de Janeiro was identified. Moving swiftly through the population, cholera had killed 2,700 persons by the end of November. By the time the epidemic had exhausted itself, less than a year later in April 1856, nearly 5,000 persons had died, more than half of them slaves. Observers were clear that among the dead blacks and "persons of the humbler walks of life" were most numerous.[9]

If in the 1850s epidemics raged with unfamiliar vengeance, other diseases on a lesser scale could readily be remembered. Smallpox and scarlet fever had intermittently struck the city from 1820 on, while, earlier, whooping cough, zamparine – a paralyzing influenza – fevers, and conjunctivitis had exacted their toll.[10] In that densely settled, ever-growing port, the population fell victim with increasing frequency to recurrent outbreaks of disease, or so it seemed to locals who reckoned the arithmetic of death by the absolute numbers of those who died. Typhoid, smallpox, malaria, "pernicious fevers," and measles followed. With fluctuations – 3,357 deaths from smallpox in 1887 or 2,056 malaria deaths in 1889, or 973 dead from typhoid fever between 1883 and 1889 – they too persisted into the next century. Pulmonary tuberculosis soon became recognized as the real killer, steady and unremitting: 1,577 deaths contrasted with only 453 from pernicious fever or 321 from typhoid in 1868. Tuberculosis claimed 1,990 lives as the single worst cause of death in 1888, and 2,000 was the average number dead from the disease each year between 1860 and 1890.[11]

The immediate presence of disease made itself felt as death became daily and wearily familiar to all. Apprehension spread, derived less from a tally of the dead than from the explanations adduced to account for the alarming prevalence of disease. The "miasmas" that fouled the air, from which disease festered, came, it was first thought, from waste – garbage left in streets and on beaches, from the slaughter-house and cemeteries, from the open ditches that carried all manner of effluents including excrement.[12] For contemporaries, their city became a filthy place where accumulated waste bred disease and spread contamination.

Such explanation prompted public officials into action. While Brazil on the eve of the yellow fever and cholera epidemics had been without "the least sanitary organization," the imperial government hurriedly established in Rio de Janeiro in 1850 the Central Board of Public Hygiene together with subordinate public health committees in each parish to battle against yellow fever.[13] The city council belatedly and minimally assumed the job of removing rubbish, or, more accurately, legislated for its removal. While well-provided householders continued to send their servants to empty waste on the beaches, others, either without servants or indifferent, still threw waste water or worse onto the street. An 1863 edict instructed that "the poor who do not have servants" should give their name and address to the inspector so that rubbish will be removed from their houses by public street cleaners. Looking toward a more modern and permanent way to rid houses and streets of filth, the government contracted the English-owned City Improvements Company in 1857 to lay an underground network of water pipes and sewerage system.[14] Both schemes were consistent with the view that removing filth would remove the source of miasma and disease.

During the 1860s, with governmental attention trained on the Paraguayan War, little new energy infused public health initiatives. Only after the soaring number of yellow fever deaths in the early 1870s – more than three and a half thousand in 1873 and more than three thousand again in 1876 when a menacing figure of Death was popularly portrayed as presiding over that year's carnaval – did the government renew efforts at making the city a healthy place.[15] Two committees set up in 1874 and 1876 requested health measures, necessary but uninspired repetitions of those twenty years earlier: potable water, street cleaning, an adequate sewerage system. Critics persuasively argued that the improvements themselves contributed to more disease. Typical of the outcry, one doctor blamed the "public sewers, the only thing that gets renewed with the lack of rain, blocking decaying matter in the pipes and spreading in the atmosphere of the streets and in the interior of houses the elements of putrid intoxication."[16] Others drew more daring conclusions. For them the very excavations dug to lay pipes explained the disease that recurrently swept the city, for they exposed the filthy and pestilent-ridden earth once used to fill the swampy areas on which Rio de Janeiro was built.[17] Thus understood, the problem became more complex and more vexing than merely extending or improving sewerage drains. The swamps had been successively buried with "refuse removed from houses and streets" and, without any scheme for removing the sub-soil water, the fill absorbed it, appearing dry on the surface but remaining humid and wet at lower depths. The high water table of partially salty water, containing bacteria and organic matter, compounded the error. Disease bred in that humid, festering soil, or so reputable and educated contemporaries believed. Their conclusion followed that "the health [of the city] depends principally on the extinction of the swamps, perennial centers of this scourge that incessantly afflicts us." The authors of that analysis boldly proposed to drain the sub-soil, a staggering engineering challenge, which never got underway.[18]

Both these threats – of abolition, and contagion – focused attention on domestic servants who not only comprised the city's largest single laboring group, but who lived in its filthiest zones, and, more significantly, entered the homes of the rich. Any disorder abolition might occasion, any miasma-bred infections belonged not only to the world of the street: they would be carried by servants into the protected spaces of domestic life.

Powerful men deemed the regulation of servants fundamental to social order because they affected "the peace, tranquility and well-being of the family, the base of all social organization."[19] In 1882 the minister of justice, arguing for a formal, legally binding contract that would regulate domestic service, urged the need to "improve the morals of the class of domestic servants and guarantee well-being to those who provide them with the means of subsistence." By calling for legally prescribed regulations, the rich intended to purchase peace of mind as much as service with the salaries they paid domestics. The minister of justice thought that the need for regulation "becomes steadily more acute" as the slave population declined.[20]

In 1889, councilors of state clearly identified the fundamental reason for urging regulation. Abolition exposed in a new light the conflicts inevitable between classes at the same time that it altered the rules that had contained those conflicts. "Among us such regulation with respect to domestic service would never have been thought necessary . . . in the regime of slavery in force until recently." The end of slavery, however, was seen to have jarred the "familiar conditions of life," causing "instability." As spokesmen for the empire the councilors readily acknowledged as proper the "unequal conditions" and as inevitable the resulting "conflicts" between the "inferior and superior classes of society." A regulation that stated mutual obligations and rights would prove no simple task, they cautioned, because of the "permanent antagonism commonly manifested by the two classes." Conflict as they described it derived from the refusal by each class to conduct itself according to its proper social place. The lower class always want "the maximum liberty and an impossible equality," while the upper class "are led by their wealth, higher birth, titles, and elevated social position" to "imperious habits."[21]

The deep-running ambivalence that had characterized traditional authority had come to be redefined as "conflict," and yet patrões remained dependent upon servants to provide their houses with every imaginable service, basic or trivial. As their own control over slaves lessened, the fondly recalled image of the favored mucama competed with a harsher one. The mucama valued "because of her more intimate contact with the family, at whose breast they had been raised and after whom they modeled their habits and inclinations," was also described as "these wretched women, and above all the slaves, who offer themselves as wet-nurses, not having any upbringing . . . their sentiments little developed."[22] At the same time that city councilmen admonished that a family treat servants "with goodwill and charity, not punishing [them], respecting their dignity . . ." and providing them with "wholesome accommodation," others saw servants as "introducing outsiders into the family almost always disposed against us," well-known for their "deceptions and lies."[23] Ironically, as the free women so sought after in earlier decades became steadily more available, employers grew restive. Servants were no longer household members but strangers whose presence was disturbing and who could not be trusted. No sooner were they hired, than they left, "alleging mistreatment" or in search of higher wages elsewhere.[24]

The end of slavery also meant that people could choose not to work. To those preoccupied with maintaining an ordered and orderly

Plate 11 An *ama de leite* and the child she once nursed, *c.* 1860

society "the great quantity of unoccupied people in this capital" was an unsettling presence,[25] as that mass of women and men lacked masters, and hence any regulated place in society. The "great number" who lived in "intermittent vagabondage," without steady work, posed a problem that required appropriate measures of control. More particularly, "vagabonds" threatened domestic security, for such unqualified persons deceivingly managed to gain work as servants. "They easily dupe the good faith of patrões by alleging false skills," authorities charged. If occasionally they took jobs, their irresponsible "desire to enjoy in leisure the salary accumulated" soon put them once again among the no-account unemployed.[26]

Anxieties were heightened as the poor in general, and servants in particular, were identified as the carriers of contagion. Such a view did not form all at once, but through the last decades of the century the old image of the cortiço as a harmful environment faded, to be replaced by one of infected slum-dwellers contaminated and endlessly contaminating the entire city population unless somehow removed: slum dwellers, not the slums, became the agents of disease. The final metamorphosis of the deprived poor into the dangerous poor occurred as physical disease became blurred in public imaginations with moral contagion. As early as 1855, the Santa Rita parish inspector had directed public attention to the cortiços where in "small rooms live a large population from the least favored classes," who threatened not only public health, but "morality of behavior." In much the same terms, the influential Baron Lavradio, president of the Central Board of Public Hygiene, in 1878, juxtaposed physical and moral contamination: conditions in cortiços were so bad, he wrote, that "many of their inhabitants are already buried alive," and cortiços "constitute centers of illness disseminated through the most crowded part of the population." Disease went in tandem with immorality: cortiços "foster the propagation of vices and crimes [that are an] affront to morality and public safety."[27]

At all levels public officials twinned disease with crime. The Society of Hygiene warned against rented rooms as the "cause of evils, whose repression depends on the police, . . . where wretchedness and filth consort for the generation of illness and crime." For the chief of police in 1867, cortiços were "the theatre of crimes, the refuge of criminals, and centers of infection."[28] The Rio de Janeiro sanitary commission urged their eradication, or they would persist as "true pigsties of misery, hideous brothels of debauchery and terrible conspiracies of crime, social dangers that aggravate . . . all contagious and epidemic disease." Officials readily singled out slum inhabitants, the poor – "workers, coachmen, day laborers, boatmen, shop-boys, laundresses, seamstresses of low clientele, common women" – as responsible for disease, crime, and immorality.[29]

The poor and their teeming slums had once belonged to the world of the street, the world kept at a distance by residents able to screen out the filth, smells, or noise with their walled gardens and shuttered windows and who relied on their servants as go-betweens, able to preserve the illusion of their own safekeeping. From mid-century those laundresses and seamstresses, and most particularly the wet-nurses, who entered private houses were identified as the carriers of disease. By the 1880s, as more families hired free women who lived out, direct ties with the cortiços could not be avoided.

Rio de Janeiro householders began to worry seriously about the slum women who took in laundry.[30] At the cortiços' communal tubs they washed, putting clothes to dry all around the central patio, on the "roof, [hanging] from windows and doors." Citizens' earlier offense at the messy sights – some even said "immoral" – around public fountains had prompted ordinances to prohibit laundresses from hanging clothes to dry in the Campo de Sant'Anna.[31] In cortiços, however, the mess came to be seen as dangerous. Lacking adequate drains, dirty, soapy water overflowed, giving off a "fetid odor." Some even claimed that the "bad smell" came from the "infected matter in the dirty clothes" as much as from waste water. In either case, it was believed that the laundering done in cortiços turned them into "true centers of miasmas," that threatened the health of the neighborhood.[32] Worse were the laundresses who, without regard to possible contamination, indiscriminately "mixed together the clothes of their [various] customers." Against these abuses, mistresses might choose "with maximum care" laundresses from outlying areas where, they believed, "water ran in abundance," and where in larger houses, the women had space for drying clothes, and – because of less pinched circumstances – used more soap. More practically, the city council moved in 1881 to prohibit the dangerous "mixing of clothes," and by 1891 had decided to allow cortiço tenants to wash only their own clothes in the shared tubs.[33] Whether the prohibitions were observed (which seems unlikely), the view of cortiço laundresses and washing sites as unhealthy had taken hold.

In its most insidious form the disease cortiço dwellers were understood to transmit penetrated to the quarters of intimate family life. Because she nurtured the newborn from the first precarious moments, the person of the wet-nurse became for patrões the most terrible and alarming carrier of disease. From mid-century, competing images of the wet-nurse emerged. No longer was she a figure of nurture and tender care; she became also a specter of hideous disease. With her body's milk she could infect the innocent with tuberculosis, even syphilis. The illnesses which patrões were duty bound to attend as the most dramatic symbol of the care owed to dependents, came to be understood as imported, carried from slums by servants, particularly wet-nurses, into once protected homes. Whatever disturbance ordinary house servants provoked by leaving, disobeying, or pilfering paled alongside the fearful presence of the wet-nurse who could contaminate.

In contrast perhaps with their plantation counterparts, city householders did not typically raise from infancy the female slaves who could later serve as wet-nurses. Despite advice to patrões as late as 1893 that they should choose as wet-nurses "women whose origins and life are well known, raised by the family, for example," urban conditions did not permit such close scrutiny. While women from the country, free of the taint of city slum life, might be especially prized, most relied on locally hired women, either slave or free. Although individual families might retain fond memories of particular women, the commonly shared view held that hired wet-nurses were "women of low class." And worse, "they live in cortiços."[34] The wet-nurse became the direct link between a sheltered and comfortable world and the disease-infected street life centered in cortiços. They came from cortiços into private homes, or in other instances, families sent their infants (or the infants of their servants) out to board with a wet-nurse, sometimes for several months, exposing them to the dangers of unknown or dirty households, and in all likelihood insuring that they shared the nursing woman's milk with other babies similarly put in her care. Wrote one doctor in 1879 "I have seen wet-nurses who nurse children of important and wealthy families . . . in cortiços."[35]

Parents rightly worried over high death rates among young children: 410 deaths for every 1,000 live births among children up to age seven in 1878 was usual for Rio de Janeiro. Among the diseases passed to children and attributed to wet-nurses were yaws, a contagious tropical skin disease with raspberry-like swellings, scrofula or tuberculosis of the lymph glands, elephantiasis, and, ugliest of all, syphilis. Parents also recognized the constant threat of pulmonary tuberculosis that could readily be passed to their babies by the women who nursed them. Besides transmitting whatever pestilence bred in cortiços, wet-nurses were believed to have infections peculiar to them, especially chronic skin diseases.[36]

The standard diseases associated with the slums had had the advantage of being blatant: the stench from their courtyards was unmistakable; yellow fever, cholera, typhoid struck quickly and identifiably. Wet-nurses, however, infected infants with diseases not at first detectable but which were thought to remain insidiously dormant, festering for years.[37]

Doctors offered detailed advice to the literate well-to-do on the ideal attributes of a wet-nurse. Although, "white wet-nurses are in all respects preferable," they were less suitable in the heat of the tropics than blacks whose "health prospers in hot regions." Thus one doctor urged choosing a "black . . . young, strong and robust, well constituted," while another thought brown-skinned women best, then whites, and only last blonde women. The milk, besides being abundant and odorless, should "spring from 5 to 8 orifices, should be sweetish, first turning watery and bluish in color, when tested, then changing to white and becoming thicker." A satisfactory wet-nurse had well developed breasts, "the nipples neither rigid nor soft, neither very pointed nor shrunken." "Pear-shaped breasts" were best; breasts too large smothered the child's face and often had too little milk; small breasts supplied milk thin in both quality and quantity. Most importantly, her breasts should be without "cracks or ulcerous sores." But such ideal figures were rare. The doctors also urged that the woman's body be scanned for a straight spine and no signs of broken bones, for lack of bodily symmetry possibly indicated rickets, spinal damage, epilepsy, the effects of syphilis or scrofula – all conditions she might pass on, causing the child a lifetime of illness.[38]

Just as the slum-dwelling poor came to be seen as contaminated in both body and spirit, wet-nurses with recognized influence over the young could endanger their moral well-being as much as their bodily health. For that reason, "no bad habits either congenital or acquired" could be allowed. A woman should possess ". . . moral qualities of such an order that they can favorably impress the little being." Yet the socially agreed-upon view of wet-nurses held that most were women "whose habits and social position did not shelter them from vices," or whose "bad customs" were attributable to their heritage as "ignorant blacks imported from Africa." Maria Graham, an English traveler to Rio de Janeiro early in the nineteenth century, wrote that caring mothers took their children to balls with them rather than leave them alone with slave amas ". . . whose manners were so depraved, and practices so immoral . . ." as to destroy the children.[39] They were also irresponsible. Some willfully contaminated their milk by using alcohol, tobacco, or certain medicines. Others ruined their milk by becoming pregnant, something "they do not always avoid but certainly always seek to hide or deny."[40] Certainly, from the 1860s and 1870s, important men made clear their point: wet-nurses were a physically polluting presence and if also immoral, as was likely, caused social pollution as well. At all times they should be looked upon with suspicion.

By the 1880s, when apprehension over intrusive disease reinforced anxiety regarding the social consequences of abolition, an old style paternalism that had permitted patrões to act toward slaves and the dependent poor with benevolence when they obeyed and rage when they refused no longer seemed a match for the grave social problems that confronted the city. The infecting and disorderly poor, packed into their cortiços, were no longer a matter for individual decision. Their presence demanded sterner and public measures. The particular solutions proposed were consistent with the dangers as contemporaries had come to identify them. As residents and officials had attempted to track down the "miasma" which fed contagion, they came to fix attention gradually and irrevocably on those corners of the city center that most trapped the dampness, where sun and wind least penetrated – on the cortiços. Wedged into the oldest and most congested part of the city, on land once wrested from mangrove swamps, the poor of the cortiços lived in "rooms made of old, used wood" and "without sanitary facilities." Humid soil high in bacteria combined with the lack of hygienic conditions to produce the "points where the first cases of infectious disease appeared and developed into epidemics."[41] A true "dread of contagion"[42] now lay hold of local imaginations, focusing apprehensions on the slums. Any solution that did not strike swiftly to eradicate the dangers appeared lamentably inadequate, almost negligent.

Anxious officials began by attempting to know how many cortiços there were in each parish, with how many tenants in how many rooms. The president of one such commission estimated that the cortiços housed as many as one third of Rio de Janeiro's population in 1879. While his own figures for one of the two districts in his parish of Santo Antonio roughly bore him out, city-wide figures put the cortiço population at 15,054 in 1867, at 21,929 in 1869, and at 46,680 in 1888 – that is, between 11 and 16 per cent of the population.[43] But if the Santo Antonio official's estimate was extravagant, his impression that the population of cortiço tenants and the sheer number of cortiços entrenched in the city center had grown dangerously large was widely shared. Undeniably the mass of slum dwellers increased in absolute numbers, more than trebling in the twenty years from 1867 to 1888, with the worst concentration of cortiços principally in the decaying area around the Campo de Sant'Anna and the Mangue Canal – still known as the Cidade Nova. The parish of Sant'Anna consistently accounted for more than a quarter to a third of the city's total cortiço population between 1867 and 1888.[44]

Tenants lived packed into small rooms, usually two or three persons to a room, although officials insisted that reported numbers undercounted actual tenancy. City regulations limited occupancy in the cortiços to two persons per room: some rooms housed seven.[45] The 54 tenants, men, women, and children, in 24 rooms of one cortiço in 1896 shared a single water tap and two latrines, while the 343 in another in 1895 had only 6 latrines and one water tap. The slum population increased, squeezing more rooms into existing cortiços. Cortiços could be concealed from public view and from inspectors behind the disguising fronts of more substantial buildings, the actual entrance being through a private house or hotel.[46] Duplicating in other parishes the pattern of Sant'Anna, the number of cortiços proliferated: 502 in 1867; 642 two years later; 1,331 by 1888.[47]

As ever more cortiços multiplied in areas already damp and unhealthy, constructed where refuse had filled in swamps, their very crowding produced more filth and dampness, so, it was thought, intensifying the miasmas.[48] Filth piled in a hole in the middle of one cortiço patio, unclean latrines, or rotting animal carcasses led, according to a complaint made to the Municipal Council by the Central Board of Public Hygiene in the summer of 1875, to the spread of yellow fever threatening all 200 tenants. Cortiços became those ". . . repugnant centers of pestilence that have been so prejudicial to the health of this unhappy capital . . ." where "from one cortiço alone on rua Formosa 15 cadavers were removed in 17 days," victims of yellow fever. Year after year local inspectors confirmed that contagious disease came if not solely, then initially and principally from slums.[49]

Toward the end of summer in 1880, police called for the complete closing of one cortiço, urging it should be "evacuated, disinfected, and the refuse removed." The health board also attempted to halt additional cortiço construction before they too became the "theatre

Plate 12 "Yellow fever now visits even the theatre," 1876

of painful scenes that appear during times of epidemics that ravage by preference the residents of the Cidade Nova."[50] Those remedies might have appeared sufficient if only the poor had suffered and died. But yellow fever indiscriminately attacked all classes, even the rich. A tarted up "yellow fever," as the *Revista Illustrada* drew her, "now visits even the theatre." And yellow fever was not the only wanton contagion. Tuberculosis "continued to cause great damage, unfortunately attacking all classes of society, not exempting any age, profession, or sex, leveling all nationalities, statuses and colors." At least one doctor allowed that the death rate among tenement dwellers exceeded that of others in his district, while public spokesmen regretted that the cortiços were always "the point of departure" as well as the place where epidemics finished, but the most urgent concern attached to the victims from "the city's richest and healthiest neighborhoods."[51] That brought to the forefront the problem of the control of servants.

Throughout the 1880s and into the 1890s, the Rio de Janeiro municipal government and those ministries of the imperial and federal governments empowered to direct city administration received and deliberated numerous proposals to register and regulate domestic servants.[52] The various proposals agreed on the basic familiar terms, although the reciprocities were at last formally defined. A servant's obligations would amount to obeying the patrão in all "legitimate" orders, offering respect, fulfilling the work "with diligence and zeal." Furthermore, a servant could be held responsible for damage or loss of property belonging to patrões. For their part, employers would have to provide "good treatment," room and board, and the agreed upon salary. If a servant suffered loss or injury defending her patrão, she was to be recompensed. The employer would provide first aid or hospital care in case a maid became ill. Each party would owe the other 15 days notice to end a contract, although in unusual circumstances either could end it immediately. A servant could be dismissed on the spot if she "committed robbery or practiced acts contrary to morality and decorum."[53] Conversely, a servant could leave without notice if an employer committed "immoral acts" or physically mistreated her. The names of all maids would be entered in a centrally kept register, wet-nurses would additionally present certificates of medical examinations, and placement agencies would be required to register themselves and prove their reliability. The work history of each servant was to be recorded in a *caderneta* or passbook where each employer would state the reasons for a servant's leaving and comment on her conduct, especially her "morality," thus enabling future employers to know the past of the "outsiders" who presented themselves for hire. Finally, contracts would secure that elusive but fundamental element of correct demeanor: a servant would "respect her master," and for any "lack of respect," or "insolence or insubordination" she could legitimately be punished or dismissed. One suggested that even the "symptoms of pregnancy" justified immediate dismissal.[54]

While the minister of justice had insisted that something be done to protect householders from exposing themselves "to the dangers of having in [their] service corrupt persons," by 1889 the councilors of state struck a cautious note. They advised that whatever measures were adopted should be readily acceptable "on the part of the population and without great disturbance to our domestic habits."[55] The risk of such unwelcome "disturbance" eventually brought attempts at regulation to a halt, but not before householders proposed further measures to eliminate the dangers of that polluting presence, the infected wet-nurse.

In 1873 José Pereira Rego, the Baron Lavradio and president of the Central Board of Public Hygiene, had declared to the Brazilian Academy of Medicine that two "momentous" health problems faced the empire: "breast-feeding by mercenary wet-nurses," and the need for a public sewerage system. By 1876 Dr. Carlos Arthur Moncorvo de Figueiredo, committed as his son would be to the question of better health for the poor, formulated the first "regulation of wet-nurses." The proposed regulation he linked to his more ambitious attempt to open the first clinic that would offer free medical examinations to wet-nurses.[56]

The example set by Moncorvo de Figueiredo and his son prompted others to action. A group of citizens formed a "Sanitation Association" in 1879. By "sanitation" they understood physical examinations for wet-nurses. In all city parishes they set up offices where women could be examined without charge. Daily newspapers announced the places and times. No one came.[57] A third effort succeeded only briefly when, in 1884, the Camara Municipal operated an "Institute of Wet-nurses." The proposal required all women, slave or free, to have a certificate based on an examination conducted by an institute doctor, valid for only three months, when a woman would then be re-examined. The institute would serve as a clearing house, keeping lists of those qualified to work as wet-nurses and recording the number of births each woman had had and the date of her last delivery. The institute foundered and after two months suspended services altogether. In the same year, a proposal went before the Camara Municipal to establish a single medical commission to examine "cattle on the hoof, slaughter houses, butcher shops, stables for milk cows, and wet-nurses."[58] A final proposal in 1907, had it passed into law, would have required compulsory examinations for any wet-nurse who resided with a family or who accepted infants into her own home, and permitted a woman to nurse only one child at a time. Seeking to insure that wet-nurses would be free of disease that could be passed to a child, doctors who proposed the law intended, for the first time, to protect the wet-nurses from contracting infection from the children they nursed by stipulating that they too should be examined.[59]

Public debate had not only aroused suspicion about the wet-nurse as a threatening figure, it also began to rearrange the image that women might have of themselves as mothers. In 1843, Dr. Imbert conceded that however preferable maternal breast feeding might be, Brazilian women, "delicate and nervous" who must struggle against the excessive tropical heat that "drains vital forces and irritates the nervous system," and who frequently married young, could not be expected to bear the "tiredness of prolonged nursing without grave detriment to their health." Later doctors and statesmen were less tolerant. They sternly blamed women who from vanity and fear of losing the beauty of their figures, or from the "caprice of fashion and social pleasures," or for being "carried away by ostentation or by desire to enjoy more easily the pleasures of life . . ." delivered their children over to hired wet-nurses. "Our women" not only "ignored their first maternal obligations," but they further subjected their children to the ". . . immense dangers of mercenary breast feeding . . . to the transmission of grave infirmities . . ." and exposed them morally to the "injection of repugnant habits. . . ."[60] By 1879 enough had been said that a new journal, *A Mãe de Família*, appeared. Aiming to influence women toward a proper carrying out of their maternal role, the journal took the line that women, born to be mothers, ought to be so committedly by making any sacrifice necessary. Somewhat later another journal that would liberate women from a merely vain and self-indulgent life, extolled motherhood as a role to be valued, one that brought satisfaction, not one to be shunned.[61]

As a result of heightened concern about wet-nurses transmitting illness and the reorientation of a woman's role, parents entrusted their children to hired wet-nurses only when unavoidable. "Cota," wrote the journalist and prominent member of parliament, Rui Barbosa, about his wife in 1880, "is on her feet but ill. Dr. Felix continues to see her daily. My little newborn daughter fares poorly and I am forced to take an *ama* here." "It is come to this," he lamented. Another mother, ill and unable to nurse her second child born in the winter of 1888, reluctantly gave him over to the hired black woman, Maria, to nurse only after trying herself for more than two weeks.[62]

The connection of contagion with the slums, the poor, and so with servants had caused local understandings of order and control to be recast as a wider and public issue lying within the jurisdiction of local government. City officials responded with reforms that would reshape both the physical and social landscape. A thoroughgoing demolition of the slums would necessarily involve local government in action that would be collective and public. Work contracts would make explicit and binding the arrangements that for so long had been informally entered into, while health examinations would institutionalize the advice that patrões and doctors had offered for years. At bottom those proposed solutions were adaptations of former ways intended to shore up the customary authority of the household and extend it to new and disturbing situations, but they too depended on local government or ministerial support to implement and enforce. If householders departed from the usual exercise of power as a private prerogative, they did so in an effort to maintain the security of house against street. They did not anticipate, however, the full consequences of the attempt to yoke public power to private purpose.

Municipal attempts in the late 1870s to clean up or demolish the slums had produced more agitation than tangible results, and what results were achieved hardly reassured a disquieted public.[63] Tenants evicted from condemned quarters, without alternatives, simply crowded into other slums, so that instead of rooms with 6 to 8 people, they then held 18 or 20 persons "cooking and sleeping in the same place." A "cortiço that had had 100 inhabitants, today has 300," reported the *Gazeta da Tarde* in 1884. And slum dwellers resisted: tenants in Sant'Anna delayed being closed down by keeping the gates locked against any who did not belong there. Another "three great cortiços . . . resisted the order [to be disinfected or close] and were not shut down by police."[64]

The famous and fearsome cortiço, "Cabeça de Porco" or Pig's Head became the symbol of cortiço resistance, defying all orders to close for some 53 years. With 4,000 inhabitants, many of them according to contemporary belief recruited from among the "assassins and criminals" and "victims of pauperism," the Cabeça de Porco consisted of an unknown number of shacks jumbled together along the old rua de Sant'Anna as it cut away from the square toward the waterfront and warehouse district. In early 1893 one of the city's first mayors under the newly established republic, Candido Barata Ribeiro, finally put an end to it. In January of that year tenants had ignored an order to close. Since they had made known their intention to impede demolition, the mayor "requested the force necessary to guarantee success." On the night of January 26, Barata Ribeiro and a team of laborers – some said 300, others said 150 – began demolition.

All night, through stifling heat, they hacked away, supposedly depositing furniture and personal possessions with their owners, while infantry surrounded the cortiço and cavalry guarded cross streets and the hill at the back. By morning they had reduced the famous cortiço to rubble. The *Rio News* reported that "this cortiço has long been a focus of infection for the whole neighborhood, and its destruction in this manner will be heartily praised."[65]

Tenants were not the only ones to impede reform. The Brazilian Academy of Medicine, never aloof from ordinary matters, lent its support for the condemnation of cortiços as "true nests of yellow fever and all infectious fevers [and] of vice and crime," pointing out that the fact that "they are still standing attests to the [illicit] protection and carelessness of the city council." Even more blame-worthy, indifferent "aristocrats" with the connivance of the municipal council acquired "fabulous incomes" from the rents they extracted at the public cost of "slowly and progressively poisoning the health of the population." The council, went the charge, more interested in the power of patronage than in the public welfare, violated its own regulations to permit a "dreadful increase in cortiços," even in the central city.[66]

City health officials, attempting to enforce renovation or demolition orders, came up short against what they sarcastically termed "worthy patronage" or "protections." The Rio de Janeiro health commission in 1896 condemned "the disposition, the habits, and the stingy impulse of urban property owners. The great proprietors even more than the small ones, resist any innovation and prefer to endure considerable losses than to agree voluntarily to the execution of health measures that would benefit no one more than they." But "to break this dominance" of city councilmen and landlords, "is neither easy nor without danger," cautioned men of the medical academy.[67]

Public intervention, it was clear, could be achieved only at private cost, and attempts to project social control as a public matter would simultaneously generate new and hence uncertainly located power. Caught in that dilemma, the impulse for renovation faltered. City residents continued to face the threat of cortiços and contagion much as they always had. During the hot and sultry summer months, the wealthy left the city, hoping to escape the worst flaring of infection. By ferry boat and train they made their way to Petrópolis, where the royal family also had their summer palace, set in the cool mountains away from the contaminated city below. Personal servants, wet-nurses or an occasional governess might accompany patrões to their summer retreats, but mostly the unlucky poor remained behind, victims in disproportionately large numbers to the disease that throve in the humid summer heat.[68]

While projects to demolish slums were being abandoned or endlessly postponed, efforts to regulate domestic servants faced other objections. The council of state concluded that the notion of work contracts was impractical, as the practice would never gain accept-ance among patrões. Householders, they recognized, would refuse to tolerate restrictions on their "domestic habits" enforced from the outside.

Furthermore, the issue of which public authority would oversee and enforce the regulations proved divisive. In the course of the 1880s some proposed that power go to the police and to local parish inspectors appointed by the chief of police. The police agreed: they ". . . have the power to revoke the passbooks . . ." from servants in cases of infractions until they could be subjected to whatever punishments were to be imposed.[69] Others were less content, especially as such an ordinance threatened the privacy of the household, the patrões' previously unchallenged sphere of domin-ance. One newspaper, commenting on attempts to register servants with the police in Buenos Aires, while conceding that "a similar regulation has many advocates" in Rio de Janeiro, condemned such supervision as "unwarranted and dangerous," an "abuse of auth-ority" that would lead to "insufferable meddling" by police. Controversy continued. The scheme briefly settled on in 1888 avoided the police, seeking instead to create a special bureau that would act on the authority of the Municipal Council.[70] A year later, when the empire ended, that city ordinance ceased to have validity.

The problem remained one of power. From early in their lengthy deliberations that ran through the 1880s, the councilors of state considered legally stipulated contracts "completely inadmissible," on the grounds that such regulation would permit dangerous excesses of public authority, its enforcement would "exceed the jurisdiction of the Municipal Council and of the police," and it would impede the "free exercise of individual activity" by restricting a person's "right to work." They condemned the proposed passbooks that would, they said, subject servants to "an odious and excessive inspection and vigilance by authorities," while further preventing a family from taking into their household and confidence whomever they chose, with or without a passbook. They found the passbooks dangerous to masters who, they insisted, should be allowed to write nothing at all in them. If they were to enter their comments, they risked being taken to court for "slander and aggression," in cases that would defy defense since the only witnesses to "occurrences that had taken place in the privacy of one's home" would be other family members who could not testify.[71]

Behind these issues lay one more deeply rooted. If the rules were to be enforced, then householders would be required to endure "domiciliary inspections and impertinent investigations" by police.[72] The very notion of a written contract implied a balance of obligations and an agreement that each party comply with the terms set down. In effect, they refused to surrender their somewhat uncertain personal supervision for more stable but mutually obliging legal agreements. More than any other single consideration, it was the violation of domestic privacy and personal authority that warned patrões away from the public regulation of servants.

In 1889 the empire crumbled, giving way to a federal republic. New voices, some less equivocal than those heard during the empire, challenged the very notion of regulation. Now using the modish language of liberalism, opponents of regulation worked to the same ends. The jurist Tristão de Alencar Araripe Junior in 1891 denied that "there exists any consideration of public order that justifies the limit of this right . . ." to work. Determined opposition crystallized around the recently established constitutional guarantee for the free exercise of any profession, an issue with deep significance in the immediate aftermath of abolition when a fledgling republic wanted to rid itself of associations with slavery and the Empire. The positivist Miguel Lemos considered the freedom to work at any chosen profession fundamental to republican society. To deny that freedom was to deny individual initiative and responsibility. "Such regulations," he argued, "only serve to aggravate and systematize the oppression of the weak by the strong, instituting a new regime of slavery."[73] In the end, philosophic arguments probably exercised less force than pragmatic considerations.

While republican leaders in the early 1890s replaced or reshaped the institutions of government, locally citizens continued their attempts to regulate servants. The police reported the "insistent complaints of public opinion" about the state of domestic service which offered guarantees to neither employer nor employee, reminding the prefect they could do nothing without a city ordinance.[74] Pressure mounted, until finally in 1896 the council made one last-ditch effort at regulation by creating a municipal register administratively under the bureau of statistics. The ordinance required that servants carry a passbook to record employers' comments and reasons for dismissal. The law passed, but it was never enforced since no government agency was willing to carry it out. Nor did the city council take up the suggestion to approve or establish private agencies that would, for a fee, assume responsibility to a family for the servants they supplied.[75]

Ministers, councilors of state, police, aldermen, lawyers, businessmen, local citizens – all had come to withdraw their proposals to formalize and fix by law the relationship between patrão and servant. Individual householders continued to rely on familiar and casual arrangements made with individual servants. Instead of a passbook, they asked for "letters of assurance or opinions from competent persons," or looked for servants known for their "good conduct" or of "assured behavior."[76] The regulation of domestic servants remained a matter of private negotiation and personal control. Initial efforts to transfer responsibility onto public authorities in a quest to reinforce order had buckled. At the same time apprehension over abolition had lessened. Although slavery no longer supplied the defining relationship for a paternal order, the overall patterns of culture had seemingly stretched to accommodate the change. Slavery's end had not cut away those fundamental notions that distinguished patrões from laboring people or the connections that tied them together. A tolerable sense of order had prevailed despite abolition.

On the issue of wet-nurses the new republic was equally unwilling to intervene. Repeating decisions made during the empire, the government defeated or ignored city requirements that wet-nurses meet prescribed health standards.[77] Moreover, compulsory health examinations of wet-nurses would require clinics, skilled staff, and even police to prosecute and fine those who refused to comply. Although both government and private citizens acknowledged that the dangers posed by sick wet-nurses warranted broader solutions than individual householders could provide by ministering to dependents or sending them away in disgust, state intervention in such intimate domestic matters, and the eclipse of private authority it would entail, were clearly unacceptable. Moncorvo de Figueiredo and other colleagues who first established clinics had misjudged public response. Although privately funded and established principally to protect the health of the well-off, their proposals nonetheless invaded zones that both masters and servants, for their different reasons, preferred to keep inviolate.

With compulsory examinations roundly defeated, voluntary free clinics partially bridged the gap. Following his father's example, Moncorvo Filho set up his own dispensary in 1901 on the rua Visconde do Rio Branco, near the Praça da Republica, in a committed effort to offer free health care and practical assistance to the poor of the city, especially children. Included in the services his clinic offered were medical examinations for wet-nurses. In order to avoid the need in the future to hire wet-nurses, however, he intended to make wholesome cow's milk (tested for tuberculosis) available whenever necessary as a substitute for maternal breast-feeding. While the father had failed to attract patients, the son met with at least modest success. Moncorvo Filho made his clinic accessible with long hours and a convenient location. More importantly, he attended the poor in general. Women went there for care during pregnancy or received sterile milk for sickly infants. Clinic doctors administered medical and surgical treatment to the sick, distributed clothes, shoes, and food, and gave vaccinations.[78]

Besides their work for the poor, between 1901 and 1908 doctors at the clinic examined 918 women who sought certificates as healthy wet-nurses. As a result of the examinations, doctors denied approval to more Brazilian than immigrant women, of whom they rejected proportionately more white women than mestizos or blacks. Among the 442 women, or 48 percent of those examined, whom doctors rejected as physically unfit to breast-feed, they identified as common symptoms or causes of ill health: vaginal discharge, then tuberculosis, urinary infections, insufficient or weak milk, syphilis, skin infections or abscesses, and anemia. "Extreme filthiness" prevented nine women from being approved; others showed signs of alcoholism or of "atrophied breast tissue." Dr. José Jayme de Almeida Pires was led to conclude that the women who would hire out as wet-nurses were themselves "victims of malnutrition and extreme poverty."[79]

Poor health proved not to be the only reason why some women went away without their certificates. Once there, 34 women refused to undergo the necessary gynecological examination.[80] Their refusal recalled the charge made by a supporter of compulsory examinations who wrote soon after abolition: "If it was already difficult to conduct a rigorous exam on the slave amas of other times, how much more difficult it becomes now that women refuse to submit to detailed inspection of the most hidden regions of their bodies. . . ."[81] Just as householders had kept aloof from meddling police inspections, so women guarded their bodies from prying examination. And in 1881, at the first clinic to offer free voluntary examinations, no women appeared. But the times, and women's attitudes changed. Between 1901 and 1908, 866 women underwent examination. One woman, "young, healthy and with milk from her first delivery," could then advertise herself for hire as a wet-nurse "with medical certificate," while another announced she had a "reference from Dr. Moncorvo." Gradually women had come to find advantage in the medical examinations that could certify them as reliable wet-nurses.[82]

If householders carried on without the legal trappings of contracts or regulations over servants or wet-nurses, questions of order and health, where morality, crime and disease were seen to overlap, nevertheless loomed as matters of troubling public concern. By 1900 apprehensions over contagion and control provoked manifest conflict between responsible citizens and the slum-dwelling poor.

To restrain that conflict and impose order, reformers turned their energies to remaking the urban landscape, impelled by a revised notion of social order. By the late 1880s, public authorities and private citizens voiced new, previously unheard concerns about drunks and thieves, roughs and vagabonds. Politicians wrote about the "rowdies who abound in this city, slaves and assassins, . . . [claiming that] the police force, hated by this class, . . . was impotent to maintain order." Or they debated laws and penalties against "the use of arms" or to contain "idlers, vagabonds, and the disorderly." Newspapers increasingly reported arrests for disorderliness or drunkenness among both men and women. Police recommended against creation of an open-air market near Sant'Anna church that would, they said, become the "corner of roughs and thieves . . . [and] the numbers game will reappear."[83] The vocabulary for describing such acts changed and both citizens and authorities sensed that public order was not secure. Crime consisted not principally of acts of personal violence or even of acts against property. Rather crime was social: disturbing public order, gambling; and most of all vagabonds – persons without legitimate occupation or known residence – were seen as a threat. Vagabondage as applied to women implied prostitution. Despite repeated attempts to prohibit prostitution, no law specifically forbade it. Instead, women suspected of being prostitutes were charged as vagabonds and with provoking disorder.[84] The social meaning of "vagabond," however, went well beyond prostitution. Once slavery had ended and a master could no longer be held accountable for dependents, "vagabond" designated the troubling class of people who had no legitimate social place, who existed outside ordered society. Reformers zealously took up the task of clearing the streets of roughs and vagabonds by arrests and especially by razing neighborhoods where the poor had long located their sense of community and where servant women continued to conduct their private lives.

Although debated for three decades, the swift and radical transformation of the city landscape finally became reality at the turn of the century when reformers finally acquired or took upon themselves the necessary powers to act. During the six months in which the most extensive demolition was accomplished, the city prefect, Francisco Pereira Passos, suspended the city council, thereby silencing whatever opposing voices might have officially spoken against his sweeping plans. He had successfully trampled on customary and long-guarded private interests in order to usurp private authority for public ends.

Something of the intent behind the changes can be gleaned from other reforms launched by Passos between 1902 and 1906. He aimed to extinguish the "deep-rooted evils that give a degrading note of backwardness to our civilization." Among those evils he included ridding the city of lottery vendors who "annoy with [their] infernal shouting, giving the city the aspect of [being] a gambling house," prohibiting "the gross customs of carnaval," preventing milk vendors from taking their cows door to door, and banning the raising of pigs in the city center or the hanging of meat in butcher shop doorways.[85] The city should instead bespeak its "civilization" and come to resemble imagined European capitals. The vulgar and unruly poor should be kept from public view. That, at least, was Passos' hope.

If some continued in their familiar ways, selling milk or raising pigs or dousing fellow revelers at carnaval, simply ignoring inconvenient ordinances, in other quarters social regulation met louder and tougher resistance. In 1902 medical researchers announced to the world the discovery that the mosquito carried yellow fever, so that the extinction of mosquito larvae would mean extinction of yellow fever.[86] In Rio de Janeiro a brigade 1,500-strong formed to inspect sewers, and open water tanks, gutters, or fish ponds, while in 1906 a team of 72 doctors aided by medical students disinfected "every house in the Federal District." The campaign against the mosquito met strong opposition. Congressmen charged that "citizens' liberties were endangered" by intruding doctors and brigade members.[87]

Congressmen proved mild opponents, however, compared with the rioters whose anger flared in 1904 against a law that made smallpox vaccinations compulsory for the first time.[88] Trouble began in the Largo do São Francisco where speakers urged non-compliance. Police tried to disperse the gathering crowd that instead swelled, by one account, to three or four thousand, including "honest workers" and "respectable" people, "members of diverse classes," until protest erupted into violence. On the fourth day the army was called out and rioting ceased.[89]

Compulsory smallpox vaccinations were announced exactly when slum demolition reached its peak, giving the poor double reason to join the rioting.[90] With the social worlds of their cortiços and neighborhoods destroyed, compulsory vaccinations invaded their bodies. They understood that vaccinations, like the earlier medical examinations for wet-nurses, threatened the last domain of private control – their bodies. The press knew how to play on popular fears with images of bodies turned into experimental laboratories for growing "colonies of bacteria," or by questioning "what type of drug is this that is going to enter the pulse of our organism?"[91] Far from seeming a welcome prevention against contagion, for the homeless poor vaccinations represented a final and intolerable invasion of their privacy, a genuine attack on "individual liberty."

Against the background of protest, whether mild or clamoring, reshaping of the city landscape went forward. Planners believed that the city's new design would prevent future contagion by opening it to cleansing sea breezes and by plans for neatly laid out residential areas. Besides the cleaned up Mangue Canal graced by a double row of royal palms, and the wholly re-built port works completed in 1911, city engineers widened some streets, straightened others, eliminated many, and cut additional ones to give new access and new buildings to the congested and crumbling Cidade Nova.[92] Catching the spirit of reform, respectable residents competed to have their streets widened. Crews dug wells to provide water for street-cleaning, landscaped parks, paved streets and public squares, and near the rua Carioca, where the old fountain had once drawn its boisterous laundresses, created a flower market. In the same section of town, the Passos administration built some 120 houses, inexpensive housing intended for working-class people.[93] Servants who did the marketing still journeyed to the old site, and the city council refused to license more convenient local markets, as "our population is not yet ready to maintain open-air markets," where, they said, experience had shown that "the authorities had to intervene constantly to keep such places clean." They nevertheless recognized that the old and dirty central market required overhauling. By 1908 a shiny new market opened, moved only a short distance and still on the bay at the far edge of the city, handy to docks but not to most city residents or their servants.[94]

As always, the wealthy would attempt to seclude and protect themselves. Where massive granite hills had once separated the bayside city from ocean beaches to the south, two tunnels now connected them. The first in 1892 and the second in 1906 joined Botafogo with Copacabana and Leme beaches enlarging greatly the potential area of the city and extending it into cooler and healthier environs.[95] Fine homes would soon appear in the seaward suburbs. In time, of course, the poor would follow to provide the servants and the services, their rickety slums perched on the surrounding hills, but for a while, residents could believe themselves safely away from infection and poverty.

But no change in Rio de Janeiro's landscape so fittingly symbolized the reformers' intent to eradicate disease and poverty as the wide Avenida Central. Stretching from the docks at the Praça Mauá to the mouth of the bay at its southern end, the avenue opened up the oldest part of the city where demolition of squalid buildings had made way for the fashionable avenue, opening the central city to daylight and sea breezes. Handsome cast iron lamps posted down the center of the avenue glowed at night, and on either side fine buildings displayed elaborate façades. Beyond where the avenue met the sea, land-fill extended the bay's edge to allow for construction of the curving Avenida Beira-Mar to the end of Botafogo. Along the avenue well-dressed women strolled in the company of well-to-do men.[96] The sumptuously beautiful Municipal Theater, inaugurated with fitting pomp in 1909, faced the sea from the beginning of the Avenida Central. Its interior stairways and pillars built from rich imported marbles, the stage and boxes accented with gold leaf, the theater was dedicated to an elite's pursuit of high culture.[97] The promiscuous jumble of the city of fifty years earlier had at last been brought to order.

By 1910 nearly 80 years had passed since the visiting French artist had presented his portrait of a Rio de Janeiro family strolling to church neatly ranked, displaying the accepted complement of servants from cook to wet-nurse, and evoking in setting and action the carefully preserved distinction between house and street. Since then, epidemic disease had showed her terrible visage, slavery had ended, and a federal republic and elected president had replaced the empire and royal family. The household of Debret's painting, although recognizable, no longer expressed the singly most ap-

Plate 13 A black woman balancing a load of laundry on her head as she walks on the Avenida Central, *c.* 1910

propriate or compelling metaphor for society. An expanded image – that of the urban landscape itself – more accurately conveyed an altered understanding of social life. More complex, the new image rendered more explicit the conflict between house and street, between rich and poor that an older notion of household had striven to deny. The webs of domestic authority and control, nowhere more visible than in the relationship between patrões and servants, strained and loosened by the changes, nonetheless endured.

Postscript

In 1961 a national meeting of The Young Domestic Servants convened in Rio de Janeiro with the aim of forming an association, the first step in becoming a legally recognized labor union. The meeting issued a "Manifesto às Patroas" in which they stated both their rights and duties, as they, the domestics, intended them to be understood. As the first of those rights, they expected to be considered with "love, respect and understanding within the houses in which we work, being considered members of the family. . . ." In return, among the duties they named, they pledged to "guard the secrets of the families of which we are considered members."

O Estado de São Paulo, 4 February 1961; *Correio da Manhã*, 4 February 1961.

Abbreviations

ACM-RJ	Arquivo da Cúria Metropolitana, Rio de Janeiro
AGC-RJ	Arquivo Geral da Cidade, Rio de Janeiro
AGC-RJ, SI	Arquivo Geral da Cidade, Rio de Janeiro, Seção Iconográfica
AIHGB	Arquivo do Instituto Histórico e Geográfico Brasileiro, Rio de Janeiro
Almanak Laemmert	*Alamanak Administrativo, Mercantil e Industrial do Rio de Janeiro*
AN	Arquivo Nacional, Rio de Janeiro
ANSPE	Arquivo Nacional, Rio de Janeiro, Seção do Poder Executivo
ANSPJ	Arquivo Nacional, Rio de Janeiro, Seção do Poder Judiciário
ANSPJ, CPO	Arquivo Nacional, Rio de Janeiro, Seção do Poder Judiciário, Cartório do Primeiro Ofício
ANSPJ, CSO	Arquivo Nacional, Rio de Janeiro, Seção do Poder Judiciário, Cartório do Segundo Ofício
Arrolamento SC, 1870	Brazil, Directoria Geral de Estatística, Arrolamento da população do Municipio da Côrte (São Cristovão) 1870, MS, Instituto Brasileiro de Geografia e Estatística, Rio de Janeiro, Departmento de Documentação e Referência
Civil Code, 1916	Joseph Wheless, trans., *The Civil Code of Brazil* [*1916*]
Código Criminal do Imperio, 1876	José Antonio de Araújo Filgueiras Junior, ed., *Código Criminal do Imperio do Brasil*
Código de Posturas, 1870	Rio de Janeiro, Camara Municipal, *Código de Posturas da Ilma. Camara Municipal do Rio de Janeiro e editaes da mesma Camara*
Código de Posturas, 1894	Rio de Janeiro, Intendencia Municipal do Districto Federal, *Código de Posturas, Leis, Decretos, Editaes e Resoluções da Intendencia Municipal do Districto Federal*
Código Penal, 1890	Antonio Bento de Faria, *Annotações theorico-praticas ao Código Penal do Brasil de accordo com a doutrina e legislação e a jurisprudencia, nacionaes e*

	estrangeiras, seguido de um appendice contendo as leis em vigor e que lhe são referentes. . . .
Código Philippino, 1870	Candido Mendes de Almeida, comp. and ed., *Código Philippino; ou Ordenações e leis do reino de Portugal, recopilados por mandado d'el-rey D. Philippe I. 14 ed. segundo a primeira de 1603 e a nona de Coimbra de 1824. Addicionada com diversas notas* . . .
Constituições Primeiras, 1853	Sebastião Monteiro da Vide, *Constituições Primeiras do Arcebispado da Bahia. Feitas e ordenadas pelo* . . . *Sebastião Monteiro da Vide, 5º Arcebispo do dito Arcebispado e do Conselho de Sua Magestade: Propostas e aceitas em o synodo Diocesano que o dito Senhor celebrou em 12 de junho do anno de 1707. Impressas em Lisboa no anno de 1719 e em Coimbra em 1720* . . .
fl. or fls.	folha or folhas
HAHR	*Hispanic American Historical Review*
JC	*Jornal do Commercio*
Leis do Brasil	Brazil, Laws, statutes, etc., *Coleção das Leis do Brasil*
Recenseamento, 1872	Brazil, Directoria Geral de Estatística, *Recenseamento da população do Imperio do Brazil a que se procedeu no dia 1º de agosto de 1872*
Recenseamento do Rio de Janeiro, 1906	Brazil, [Directoria Geral de Estatística], *Recenseamento do Rio de Janeiro (Districto Federal) realizado em 20 de setembro de 1906*
Relatorio, 1870	Brazil, Directoria Geral de Estatística, *Relatorio apresentado ao Ministro e Secretario d'Estado dos Negocios do Imperio pela Commissão encarregada da direcção dos trabalhos do arrolamento da população do Municipio da Côrte a que se procedeu em abril de 1870*
RIHGB	*Revista do Instituto Histórico e Geográfico Brasileiro*

Notes

Introduction

1 Clifford Geertz, "Thick description: toward an interpretive theory of culture," in *The Interpretation of Cultures, Selected Essays* (New York: Basic Books, 1973), p. 5.

2 For an intellectual history of English paternalism and its public projections, see David Roberts, *Paternalism in Early Victorian England* (New Brunswick, NJ: Rutgers University Press, 1979); in the relationship between law and custom, Brazil differs profoundly from the American South described by Eugene Genovese, *Roll, Jordan, Roll: The World the Slaves Made* (New York: Pantheon, 1974), where law and custom were distinct, alternatives to which both masters and slaves might have recourse. Challenging Genovese, James Oakes, *The Ruling Race: A History of American Slaveholders* (New York: Alfred A. Knopf, 1982), does not distinguish between law and custom, but between a benevolent paternalism of older, more aristocratic areas and an increasingly harsh one as slavery spread west under newer and rougher planters.

3 Brazil, Directoria Geral de Estatística, *Recenseamento da população do Imperio do Brazil a que se procedeu no dia 1º de agosto de 1872* (Rio de Janeiro: Leuzinger, 1873–1876), Municipio Neutro, pp. 1–33 (hereafter cited as *Recenseamento, 1872);* Brazil, [Directoria Geral de Estatística], *Recenseamento do Rio de Janeiro (Districto Federal) realizado em 20 de setembro de 1906* (Rio de Janeiro: Officina da Estatística, 1907), pp. 181–317 (hereafter cited as *Recenseamento do Rio de Janeiro, 1906).*

4 Summary figures for 1870 are based on a household-by-household census of the city. So far manuscript lists have been located for only one parish. As the first to analyze those manuscripts, I draw on that evidence throughout the book.

5 An observer in 1891 estimated that manufacturing in Rio de Janeiro employed 2,000 women. One cotton and woolen factory, for example, engaged 60 women and 47 children as operatives. In its annual report in 1878 a textile mill listed 65 women and girls among its 343 workers. The number of women increased to 145 out of a total of 451 workers there in 1882, and by 1891, 392 of the 928 operatives were women and girls. By 1907, manufacturing establishments in Rio de Janeiro totaled 671, including 22 textile factories. Centro Industrial do Brasil, *Le Brésil: Ses richesses naturelles, ses industries,* vol. III: *Industrie manufacturière* (Rio de Janeiro: Imprimerie M. Orosco, 1909), pp. xvii–xix, 36–37; Christopher Columbus Andrews, *Brazil: Its Condition and Prospects,* 3rd edn. (New York: D. Appleton & Co., 1891), p. 39; Companhia Brasil Industrial, *Relatorio . . . 1878* (Rio de Janeiro:

Moreira, Maximino, 1878), p. 8; *Relatorio . . . 1882* (Rio de Janeiro: Moreira, Maximino, 1882), p. 8; Companhia de Fiação e Tecelagem Brazil Industrial, *Relatorio . . . 1891* (Rio de Janeiro: Leuzinger, 1891), p. 6; on conditions for textile workers, including women, see Stanley Stein, *The Brazilian Cotton Manufacture: Textile Enterprise in an Underdeveloped Area, 1850–1950* (Cambridge: Harvard University Press, 1957), pp. 51–65; Eulália Maria Lahmeyer Lobo, *História do Rio de Janeiro: do capital comercial ao capital industrial e financeiro*, 2 vols. (Rio de Janeiro: IBMEC, 1978), provides a detailed statistical profile of the city over the last decades of the nineteenth century that includes transformations in the labor force.

6 Brazil, Directoria Geral de Estatística, *Relatorio apresentado ao Ministro e Secretário d'Estado dos Negocios do Imperio pela Commissão encarregada da direcção dos trabalhos do arrolamento da população do Municipio da Côrte a que se procedeu em abril de 1870* (Rio de Janeiro: Perseverança, 1871), Mappas A–K, n.p. (hereafter cited as *Relatorio, 1870); Recenseamento, 1872*, Municipio Neutro, pp. 1–33; *Recenseamento do Rio de Janeiro, 1906*, pp. 174–317. Nor does nineteenth-century Rio de Janeiro, with its preponderance of servant women, appear unusual. In the United States, as late as 1870, 50 percent of employed women were servants, while in England one of every six women was a domestic and among single women, one of every five. Daniel E. Sutherland, *Americans and Their Servants: Domestic Service in the United States from 1800 to 1920* (Baton Rouge and London: Louisiana State University Press, 1981), p. 45; Theresa M. McBride, *The Domestic Revolution: The Modernization of Household Service in England and France, 1820–1920* (New York: Holmes & Meier, 1976), p. 34. Sarah C. Maza shows that in late eighteenth-century France women became increasingly dominant among household servants who counted for as many as one-fifth of the adult workforce, *Servants and Masters in Eighteenth-Century France: The Uses of Loyalty* (Princeton University Press, 1983), pp. 25, 277–278. See also, Cissie Fairchilds, *Domestic Enemies: Servants and Their Masters in Old Regime France* (Baltimore: The Johns Hopkins University Press, 1983).

7 John V. Lombardi's rejection of a legal definition of slave status as necessarily a meaningful category for the description or explanation of social experience in favor of other categories such as race or occupation fundamentally influenced this study and the conclusions I reached. See "Comparative slave systems in the Americas: a critical review," in Richard Graham and Peter H. Smith (eds.), *New Approaches to Latin American History* (Austin: University of Texas Press, 1974), pp. 156–174. In a different vein, João José Reis argues persuasively that ethnicity, and, to an extent, religious identity rather than slave or free status *per se* produced the allegiances and hence the rebellion he analyzed, "Slave Rebellion in Brazil: The African Muslim Uprising in Bahia, 1835," (Ph.D. diss., University of Minnesota, 1983). Writing about the sugar society of colonial Brazil and the economic connotations of status, Stuart B. Schwartz, *Sugar Plantations in the Formation of Brazilian Society,* Cambridge Latin American Series, 52 (Cambridge University Press, 1985), pp. 252–253, similarly concludes that what it meant to be a slave or free person of color ranged along a continuum of situations and experiences that variously permitted, denied, or qualified actual freedoms, distinctions not only perceived by slaves, but recognized by masters.

8 Emília Viotti da Costa, *Da senzala à colonia*, Corpo e Alma do Brasil, 19 (São Paulo: Difusão Européia do Livro, 1966), pp. 456–467; for a qualification of that earlier

view, see her *The Brazilian Empire* (University of Chicago Press, 1985), p. 171; Maria Odila Leite da Silva Dias, *Quotidiano e poder em São Paulo no século XIX—Ana Gertrudes de Jesus* (São Paulo: Brasiliense, 1984), pp. 10, 125; Florestan Fernandes, *The Negro in Brazilian Society*, trans. Jacqueline D. Skiles, A. Brunel, and Arthur Rothwell, ed. Phillis B. Eveleth (New York: Columbia University Press, 1969), pp. 1–54; Raymundo Faoro, *Os donos do poder: Formação do patronanto político brasileiro*, 2 vols., 2nd edn. (Porto Alegre: Globo, and São Paulo: Editôra da Universidade de São Paulo, 1975), II, 452–470.

9 See, for example, Stanley Stein, *Vassouras: A Brazilian Coffee County, 1850–1900* (Cambridge: Harvard University Press, 1957), pp. 250–276; Warren Dean, *Rio Claro: A Brazilian Plantation System, 1820–1920* (Stanford University Press, 1976), pp. 88–193; Jacob Gorender, *O escravismo colonial* (São Paulo: Editôra Ática, 1978), pp. 555–572; Costa, *Da senzala*, pp. 446–455; Richard Graham, "Causes for the abolition of negro slavery in Brazil: an interpretive essay," *Hispanic American Historical Review* 46 (May 1966), 123–137 (hereafter cited as *HAHR*).

10 Here I follow Tony Judt, "A clown in royal purple: social history and the historians," *History Workshop* 7 (Spring 1979), 66–94, in insisting that social history can and should be placed in context of the larger events of economics or politics.

1 The social landscape of house and street

1 Debret came to Brazil in 1816, a member of the French cultural mission invited by the Portuguese king Dom João VI resident in the colony since 1808. Jean Baptiste Debret, *Voyage pittoresque et historique au Brésil, ou Séjour d'un artiste français au Brésil*, 3 vols. (Paris: Firmin Didot Frères, Imprimeurs de L'Institut de France, 1834–1839), II, Planche 5 and pp. 31–32.

2 The law did not repeat what tradition ensured, and set only those limits on the authority of the *cabeça de casal* that were consistent with protecting the property rights of wife and children. The restrictions appear scattered through the code, see Candido Mendes de Almeida, comp. and ed., *Código Philippino; ou Ordenações e leis do reino de Portugal, recopilados por mandado d'el-rey D. Philippe I. 14 ed. segundo a primeira de 1603 e a nona de Coimbra de 1824. Addicionada com diversas notas . . .* (Rio de Janeiro: Typ. do Instituto Philomathico, 1870), Liv. 1, Tit. LXXXVIII, par. 6; Liv. 4, Tit. XCV, nn. 2 and 5; Liv. 5, Tit. XXII (hereafter cited as *Código Philippino, 1870*). I cite the 1870 edition because Almeida's notes explain or qualify Portuguese law as practiced in Brazil; this edition further includes many of the Portuguese and Brazilian laws that modified the 1603 code. The Philippine Code remained the basis for civil law in Brazil until 1916 when Brazil promulgated its own civil code. The new code incorporated the old restraints on the power of the cabeça de casal. Joseph Wheless, trans., *The Civil Code of Brazil [1916]* (St. Louis: Thomas Law Book Co., 1920), Special Part, Book 1, Title II, ch. II, art. 233 (hereafter cited as *Civil Code, 1916*); the head of a household or family might also be referred to as the *senhor* or *senhora*, or as the *amo* who provided for his dependents.

3 *Código Philippino, 1870*, Liv. 5, Tit. XXXVI, par. 1. The right to castigate was restated in Brazilian criminal law. [José Antonio de] Araújo Filgueiras Junior, ed., *Código Criminal do Imperio do Brasil*, 2nd edn. (Rio de Janeiro: Laemmert, 1876), Art. 14, par. 6 (hereafter cited as *Código Criminal do Imperio, 1876*).

4 *Código Philippino, 1870,* Liv. 5, Tit. xxiv.

5 Only in 1867 did Agostinho Marques Perdigão Malheiro publish his *A escravidão no Brasil: ensaio histórico-jurídico-social,* 3 parts in 1 vol. (Rio de Janeiro: Typ. Nacional, 1866–1867), an outline for a code of law that would regulate slavery based on Roman law, civil and criminal law as practiced in Brazil, and local custom. No such code resulted, but parliament did pass some particular laws. Notably, a law in 1869 forbade the separation of husband from wife or children from parents as well as the sale of slaves at auction, while in 1871 the Rio Branco Law, or Law of the Free Womb, declared all children henceforth born of slave women to be born free. Brazil, Laws, statutes, etc., *Coleção das Leis do Brasil,* Lei 1695, 15 September 1869, Art. 11 and 1, and Lei 2040, 28 September 1871, Art. 1 (hereafter cited as *Leis do Brasil*).

6 Decisão 57, Reino, 19 June 1822, Cap. 1, par. 8, presented in Francisco Belisário Soares de Souza, *O sistema eleitoral no Império,* 2nd edn., Coleção Bernardo Pereira de Vasconcelos, Série Estudos Jurídicos, 18 (Brasília: Senado Federal, 1979), pp. 178–179; *Leis do Brasil,* Lei 387, 19 August 1846, Tit. 1, Cap. 11, art. 3 and 5. Theresa M. McBride, *The Domestic Revolution: The Modernization of Household Service in England and France, 1820–1920* (New York: Holmes & Meier, 1976), p. 15 describes a similar situation for servants in France and England in the nineteenth century; servants in both societies were the last groups to be franchised.

7 *Leis do Brasil,* Lei 387, 19 August 1846, art. 107.

8 *Relatorio, 1870,* p. 4; *Leis do Brasil,* Decreto 4856, 30 December 1871, Regulamento, Cap. 1, Art. 3, par. 1; Rio de Janeiro, Camara Municipal, *Código de Posturas de Ilma. Camara Municipal do Rio de Janeiro e editaes da mesma Camara* (Rio de Janeiro: Laemmert, 1870), Secção Segunda, Policia, Tit. ix, par. 3 (hereafter cited as *Código de Posturas, 1870*); *Recenseamento do Rio de Janeiro, 1906,* pp. 10, 33 and for examples, pp. 36–37. The multi-faceted meaning of household, or *fogo,* literally meaning hearth, in Brazil resembles the key concepts *domus* and *hostal* where each meant both family and house and contained elements of kitchen, fire, goods and lands, children, and conjugal alliance described by Emmanuel Le Roy Ladurie, in *Montaillou: The Promised Land of Error,* trans. Barbara Bray (New York: Braziller, 1978), pp. 24–52, 179.

9 Dr. Antonio Joaquim Fortes Bustamante, household head, casa n. 21 a 25, rua do Retiro Saudoso, 14° quarteiraõ, and José Maria Chaves, household head, casa n. 41, Praça de D. Pedro I, 8° quarteiraõ, and Maria José Quintella, household head, casa n. 6, Estalagem Mauá, rua do Costume, 2° quarteiraõ, Brazil, Directoria Geral de Estatística, Arrolamento da população do Municipio da Côrte (São Cristovão) 1870, MS, Instituto Brasileiro de Geografia e Estatística, Rio de Janeiro, Departmento de Documentação e Referência, (hereafter cited as Arrolamento SC, 1870).

10 *Recenseamento do Rio de Janeiro, 1906,* p. 10.

11 For example, *Jornal do Commercio,* 28 August 1872, 2 July 1862 (hereafter cited as *JC*).

12 *JC,* 26 July 1882; among the São Cristovão women who lived independently and did domestic work, 70 percent were seamstresses and 23 percent did washing or ironing. Arrolamento SC, 1870.

13 D. Joaquina Roza de Souza, household head, casa n. C, rua Bella de São João, 5° quarteirão, and Americo Brazilio Pacheco, household head, casa n. 8, rua Bella de São João, 3° quarteirão, Arrolamento SC, 1870.

14 Anphilophio Botelho Freire de Carvalho to João Mauricio Wanderley, Barão de Cotegipe, São João da Barra, 16 September 1885, Arquivo do Instituto Histórico e Geográfico Brasileiro, Coleção Cotegipe, L. 13, P. 46 (hereafter cited as AIHGB).

15 "A educação da mulher," *A Mãe de Familia*, January 1881, p. 19; Júlia Lopes de Almeida, *Livro das noivas*, 3rd edn. (Rio de Janeiro: Companhia Nacional Editora, 1896), p. 157.

16 Louis François de Tollenare, *Notas dominicaes. Tomadas durante uma residencia em Portugal e no Brasil nos annos de 1816, 1817, e 1818.* . . . (Recife: "Jornal do Recife," 1905), p. 248; Robert Walsh, *Notices of Brazil in 1828 and 1829*, 2 vols. (London: Frederick Westley and A. H. Davis, 1830), 1, 467; Daniel P. Kidder and James C. Fletcher, *Brazil and the Brazilians Portrayed in Historical and Descriptive Sketches*, 9th edn. rev. (London: Sampson Low, Marston, Searle, and Rivington, 1879), p. 169.

17 Louis Couty, *L'Esclavage au Brésil* (Paris: Guillaumen, 1881), p. 43; D. Isabel Maria d'Almeida, household head, casa n. 2A, rua de Maruhy, 6° quarteirão, Arrolamento SC, 1870; *JC*, 1 July 1882.

18 Juizo de Direito da Iª Vara Civel, defendant, Serafina (preta), Rio de Janeiro, 1882, Arquivo Nacional, Rio de Janeiro, Seção do Poder Judiciário, Maço 555, N. 3498, fl. 22 (hereafter cited as ANSPJ); D. Rosinda Roza Ferreira de Almeida, household head, casa n. 3, Travessa de São Luiz, 2° quarteirão Arrolamento SC, 1870.

19 Couty, *L'Esclavage*, p. 43; Léo de Affonseca Junior, *O custo da vida na cidade do Rio de Janeiro* (Rio de Janeiro: Imprensa Nacional, 1920), pp. 4, 14, 16, 18.

20 Wages remained noticeably stable over the period 1860 to 1910 despite periods of marked inflation. Those cited here included room and board. *JC*, 2 July 1862, 28 August 1872, 4 and 11 July 1877, 1 July 1882, 13 July 1887, 2 and 16 July 1890, 2 September 1905, 5 October 1909; *Gazeta da Tarde*, 5 January 1881, cited in Robert Conrad, *The Destruction of Brazilian Slavery, 1850–1888* (Berkeley: University of California Press, 1972), p. 50n. See also, Appendix IV, "Salaries and Cost of Living, Rio de Janeiro," in J. C. Oakenfull, *Brazil in 1912* (London: Atkinson, 1913), pp. 436–437. Throughout, exchange values are calculated using "Appendix: Statistical tables: exchange value of the milreis in U.S. dollars, 1821–1930," in Julian Smith Duncan, *Public and Private Operation of the Railways in Brazil*, Studies in History, Economics and Public Law, 367 (New York: Colombia University Press, 1932), p. 183.

21 *JC*, 2 July 1862; "Table 19: Rio de Janeiro all slave monthly hire rates, 1835–1888," in Pedro Carvalho de Mello, "The economics of labor in Brazilian coffee plantations, 1850–1888" (Ph.D. diss., University of Chicago, 1977), p. 66.

22 Although the 1870 census was conducted in all parishes of the city, manuscript returns only for the parish of São Cristovão have so far been located. The figures, tables, and discussion I present here are based on my analysis of those household lists. For census-taking purposes, the parish was divided into 16 *quarteirões* or blocks (actually, uneven groupings of streets), two of which are missing, causing my totals to differ from those in the published summary of the census. At the beginning of the returns for each quarteirão, a list appears of all streets and addresses indicating commercial establishments and public buildings as well as private dwellings. Arrolamento SC, 1870; *Relatorio, 1870*.

23 Antonio Dias da Silva, household head, casa n. [illegible], rua São Luiz Gonzaga, 10° quarteirão, and João Teixeira Ribro[?], household head, casa n. 75, rua São Luiz Gonzaga, 10° quarteirão, and D. Maria Thomazia Pereira da Silva, casa n. 1, rua da Alegria, 13° quarteirão, Arrolamento SC, 1870.

24 Gilberto Freyre, *Sobrados e mucambos; decadência do patriarcado rural e desenvolvimento do urbano*, 3rd edn., 2 vols. (Rio de Janeiro: José Olympio, 1961), I, 33–48, first suggested the duality of "house and street." I have drawn on Roberto Da Matta's elaboration of the concepts for contemporary Brazil, *Carnavais, malandros e heróis: para uma sociologia do dilema brasileiro*, 2nd edn. (Rio de Janeiro: Zahar, 1981), pp. 71–75, applying them to nineteenth-century Rio de Janeiro.

25 Louis Agassiz and Elizabeth Cary Agassiz, *A Journey in Brazil*, 2nd edn. (Boston: Ticknor and Fields, 1868), p. 53; Kidder and Fletcher, *Brazil*, pp. 101–102, 163; Adolfo Morales de los Rios Filho, *O Rio de Janeiro imperial* (Rio de Janeiro: Editôra "A Noite," 1946), pp. 21–22.

26 Kidder and Fletcher, *Brazil*, p. 27; Inventory, Anna Angelica do Sacramento Bastos, Rio de Janeiro, 1873, ANSPJ, Caixa 82, N. 400, fls. 9–15; Inventory, Antonia Maria do Espirito Santo Albuquerque, Rio de Janeiro, 1871, ANSPJ, Maço 448, N. 6261, fl. 6; Karl Hermann Konrad Burmeister, *Viagem ao Brasil através das províncias do Rio de Janeiro e Minas Gerais, visando especialmente a história natural dos distritos auridiamentíferos*, trans. Manoel Salvaterra and Hubert Schoenfeldt, Biblioteca Histórica Brasileira, 19, first published 1853 (São Paulo: Martins, 1952), p. 47; Thomas Ewbank, *Life in Brazil: or a Journal of a Visit to the Land of the Cocoa and the Palm* (1856; rpt. Detroit: Blaine Ethridge Books, 1971), p. 286; Debret, *Voyage*, III, Planche 14.

27 "Planta de uma casa de chácara do Rio de Janeiro na segunda metade do século XIX," in Freyre, *Sobrados e mucambos*, I, pp. 169, 175, 189; "A Mãe escrava," *A Mãe de Familia*, November 1879, p. 174.

28 Ewbank, *Life in Brazil*, p. 85; Antonio Martins de Azevedo Pimentel, *Quaes os melhoramentos hygienicos que devem ser introduzidos no Rio de Janeiro, para tornar esta cidade mais saudavel* . . . (Rio de Janeiro: Moreira Maximino, 1884), p. 111; Debret, *Voyage*, III, Planche 42 and pp. 213–214, Planche 43 and p. 216; Kidder and Fletcher, *Brazil*, p. 162; B. Ribeiro de Freitas, "Hygiene da Habitação: os corredores longos e as alcovas das casas do Rio de Janeiro," *Revista dos Constructores*, no. 7 (August 1886), pp. 110–111; Carlos A. C. Lemos, *Cozinhas, etc. Um estudo sobre as zonas de serviço da casa paulista*, Debates, 94 (São Paulo: Perspectiva, 1976), pp. 105–149.

29 Burmeister, *Viagem*, p. 47; Debret, Voyage, III, Planche 42 and pp. 213–215; Pimentel, *Quaes os melhoramentos*, p. 111; Ewbank, *Life in Brazil*, pp. 86–87; Ina von Binzer (pseud. Ulla Von Eck?), *Alegrias e tristezas de uma educadora alemã no Brasil*, trans. Alice Rossi and Luisita de Gama Cerqueiro (São Paulo: Anhembí, 1956), pp. 22, 55–56; photographs, Teixeira house, Rio de Janeiro, 1918, Arquivo Geral da Cidade do Rio de Janeiro, Coleção da Família Carneiro Leão Teixeira (hereafter cited as AGC-RJ).

30 President, Commissão Sanitaria . . . Santo Antonio to President of the Junta Central de Hygiene Pública, Rio de Janeiro, 23 December 1879, AGC-RJ, Relatorios sobre assumptos de hygiene, Cod. 38-2-32, fl. 49; Fiscal of Santo Antonio to Camara Municipal, Rio de Janeiro, AGC-RJ, Estalagens e cortiços; Requerimentos e outros papeis relativos á existencia e á fiscalização sanitaria e de costumes dessas habitações collectivas, 1834–1880, Cod. 43-1-25, fl. 88v; Relação

das casas de commodos e estalagem, Rio de Janeiro, 1896, AGC-RJ, Documentação Avulsa; Habitações collectivas, 1901–1906, Cod. 44-2-11; Mappa [São José], AGC-RJ, Habitações collectivas; Notas estatísticas, 1–10 September 1895, Cod. 44-2-10, fl. 1; *Código de Posturas, 1870*, Secção Segunda, Policia, Tit. IV, par. 5.

31 President, Commissão Sanitaria . . . Santo Antonio to President of the Junta Central de Hygiene Pública, Rio de Janeiro, 23 December 1879, AGC-RJ, Relatorios sobre assumptos de hygiene, Cod. 38-2-32, fl. 30.

32 *Código Philippino, 1870*, Liv. 1, Tit. LXV, par. 14 and n. 3; *Código de Posturas, 1870*, Secção Segunda, Policia, Tit. IX, par. 20 and Tit. IV, par. 1; for an example of a slave accompanied on the street because it was past curfew see, 6º Distrito Criminal, Furto de escravo, defendant, Severiana Maria da Conceição, Rio de Janeiro, 1882, ANSPJ, Caixa 1736, N. 5191, fl. 10v; Juizo do Supremo Tribunal, Revista Civel, defendant, Maria Elenteria de Albuquerque, Rio de Janeiro, 1872, ANSPJ, Maço 23, N. 472, fl. 80, 82v; J. F. de Mello Barreto and Hermeto Lima, *História da polícia do Rio de Janeiro: aspectos da cidade e da vida carioca, 1831–1870*, 3 vols. (Rio de Janeiro: Editôra "A Noite," 1942), III, 102–103; the charge against violators was made in September 1877 by a policeman on his nightly rounds, "Infracção de Posturas. Sacramento. 1870–1879," AGC-RJ, Cod. 9-2-35, fl. 51.

33 Gilberto Freyre, "Social life in Brazil in the middle of the nineteenth century," *HAHR* 5 (1922), 612; Ewbank, *Life in Brazil*, pp. 89–91; Kidder and Fletcher, *Brazil*, pp. 88–89.

34 *JC*, 2 July 1851; Eugenio Rebello, "Da vida sedentaria e de seus inconvenientes anti-hygienicos," *Revista de Hygiene*, September 1886, p. 188.

35 Joaquim Elisio Pereira Marinho to João Mauricio Wanderley, Barão de Cotegipe, Bahia, 11 November 1882, AIHGB, Coleção Cotegipe, L. 37, D. 163; *JC*, 19 July 1882.

36 For examples see, *Correio Mercantil*, 15 December 1857; *JC*, 4 July 1855, 2 July 1862, 28 August 1872, 25 July 1877; Bernardo José Fernandes, household head, casa n. 2-H, rua de Maruhy, 6º quarteirão, Arrolamento SC, 1870; *Código Philippino, 1870*, Liv. 5, Tit. XXIV.

37 Doação de escravos, Rio de Janeiro, 1867, ANSPJ, Cartório do Primeiro Ofício, Escrituras, Liv. 300, fls. 86, 67 (hereafter cited as ANSPJ, CPO).

38 Juizo de Direito da 1ª Vara Civel, defendant, Serafina (preta), Rio de Janeiro, 1882, ANSPJ, Maço 555, N. 3498, fls. 4v, 71–71v, 123–123v.

39 Kidder and Fletcher, *Brazil*, p. 169.

40 *JC*, 7 August 1872, 5 July 1884, 4 July 1895, 21 July 1851.

41 *JC*, 18 July 1877.

42 Charles Expilly, *Le Brésil tel qu'il est*, 3rd edn. (Paris: Charlieu et Huillery, 1864), p. 183. In fact, newspaper advertisements were increasingly used by all who participated in the exchange of domestic labor: prospective employers, individual slave owners, commercial slave dealers, rental agents, and servant women themselves. On any one day the principal paper, the *Jornal do Commercio* with a circulation of 15,000 readers in 1875, ran as many as 170 notices concerning female servants, while in 1851 the number had been 28 and in 1864, 134. *The Empire of Brazil at the Universal Exhibition of 1876 in Philadelphia* (Rio de Janeiro: Imperial Instituto Artistico, 1876), p. 225; Waldir Ribeiro do Val, *Geografia de Machado de Assis* (Rio de Janeiro: São José, 1977), p. 88.

43 For licensing requests see: AGC-RJ, Escravidão e Escravos ao ganho, 1863 a 1867, Cod. 6-1-54.

44 *JC*, 11 July 1877; "A educação da mulher," *A Mãe de Familia*, February 1881, p. 29; *JC*, 5 May 1900; Expilly, *Le Brésil*, pp. 172–173, 179, 182–183; *JC*, 4 July 1877.

45 President, Commissão Sanitaria . . . Santo Antonio to President of the Junta Central de Hygiene Pública, Rio de Janeiro, 23 December 1879, ACG-RJ, Relatorios sobre assumptos de hygiene, Cod. 38-2-32, fls. 41–41v, 47; *JC*, 2 July 1862.

46 Joaquim da Fonseca Barbosa to Luiz Ribeiro da Cunha, Rio de Janeiro, 9 February 1879, 1 February 1879, and Luiz Ribeiro da Cunha to Joaquim da Fonseca Barbosa, Fortaleza, 25 February 1879, in Joaquim da Fonseca Barbosa, Copy Book, 28 March 1878–4 October 1879; Death Certificates, Santa Casa de Misericórdia, Rio de Janeiro, 1878–1879, all in Juiz do Comercio da 1ª Vara, defendant, Duarte, Fonseca & Cia., Rio de Janeiro, 1881, ANSPJ, Maço 3149, N. 4530. Each agent accused the other of poor business practices: Fonseca of poor care and slave sale, his associate of having sent sick slaves. In 1881 their case was sent to Maranhão to an appellate court.

47 Proposal from João [Branho?] Muniz to Conselho de Intendência da Capital Federal, Rio de Janeiro [*c.* 1892], AGC-RJ, Documentação Avulsa, Serviço Domestico, 1882–1904; Serrarias, 1875–1911, Cod. 50-1-41.

48 Rental Agreement between José Thomas Nabuco de Araújo and Casa Narcizo e Silva, Rio de Janeiro, 21 January 1856, AIHGB, Coleção Senador Nabuco, L. 383 [new cataloguing]; Expilly, *Le Brésil*, p. 172.

49 *Almanak administrativo, mercantil e industrial . . . do Rio de Janeiro* (Rio de Janeiro: Laemmert, 1860), pp. 669, 672 (hereafter cited as *Almanak Laemmert*); *JC*, 7 August 1872, 4 July 1877, 7 August 1872, 28 August 1872. The phrase "just arrived" appeared frequently in advertisements for ordinary goods – textiles, shoes, etc. – as it had earlier for slaves, underscoring the perception of both as merchandise.

50 *JC*, 5 May 1900.

51 President, Commissáo Sanitaria . . . Santo Antonio to President of the Junta Central de Hygiene Pública, Rio de Janeiro, 23 December 1879, AGC-RJ, Relatorios sobre assumptos de hygiene, Cod. 38-2-32, fl. 41; *Almanak Laemmert*, 1885, p. 536; 1890, pp. 641, 1, 915; 1895, p. 694; 1900, p. 483; 1910, p. 837.

52 Although no census specified occupation by color, we can form an approximate idea of the proportion of white or black women by noting the nationalities of women generally and the birthplaces of servant women, in particular, see Tables 6, 7, and 8.

53 João Baptista A. Imbert, *Guia medico das mães de familia, ou a infancia considerada na sua hygiene, suas molestias e tratamentos* (Rio de Janeiro: Typ. Franceza, 1843), p. 51; Almeida, *Livro das noivas*, p. 157.

54 *JC*, 7 August 1872.

55 Juizo de Direito da 1ª Vara Civel, defendant, Serafina (preta), Rio de Janeiro, 1882, ANSPJ, Maço 555, N. 3498, fl. 22; D. Olympia Amalia Monteiro, casa n. 10, rua de São Januario, 8º quarteirão, Arrolamento SC, 1870; *JC*, 25 July 1877, 16 July 1890, 5 May 1900, 4 July 1895, 13 September 1905.

56 *JC*, 4 July and 11 July 1877, 1 July 1882, 2 September 1905.

57 Fernando Nascimento Silva, "Dados de geografia carioca," and the accompanying map by Eduardo Canabrava Barreiros, "Cartograma conjectural da cidade do Rio de Janeiro na época de sua fundação," pp. 29–38 and [393], and Lygia Maria Cavalcanti Bernardes, "Posição geográfica do Rio de Janeiro," pp. 19–28, and

Cláudio Bardy, "O século XVI (da fundação até o fim)," p. 60, all in Fernando Nascimento Silva, ed., *Rio de Janeiro em seus quatrocentos anos: formação e desenvolvimento da cidade* (Rio de Janeiro: Distribuidora Record, 1965).

58 Gilberto Ferrez, *A Praça 15 de Novembro, antigo Largo do Carmo* (Rio de Janeiro: Riotur Empresa de Turismo do Município do Rio de Janeiro, 1978), pp. 9–10 and Estampas 1–6; Francisco Agenor de Noronha Santos, "Anotações," in Luiz Gonçalves dos Santos [Padre Perereca], *Memórias para servir à história do reino do Brasil*, 2 vols., Reconquista do Brasil, n.s., nos. 36 and 37, first published 1825 (Belo Horizonte and São Paulo: Itatiaia and University of São Paulo, 1981), 1, 88; Preston James, "Rio de Janeiro and São Paulo," *Geographical Review* 23 (1933), 283.

59 Edna Mascarenhas Sant'Anna, "Anexo 1: As transformações ocorridas no trecho ocupado atualmente pela área central," in Brazil, Instituto Brasileiro de Geografia e Estatística, Conselho Nacional de Geografia, Serviço Nacional de Recenseamento, Divisão de Geografia, *A área central da cidade do Rio de Janeiro* (Rio de Janeiro: Instituto Brasileiro de Geografia e Estatística, 1967), pp. 45–47; Torquato Xavier Monteiro Tapajós, . . . *Estudos de hygiene; a cidade do Rio de Janeiro; primeira parte; terras, aguas, e ares; idéias finaes* (Rio de Janeiro: Imprensa Nacional, 1895), pp. 44–46.

60 As late as the 1860s, the city was still draining that "vast swamp," the Campo de Sant'Anna, see Adolpho Bezerra de Menezes, *O Governo e a Camara Municipal da Côrte. Artigos publicados na "Reforma"* (Rio de Janeiro: Typ. da "Reforma," 1873), pp. 53–54.

61 *The British and American Mail*, 8 January 1879, p. 2; Rio de Janeiro, Prefeitura da Cidade do Rio de Janeiro, *O Rio de Janeiro e seus prefeitos*, vol. 3, *Evolução urbanista da cidade* (Rio de Janeiro: Prefeitura da Cidade do Rio de Janeiro, 1977), 26; Junta Central de Hygiene Pública to Ministerio do Imperio, Rio de Janeiro, 20 March 1878, AGC-RJ, Abastecimento d'Agua; Canalização Geral, 1832–1903, Cod. 51-1-14, fls. 39–40.

62 Rosauro Mariano da Silva, "A luta pela água," in Silva, *Rio de Janeiro em seus quatrocentos anos*, pp. 311–337; Maria Graham, *Journal of a Voyage to Brazil and Residence There, During Part of the Years 1821, 1822, 1823* (1824; rpt. New York: Praeger, 1969), pp. 167, 169; Noronha Santos, "Anotações," in Santos, *Mémorias para servir à história*, 1, 97; Walsh, *Notices of Brazil*, 1, 506–507; Burmeister, *Viagem*, p. 51; Rios Filho, *O Rio de Janeiro*, p. 77.

63 John Luccock, *Notes on Rio de Janeiro and the Southern Parts of Brazil; Taken During a Residence of Ten Years in that Country, from 1808 to 1818* (London: Samuel Leigh, 1820), p. 41; "Mappa da População do Municipio da Côerte, Mappa das 8 Freguezias da Cidade, 1838," Ministerio do Reino e Imperio (Mappas da População), Arquivo Nacional, Rio de Janeiro, Caixa 761, Pacote 1 (hereafter cited as AN); *Recenseamento, 1872*, Municipio Neutro, "Quadros Gerais," pp. 58–61; Brazil, Directoria Geral de Estatística, *Recenseamento Geral da Republica dos Estados Unidos do Brazil em 31 dezembro 1890: Districto Federal (cidade do Rio de Janeiro)* (Rio de Janeiro: Typ. Leuzinger, 1895), pp. 401, 423–425; *Recenseamento do Rio de Janeiro, 1906*, pp. 178–306, 390–391; the now missing 1849 census was reprinted under the heading "Recenseamento da população existente no Municipio Neutro no fim do anno de 1849, organisado por freguezias, seus fogos, districtos e quarteirões; e nestes distribuidos por classes de sexo, condição, naturalidade, idade e estado, não se incluindo nestas duas ultimas a população

escrava; pelo Dr. Roberto Haddock Lobo," in *Correio Mercantil,* 7 January 1851, p. 4; on European immigration to Brazil, see also Thomas W. Merrick and Douglas H. Graham, *Population and Economic Development in Brazil, 1800 to the Present* (Baltimore: The Johns Hopkins University Press, 1979), pp. 37, 90–91.

64 Antonio Martins de Azevedo Pimentel, *Subsidios para o estudo da hygiene do Rio de Janeiro* (Rio de Janeiro: Gaspar da Silva, 1890), pp. 179, 273; Ministerio da Agricultura, Commercio e Obras Publicas, *Relatorio,* 1883, p. 112; Federico Lisboa de Mara, *Histórico sobre o abastecimento de agua á Capital do Imperio desde 1861–1889* (Rio de Janeiro: Imprensa Nacional, 1889), p. 19; Marc Ferrez, Abastecimento d'agua, [*c.* 1890], Arquivo Geral da Cidade, Rio de Janeiro, Seção Iconográfica (hereafter cited as AGC-RJ, SI), is a photographic essay depicting Rio's improved water supply – sources, conduits, and storage areas. One historian has argued that the "privilege of receiving piped water," limited for many years to a few residents, was extended only when new sources of water became available. Silva, "A luta pela agua," in Silva, *Rio de Janeiro em seus quatrocentos anos,* p. 320.

65 "Nova planta indicadora da cidade do Rio de Janeiro e suburbios," organized by Alexandre Speltz, 1877; "Planta da Cidade do Rio de Janeiro e de uma parte dos suburbios," organized by Major E. de Maschek [post. 1885]; "Mappa das linhas da Companhia Botanical Garden Rail Road, . . . [*c.* 1890]," in Rio de Janeiro, Biblioteca Nacional, *Album Cartográfico do Rio de Janeiro, séculos XVIII e XIX,* organized by Lygia da Fonseca Fernandes da Cunha (Rio de Janeiro: Biblioteca Nacional, 1971); *The Empire of Brazil at the Universal Exhibition,* pp. 334–336; Agenor Francisco Noronha Santos provides a detailed and extensively documented history of Rio de Janeiro transportation, *Meios de transporte no Rio de Janeiro. História e legislação,* 2 vols. in 1 (Rio de Janeiro: Typ. do "Jornal do Commercio," Rodrigues & C., 1934), especially the section on city tramlines, 1, 257–464; for a shorter, popular account based on Santos, see Charles Julius Dunlop, *Os meios de transporte do Rio antigo* (Rio de Janeiro: Grupo de Planejamento Gráfico, 1973), pp. 30–39.

66 Santos, *Meios de transporte,* 1, 213–233, 395–411; 11, 257–266; Mule-drawn gôndolas, with steps and a door at the rear, were photographed by Marc Ferrez, "Largo do São Francisco de Paula, *c.* 1865," in Gilberto Ferrez, ed., *O Rio antigo do fotografo Marc Ferrez; Paisagens e tipos humanos do Rio de Janeiro, 1865–1918* (São Paulo: Ex Libris Ltda., 1984), p. 140.

67 Mappa N. 12, "Relação dos cortiços existentes na Côrte, com designação de seu numero e população, por sexos, estados, nacionalidades e profissões," in Relatorio do Chefe de Policia da Côrte, Annexo D, Brazil, Ministerio da Justiça, *Relatorio,* 1856, n.p.; Mappa 7, "Mappa demonstrativo do numero de cortiços e moradores dos mesmos, existentes nas freguezias da Côrte," in Relatorio do Chefe de Policia da Côrte, Annexo B, Relatorios de Diversas Autoridades, Brazil, Ministerio da Justiça, *Relatorio,* 1867, p. 69; Pimentel, *Subsidios,* pp. 187–188.

68 Relatorio do Chefe de Policia da Côrte, Annexo D, Brazil, Ministerio da Justiça, *Relatorio,* 1856, n. p.

69 Santos, *Meios de transporte,* 1, 108–119, 153–156; Charles Hastings Dent, *A Year in Brazil with Notes on Abolition of Slavery, the Finances of the Empire, Religion, Meteorology, Natural History, Etc.* (London: K. Paul, Trench, 1886), pp. 236–237; Ewbank, *Life in Brazil,* p. 63; Dunlop, *Os meios,* pp. 19–24, 36.

70 Joaquim Elisio Pereira Marinho to João Mauricio Wanderley, Barão de

Cotegipe, Bahia, 11 November 1882, AIGHB, Coleção Cotegipe, L. 37, D. 163.

71 Gilberto Freyre, *Ordem e progresso*, 2 vols. (Rio de Janeiro: José Olympio, 1959), I, 94; José Lopes da Silva Trovão, *Discurso proferido na sessão do Senado Federal de 11 de setembro de 1895 sobre o trabalho das crianças* (Rio de Janeiro: Imprensa Nacional, 1896), p. 24.

72 James McFadden Gaston, *Hunting a Home in Brazil. The Agricultural Resources and other Characteristics of the Country; also, the Manners and Customs of the Inhabitants* (Philadelphia: King and Baird Printers, 1867), pp. 19–20.

2 The work

1 Louis Agassiz and Elizabeth Cary Agassiz, *A Journey in Brazil*, 2nd edn. (Boston: Ticknor and Fields, 1868), pp. 72–73; Antonio Martins de Azevedo Pimentel, *Quaes os melhoramentos hygienicos que devem ser introduzidos no Rio de Janeiro, para tornar esta cidade mais saudavel* . . . (Rio de Janeiro: Moreira Maximino, 1884), p. 130; Charles Expilly, *Le Brésil tel qu'il est*, 3rd edn. (Paris: Charlieu et Huillery, 1864), p. 173; A.S.Q., *O cozinheiro e doceiro popular* (Rio de Janeiro: Editôra Quaresma, 1927), p. 373; Daniel P. Kidder and James C. Fletcher, *Brazil and the Brazilians Portrayed in Historical and Descriptive Sketches*, 9th edn. rev. (London: Sampson Low, Marston, Searle, and Rivington, 1879), p. 173.

2 Carolina Nabuco, *Meu livro de cozinha* (Rio de Janeiro: Editôra Nova Fronteira, 1977), pp. 27–28; Thomas Ewbank, *Life in Brazil: or a Journal of a Visit to the Land of the Cocoa and the Palm* (1856; rpt. Detroit: Blaine Ethridge Books, 1971), p. 136; Carlos Delgado de Carvalho, *História da cidade do Rio de Janeiro* (Rio de Janeiro: F. Alves, 1926), p. 109.

3 A.S.Q., *O cozinheiro e doceiro popular*, p. 373.

4 *JC*, 1 January 1871; Richard Graham, *Britain and the Onset of Modernization in Brazil, 1850–1914*, Cambridge Latin American Studies, 4 (Cambridge University Press, 1968), pp. 112–113; *Rio News*, 24 January 1883.

5 Nabuco, *Meu livro*, p. 23; Carolina Nabuco, *The Life of Joaquim Nabuco*, trans. and ed. Ronald Hilton, first published 1928 (Stanford University Press, 1950), p. 195.

6 Ewbank, *Life in Brazil*, p. 286; Felippe Neri Collaço, *O conselheiro da familia brasileira* (Rio de Janeiro: Garnier, 1883), p. 43; Nabuco, *Meu livro*, p. 19; *JC*, 7 August 1872.

7 Charles Julius Dunlop, *Subsídios para a história do Rio de Janeiro* (Rio de Janeiro: Editôra Rio Antigo, 1957), p. 145; Júlia Lopes de Almeida, *Livro das noivas*, 3rd edn. (Rio de Janeiro: Typ. da Companhia Nacional Editora, 1896), p. 99; *JC*, 4 September 1860, 5 February 1882.

8 Almeida, *Livro das noivas*, p. 165; Exposição "A cozinha no Rio antigo," Museu Histórico da Cidade, Rio de Janeiro, 4 July–3 August 1980.

9 Collaço, *Conselheiro*, pp. 44–45; Ewbank, *Life in Brazil*, pp. 286, 359–360; Inventory, Aguida Maria da Conceição, Rio de Janeiro, 1859, ANSPJ, Caixa 78, N. 332, fl. 3v; Exposição, "A cozinha no Rio antigo."

10 Ewbank, *Life in Brazil*, pp. 357–360; Exposição, "A cozinha no Rio antigo."

11 Henry Koster, *Travels in Brazil*, ed. and intro. C. Harvey Gardiner, first published 1817 (Carbondale, Ill.: Southern Illinois University Press, 1966), pp. 17, 97–98.

12 Photographs of the interior of the Carneiro Leão Teixeira house, Rio de Janeiro, 1918, AGC-RJ, Coleção da Família Carneiro Leão Teixeira; Inventory, Anna Angelica do Sacramento Bastos, Rio de Janeiro, 1873, ANSPJ, Caixa 82, N. 400, fls. 3v–4.

13 Inventory, Aguida Maria da Conceição, Rio de Janeiro, 1859, ANSPJ, Caixa 78, N. 332, fl. 3v; Inventory, Alexandrina Maria da Conceição, Rio de Janeiro, 1863, ANSPJ, Caixa 83, N. 416, fl. 77; Inventory, Anna Angelica do Sacramento Bastos, Rio de Janeiro, 1873, ANSPJ, Caixa 82, N. 400, fls. 3–3v, 11, 32v; J. Wasth Rodrigues, *Mobiliário do Brasil antigo (Evolução de cadeiras luso-brasileiras)* (São Paulo: Companhia Editôra Nacional, 1958), Estampas 40–42; Photographs, Teixeira house, Rio de Janeiro, 1918, AGC-RJ, Coleção da Família Carneiro Leão Teixeira.

14 Almeida, *Livro das noivas*, pp. 158–160; Marc Ferrez, Photographs of the interior of the Countess d'Eu villa, Rio de Janeiro, 1886, Gilberto Ferrez and Weston J. Naef, *Pioneer Photographers of Brazil, 1840–1920* (New York: The Center for Inter-American Relations, 1976), pp. 132–133; cane furniture from the nineteenth century exhibited at the Museu da Cidade, Rio de Janeiro and at the Museu da Fundação Carlos Costa Pinto, Salvador, Bahia.

15 Ewbank, *Life in Brazil*, pp. 59, 86; Karl Hermann Konrad Burmeister, *Viagem ao Brazil através das províncias do Rio de Janeiro e Minas Gerais, visando especialmente a história natural dos distritos auridiamantíferos*, trans. Manoel Salvaterra and Hubert Schoenfeldt, Biblioteca Histórica Brasileira, 19, first published 1853 (São Paulo: Martins, 1952), p. 47; Augusto César Malta, Photograph of the office-bedroom of the Baron Rio Branco, 1912, Ferrez and Naef, *Pioneer Photographers*, p. 140; Photographs, Teixeria house, Rio de Janeiro, 1918, AGC-RJ, Coleção da Família Carneiro Leão Teixeira; examples of decoratively painted walls depicting fruit, birds, rural landscapes, and Brazilian Indians can be seen at Catete Palace, Rio de Janeiro, once the home of Antonio Clemente Pinto, Baron Nova Friburgo, built about 1860; Collaço, *Conselheiro*, p. 43.

16 Myriam Ellis, *A baléia no Brasil colonial* (São Paulo: Melhoramentos, 1969), pp. 136–143; Dunlop, *Subsídios*, pp. 11, 22–23, 34, 38–39; Max Fleiuss, *História da cidade do Rio de Janeiro (Distrito Federal), resumo didáctico* (São Paulo: Melhoramentos, [1928]), p. 190; globes exhibited at the Museu da Fundação Carlos Costa Pinto, Salvador, Bahia.

17 AGC-RJ, Illuminação Particular; Requerimentos de particulares solicitando canalização do gaz para illuminação domiciliares, 1861–1863 e 1864, Cod. 9-1-7, fls. 2–5, 6, 10–11, 16, and Electricidade; Fiscalização, 1906, Cod. 42-3-75, fls. 28, 57–58, 61, 63, 72; Dunlop, *Subsídios*, pp. 67–68, 150–151; *Revista dos Constructores*, no. 6 (July 1886), p. 90; *JC*, 20 March 1875.

18 *A Mãe de Familia*, March 1879, p. 44; ibid., May 1879, pp. 65–66; Speech of Alvaro Baptista, 29 July 1921, in Brazil, Congresso, Câmara dos Deputados, *Anais*, 1921, VI, 633; Emiliano di Cavalcanti, *Viagem da minha vida* (Rio de Janeiro: Civilização Brasileira, 1955), p. 27; José Modesto de Souza Junior, *Do regimen alimentar dos recem-nascidos . . .* (Rio de Janeiro: Imprensa Gutenberg, 1895), p. 45. Commercial wet-nursing was not unique to Brazil, see George D. Sussman, "The wet-nursing business in nineteenth-century France," *French Historical Studies* 9 (1975), 302–328; and his *Selling Mother's Milk: The Wet-Nursing Business in France, 1715–1914* (Urbana: University of Illinois, 1982).

19 Travelers and historians agree that only from the 1850s and 1860s did Rio de Janeiro women of position leave their houses to attend public diversions or to stroll in the Passeio Publico or to sea-bathe. See Pedro Calmon, *História social do Brasil*, Série 5ᵃ, Brasiliana, 83 (São Paulo: Companhia Editôra Nacional, 1940), p. 234; Ewbank, *Life in Brazil*, pp. 81, 88–89; Kidder and Fletcher, *Brazil*, pp. 88–89, 91; Eugenio Rebello, "Da vida sedentaria e de seus inconvenientes anti-

hygienicos," *Revista de Hygiene*, September 1886, p. 188; Côrte de Apelação, Acção de Liberdade pela Belmira por seu curador, defendant, Francisco da Veiga Abreu, Rio de Janeiro, 1872, ANSPJ, Maço 216, N. 1740, fl. 40v.

20 Inventory, Anna Angelica do Sacramento Bastos, Rio de Janeiro, 1873, ANSPJ, Caixa 82, N. 400, fls. 4, 10v, 13–13v, 38; Museu da Fundação Carlos Costa Pinto, Salvador, Bahia; Gilberto Freyre, "Social life in Brazil in the middle of the nineteenth century," *HAHR* 5 (1922), 627; Charles Expilly, *Mulheres e costumes do Brasil*, trans. Gastão Penalva, 2nd edn., Série 5ª, Brasiliana, 56, first published 1863 (São Paulo: Companhia Editôra Nacional, 1977), pp. 366–367; Adele Toussaint-Samson, *Une Parisienne au Brésil avec photographies originales* (Paris: Paul Ollendorff, 1883), p. 58; *JC*, 2 July 1862, 7 August 1872.

21 *A Estação*, 15 May 1879, p. 1; Kidder and Fletcher, *Brazil*, p. 168; *JC*, 2 January 1871, 28 August 1872, 20 March 1875, 4 July 1877, 25 July 1877, 13 July 1887, 2 July 1890.

22 The three sites are indicated on the map, "A cidade do Rio de Janeiro nos meados do século xix, baseada na Planta Garnier de 1852," in Eduardo Canabrava Barreiros, *Atlas da evolução urbana da cidade do Rio de Janeiro: ensaio, 1565–1965* (Rio de Janeiro: Instituto Histórico e Geográfico Brasileiro, 1965), Prancha 16, p. 21.

23 Inventory, Anna Angelica do Sacramento Bastos, Rio de Janeiro, 1873, ANSPJ, Caixa 82, N. 400, fl. 4; Almeida, *Livro das noivas*, pp. 25–26; Collaço, *Conselheiro*, pp. 65–68; Nabuco, *Meu livro*, p. 27.

24 Kidder and Fletcher, *Brazil*, p. 102; Ewbank, *Life in Brazil*, 73; Jean Baptiste Debret, *Voyage pittoresque et historique au Brésil, ou Séjour d'un artiste français au Brésil*, 3 vols. (Paris: Firmin Didot Frères, Imprimeurs de L'Institut de France, 1834–1839), 1, Planche 22 and p. 39; 11, Planche 48 and pp. 147–148.

25 Maria Graham, *Journal of a Voyage to Brazil and Residence There, During Part of the Years 1821, 1822, 1823* (1824; rpt. New York: Praeger, 1969), pp. 167–169; Burmeister, *Viagem*, pp. 28, 42, 51; Ewbank, *Life in Brazil*, pp. 113–114; P. G. Bertichem, *O Rio de Janeiro e seus arrabaldes, 1856*, intro. and notes by Gilberto Ferrez (Rio de Janeiro: Kosmos, 1976), p. 43; Adolfo Morales de los Rios Filho, *O Rio de Janeiro imperial* (Rio de Janeiro: Editôra "A Noite," 1946), pp. 77–79.

26 "Planta de uma casa de chácara do Rio de Janeiro na segunda metade do século xix," in Gilberto Freyre, *Sobrados e mucambos; decadência do patriarcado rural e desenvolvimento do urbano*, 3rd edn., 2 vols. (Rio de Janeiro: José Olympio, 1961), 1, 189; Max Fleiuss, *História administrativa do Brasil*, 2nd edn. (Rio de Janeiro: Melhoramentos [1925]), p. 206; see, for example, the laundry area at the Casa de Rui Barbosa, 134 rua São Clemente, Rio de Janeiro; Junta Central de Hygiene Pública to Ministerio do Imperio, Rio de Janeiro, 20 March 1878, AGC-RJ, Abastecimento d'Agua; Canalização Geral, 1832–1903, Cod. 51-1-14, fls. 39–40.

27 Ewbank, *Life in Brazil*, pp. 280–281; Rios Filho, *Rio de Janeiro*, p. 78; Herbert H. Smith, *Brazil: The Amazon and the Coast* (New York: Scribner's, 1879), p. 497; Charles Hastings Dent, *A Year in Brazil with Notes on Abolition of Slavery, the Finances of the Empire, Religion, Meteorology, Natural History, Etc.* (London: K. Paul, Trench, 1886), p. 237; photograph of the Largo da Carioca, Luiz Edmundo da Costa, *O Rio de Janeiro do meu tempo*, 3 vols. (Rio de Janeiro: Imprensa Nacional, 1938), 11, 705; AGJ-RJ, Abastecimento d'Agua; Venda publica, . . . 1869–1881, Cod. 51-1-31, fls. 6, 10; Juizo do Supremo Tribunal de Justiça, Revista Civel, defendant, Maria Elenteria de Albuquerque, Rio de Janeiro, 1872, ANSPJ, Maço 23, N. 472, fl. 84v; Inventory, Aguida Maria da Conceição, Rio de Janeiro, 1859, ANSPJ, Caixa 78, N. 332, fl. 3v.

28 José Pereira Rego, *Esboço historico das epidemias que tem grassado na cidade do Rio de Janeiro desde 1830 a 1870* (Rio de Janeiro: Typ. Nacional, 1872), pp. 207–208; Antonio Martins de Azevedo Pimentel, *Subsidios para o estudo da hygiene do Rio de Janeiro* (Rio de Janeiro: Gaspar da Silva, 1890), pp. 165, 224; Vicente Rodrigues to Camara Municipal, Rio de Janeiro, 28 January 1856, AGC–R J, Limpeza publica, 1856–1861, Cod. 31-1-37, fl. 2; Edital, 13 February 1863, *Código de Posturas, 1870*, permitted emptying fecal matter on the beaches only after six in the afternoon; private companies that would remove garbage, waste water and fecal matter listed themselves in the *Almanak Laemmert*, 1860, p. 747, for example.

29 Rio de Janeiro, Intendencia Municipal do Districto Federal, *Código de Posturas, Leis, Decretos, Editaes e Resoluções da Intendencia Municipal do Districto Federal* (Rio de Janeiro: Mont'Averne, 1894), Secção Segunda, Policia, Tit. II, par. 11 (hereafter cited as *Código de Posturas, 1894*; Proposal by Alexis Gary Cia., 18 August 1885, AGC-R J, Limpeza Publica e Incineração de lixo, 1878–1886, Cod. 31-2-8, fl. 9; Relatorio de Serviço da Limpeza, 1893, AGC-R J, Cod. 38-3-41, fl. 8.

30 Smith, *Brazil*, pp. 485–486; Ewbank, *Life in Brazil*, p. 87; Agassiz and Agassiz, *A Journey*, p. 82; Kidder and Fletcher, *Brazil*, p. 170; Maria Yedda Leite Linhares, *História do abastecimento; uma problemática em questão, (1530–1918)*, Coleção Estudos sobre o Desenvolvimento Agrícola, vol. 5 (Brasília: BINAGRI Edições, 1979), pp. 159–174, 194–213; the Marc Ferrez photograph, "Doca e mercado da Praia do Peixe, *c.* 1880," taken from the water shows the one-masted boats that brought produce across the bay to market and, on the shore, the shoppers, in Gilberto Ferrez, ed., *O Rio antigo do fotografo Marc Ferrez: Paisagens e tipos humanos do Rio de Janeiro, 1865–1918* (São Paulo: Ex Libris Ltda., 1984), p. 36.

31 Secretaria, Ministerio da Justiça, Consultas, Conselho de Estado, Secção de Justiça, Rio de Janeiro, 25 July 1881, Arquivo Nacional, Seção do Poder Executivo, Caixa 558, Pac. 3 (hereafter cited as ANSPE); AGC-R J, Carnes . . . Volantes de Carnes e Miudos, 1855–1903, Cod. 53-4-12, fls. 9, 42, 77, 83, 93; for photographs of street vendors posed for the popular *cartes de visite*, see those by Marc Ferrez in Ferrez, *O Rio antigo do fotografo Marc Ferrez*, pp. 91–107, especially "Vendedora de miudezas," p. 99 and "Baianas," pp. 106 and 107; petition from several bakers to Camara Municipal, Rio de Janeiro, 14 February 1861, and accompanying comment, 19 March 1861, AGC-R J, Commercio de Pão, 1841–1907, Cod. 58-4-36, fls. 34–35; Fiscal to Camara Municipal, Rio de Janeiro, 11 March 1870, AGC-R J, Infracção de Posturas; Sacramento, 1870–1879, Cod. 9-2-35, fls. 2–2v; AGC-R J, Commercio de Leite, 1850–1879, Cod. 58-4-45, fl. 21; José Alípio Goulart, "Alguns dados sôbre o comércio ambulante do leite no Rio de Janeiro do século XIX," *Revista do Instituto Histórico e Geográfico Brasileiro*, 263 (April–June 1964), 31 (hereafter cited as RIHGB).

32 Rio de Janeiro, Prefeitura do Districto Federal, *Codificação Sanitária 1884–1913* (Rio de Janeiro: Officina do "Paiz," 1913), p. 44; Brazil, Conselho Nacional de Estatística, *Anuário estatístico do Brasil, 1908–1912*, 2 vols. (Rio de Janeiro: Typ. da Estatística, 1916–1917), II, 136; Ewbank, *Life in Brazil*, pp. 93, 95–96, 324; Expilly, *Mulheres*, p. 81; Touissant-Samson, *Une Parisienne*, p. 47; Agassiz and Agassiz, *A Journey*, pp. 82–83; AGC-R J, Commercio de Café, 1848 a 1887, Cod. 58-4-42, fls. 17, 19, 38; AGC-R J, Commercio de Gêlo, 1847–1862, Cod. 58-4-41, fl. 18; Costa, *O Rio*, I, 48, 80, 96.

33 Kidder and Fletcher, *Brazil*, p. 167; Dent, *A Year in Brazil*, p. 187.

34 Toussaint-Samson, *Une Parisienne*, p. 61; Kidder and Fletcher, *Brazil*, p. 125;

Juizo do Supremo Tribunal de Justiça, Revista Civel, defendant, Maria Elenteria de Albuquerque, Rio de Janeiro, 1872, ANSPJ, Maço, 23, N. 472, fl. 65v.

35 Ewbank, *Life in Brazil*, pp. 84–85; AGC-RJ, SI, Ruas e Praças do Centro, 1904 [photograph n. 69]; Dent, *A Year in Brazil*, p. 22; Kidder and Fletcher, *Brazil*, pp. 28–30 and 38–39; Christopher Columbus Andrews, *Brazil: Its Condition and Prospects*, 3rd edn. (New York: D. Appleton & Co., 1891), p. 32; James McFadden Gaston, *Hunting a Home in Brazil. The Agricultural Resources and other Characteristics of the Country; also, the Manners and Customs of the Inhabitants* (Philadelphia: King and Baird Printers, 1867), pp. 10–12; see the photographs by Marc Ferrez, "O centro do Rio de Janeiro, *c.* 1885," showing the density of buildings and narrow streets, "Rua do Ouvidor, *c.* 1890," and "Rua Direita, *c.* 1870, 1880, 1890," in Ferrez, *O Rio antigo do fotografo Marc Ferrez*, pp. 54–55, 56, and 51–53.

36 Ida Pfeiffer, *A Woman's Journey Round the World, from Vienna to Brazil, Chili, Tahiti, China, Hindostan, Persia, and Asia Minor*, 2nd edn. (London: [Office of the National Illustrated Library, 1852], p.16; Agassiz and Agassiz, *A Journey*, p. 50; Junta Central de Hygiene Pública to Camara Municipal, Rio de Janeiro, 17 February 1876, AGC-RJ, Carnes e Matadouros; Serviço Sanitario, 1853–1909, Cod. 53-4-10, fl. 45 *O Auxiliador da undustria Nacional*, 9 (February 1881), 328.

37 L. A. Silva, "A remoção do lixo," *Revista de Hygiene*, June 1886, p. 49; AGC-RJ, Relatorio de Serviço da Limpeza, Rio de Janeiro, 1893, Cod. 38-3-41, fls. 6v, 8v; Marc Ferrez, View of rua do Ouvidor, AGC-RJ, SI, Coleção Emilio Brondi, 1; Pfeiffer, *A Woman's Journey*, p. 19; Touissant-Samson, *Une Parisienne*, p. 62.

38 Kidder and Fletcher, *Brazil*, p. 27; Francisco Agenor de Noronha Santos, *Chorographia do Districto Federal (cidade do Rio de Janeiro)*, 3rd edn. (Rio de Janeiro: Benjamin de Aguila, 1913), p. 363.

39 Kidder and Fletcher, *Brazil*, pp. 125, 133; *Código de Posturas, 1870*, Secção Segunda, Policia, Tit. IV, art 6.

40 L. Cruls, *O clima do Rio de Janeiro* (Rio de Janeiro: H. Lombaerts & Comp., Impressores do Observatorio, 1892), p. 24; Edital, 25 November 1885, *Código de Posturas, 1894*; Almeida, *Livro das noivas*, p. 92; untitled report on public health, *c.* 1893, AGC-RJ, Relatorios sobre assumptos de hygiene, Cod. 38-2-32, fls. 93, 95; Rio de Janeiro, Camara Municipal, Sessão 36, 8 November 1879, *Boletim da Illustrissima Camara Municipal da Côrte*, 1879, p. 28.

41 Pimentel, *Subsidios*, p. 172; Ewbank, *Life in Brazil*, p. 87.

42 Pimentel, *Quaes os melhoramentos*, p. 107; Cruls, *O clima*, pp. 23, 54–55.

43 Miguel de Piero Machado and Francisco Pinto de Santa Valle to Camara Municipal, Rio de Janeiro, 5 November 1890, AGC-RJ, Diversos Mercados, 1843–1902, Cod. 61-1-24, fl. 14; Rio de Janeiro, *Codificação Sanitária*, Postura, 1899, p. 6.

44 Juizo do 4° Distrito Criminal, defendant, Luiz Ferreira de Almeida, Rio de Janeiro, 1873, ANSPJ, Caixa 1747, No. 5564, fl. 2; Juizo Municipal da 1ª Vara, defendant, Josefina Carolina das Dores, Rio de Janeiro, 1865, ANSPJ, Maço 791, N. 16027, fls. 2v–3.

45 For examples, see *Cidade do Rio* for January and February 1889, especially 7 February 1889, and 16 February 1889; Subdelegado de Policia, 1° Districto do Engenho Velho, defendant, Lauriana Maria da Conceição, Rio de Janeiro, 1890, ANSPJ, Maço 80, N. 1584, fls. 7–7v, 12v; Juizo da 20ª Pretoria, defendant, Olinda Maria da Conceição, Rio de Janeiro, 1895, ANSPJ, Caixa 1372, N. 9649, fls. 2, 5–5v, 7.

46 Juizo Municipal da 2ª Vara Civel, defendant, Emilia Julia da Conceição, Rio de

Janeiro, 1870, ANSPJ, Maço 885, N. 833, fl. 12; Juizo da 20ª Pretoria, defendant, Olinda Maria da Conceição, Rio de Janeiro, 1895, ANSPJ, Caixa 1372, N. 9649, fl. 5.

47 Chefe da Delegacia de Policia to Camara Municipal, Rio de Janeiro, 13 November 1888, AGC-RJ, Cod. 48-4-61, fl. 1; Chefe de Policia to Prefeito, Rio de Janeiro, 10 January 1900, AGC-RJ, Cod. 48-4-62, fl. 1—IV; Petition to Camara dos Deputados, Rio de Janeiro, 2 June 1879, carried 759 signatures, AGC-RJ, Cod. 48-4-63, fl. 2; Parecer da Commissão de Saude Pública, Rio de Janeiro, 19 August 1879, AGC-RJ, Cod. 48-4-63, fl. 3; "Annexo H: Relatorio do Presidente da Junta de Hygiene Pública," in Brazil, Ministerio do Imperio, Relatorio, 1870, p. 7 and n.

48 Subdelegado de Policia, 1º Districto do Engenho Velho, defendant, Lauriana Maria da Conceição, Rio de Janeiro, 1890, ANSPJ, Maço 80, N. 1584, fls. 7—7v, 12v; Juizo da 20ª Pretoria, defendant, Olinda Maria da Conceição, Rio de Janeiro, 1895, ANSPJ, Caixa 1372, N. 9649, fls. 2, 5—5v, 7.

49 Côrte de Apelação, Acção de Liberdade pela Belmira por seu curador, defendant, Francisco da Veiga Abreu, Rio de Janeiro, 1872, ANSPJ, Maço 216, N. 1740, fl. 33v.

50 From "Regras de servir a mesa," *Cozinheiro Nacional* (Rio de Janeiro: Garnier [c. 1900]), quoted in Luis da Camara Cascudo, ed., *Antologia da alimentação no Brasil* (Rio de Janeiro: Livros Técnicos e Científicos Editôra, 1977), pp. 27—30; Alexandre José Melo Morais Filho, *Festas e tradições populares do Brasil*, 3rd edn. rev., notes by Luis da Camara Cascudo, first published 1888 (Rio de Janeiro: Briguiet, 1946), p. 21; Ina von Binzer (pseud. Ulla Von Eck?), *Alegrias e tristezas de uma educadora alemã no Brasil*, trans. Alice Rossi and Luisita de Gama Cerqueira (São Paulo: Anhembí, 1956), p. 25.

51 Maurice Rugendas, *Voyage pittoresque dans le Brésil*, trans. M. de Golbery (Paris: Engelmann, 1835), 2e Div., Planche 7, "Négresses de Rio-Janeiro"; Augusto José Pereira das Neves, Meu nascimento e factos mais notaveis da minha vida [1835—1909], MS, in the possession of Guilherme Paulo Castagnoli Pereira das Neves, Rio de Janeiro, and kindly lent me, entry for January 1891, fl. 162; Debret, *Voyage*, II, Planche 6; Souza Junior, *Do regimen alimentar*, p. 44; Carta de Liberdade, Rio de Janeiro, 1875, ANSPJ, CSO, Escrituras, Liv. 114, fl. 62v; Kidder and Fletcher, *Brazil*, p. 134.

52 Pfeiffer, *A Woman's Journey*, p. 42; Collaço, *Conselheiro*, p. 44; Nabuco, *Meu livro*, p. 9.

53 Almeida, *Livro das noivas*, pp. 165—166; Ewbank, *Life in Brazil*, p. 287; Inventory, Aguida Maria da Conceição, Rio de Janeiro, 1859, ANSPJ, Caixa 78, N. 332, fl. 372v; Francisco de Paula Candido, *Relatorio sobre as medidas da salubridade reclamadas pela cidade do Rio de Janeiro* (Rio de Janeiro, 1851), n.p., quoted in Freyre, *Sobrados e mucambos*, I, 208; Pimentel, *Subsidios*, p. 181.

54 Rio de Janeiro, Inspectoria geral da illuminação da Côrte, *Tabela das horas de acender e apagar os combustadores publicos* (Rio de Janeiro: Imprensa Nacional, 1889), p. 15; Goulart, "Alguns dados," *RIHGB*, 31; Carvalho, *História da cidade*, p. 109; João Mauricio Wanderley, Barão de Cotegipe, to João Alfredo Correia de Oliveira, Rio de Janeiro, 3 July [1875], typescript copy, AIHGB, Coleção Cotegipe, L. 50, D. 108; João José de Oliveira Junqueira to João Mauricio Wanderley, Barão de Cotegipe, Rio de Janeiro, 20 February 1873, AIHGB, Coleção Cotegipe, L. 31, D. 45.

55 Brazil, Congresso, Câmara dos Deputados, *Manual parlamentar, regimento interno da*

Camara dos Deputados . . . (Rio de Janeiro: Imprensa Nacional, 1887), Art. 57, p. 22; ch. vii, "Organização judiciária," in Brazil, Ministerio da Justiça, *Notícia histórica dos serviços, instituições e estabelecimentos pertencentes a esta repartição, elaborada por ordem do respectivo ministro, Dr. Amaro Cavalcanti* (Rio de Janeiro: Imprensa Nacional, 1898), p. 40; Nabuco, *Meu livro*, p. 27.

56 Almeida, *Livro das noivas*, pp. 78–79.

57 Bernardo Guimarães, *A escrava Isaura*, first published 1875 (Belo Horizonte: Itatiaia, 1977), pp. 37, 74.

58 However frequent, violence against household servants is difficult to document except when aberrant enough by contemporary standards for neighbors and the courts to have intervened, for example see Juizo da 5ª Circumscripção, Inquerito, defendant, Stella Bandeira, Rio de Janeiro, 1896, ANSPJ, Maço 2279, n. 1334, fls. 2v–4, 10v–11, 18. Actual incidents of theft by servants are difficult to document, for employers despite their accusations, seldom thought it worthwhile to take servants to court, but for examples of standard accusations, see João [Branho?] Muniz to Conselho de Intendencia da Capital Federal, Rio de Janeiro [*c.* 1892], AGC-RJ, Documentação Avulsa; Serviço Domestico, 1882–1904; Serrarias, 1875–1911, Cod. 50-1-41; "Serviço domestico," *O Commentario*, ser. iii, n. 10 (February 1906), p. 149; *Rio News*, 24 January 1893, p. 4.

59 Juizo da 3ª Pretoria Criminal, Inquerito sobre defloramento da menor, defendant [sic], Maria dos Anjos Almeida, Rio de Janeiro, 1900, ANSPJ, Maço 958, n. 6012, fls. 8–8v, 10; Expilly, *Mulheres*, pp. 84–85; "A Mãe escrava," *A Mãe de Familia*, May 1880, p. 77; Paulo Barreto (pseud. João do Rio), *As religiões do Rio* (1906; rpt. Rio de Janeiro: Organização Simões, 1951), p. 36; Juizo da 9ª Pretoria, defendant, Carolina Alves, Rio de Janeiro, 1906, ANSPJ, Maço 1015, n. 2138, fls. 3, 4v; Côrte de Apelação, Acção de Liberdade pela Belmira por seu curador, defendant, Francisco da Veiga Abreu, Rio de Janeiro, 1872, ANSPJ, Maço 216, n. 1740, fl. 37.

60 Between 1860 and 1863 only two women, peddlers of notions and nicknacks, acquired new licenses. Felix Martins Corrêa to Camara Municipal, Rio de Janeiro, 1861, AGC-RJ, Escravos ao ganho, 1860 e 1861, Cod. 6-1-52, fl. 146; Rosalina Soares to Camara Municipal, Rio de Janeiro, 1863, AGC-RJ, Escravidão e Escravos ao ganho, 1863–1867, Cod. 6-1-54, fl. 71.

61 AGC-RJ, Mercado da Candelaria, 1870–1879, Cod. 61-2-17, fls. 101–102; AGC-RJ, Barracas, Barracões e Barraquinhos, 1846 . . . 1863–1865, Cod. 58-3-36, fl. 25.

62 Kidder and Fletcher, *Brazil*, p. 167; in São Cristovão 32 free women and 8 slave women worked as *quitandeiras*, Arrolamento SC, 1870; "Vendedora de miudezas," in Costa, *O Rio*, i, 128.

63 Kidder and Fletcher, *Brazil*, p. 172.

64 Proposals for regulating the sale of bread to Camara Municipal, Rio de Janeiro, 1861 and 1892, AGC-RJ, Commercio de pão, 1841–1907, Cod. 58-4-36, fls. 38, 129; Accused to Camara Municipal, Rio de Janeiro, 10 March 1879, AGC-RJ, Infracção de Posturas, Sacramento, 1870–1879, Cod. 9-2-35, fl. 29; José Luiz Sayão de Bulhões Carvalho, *A verdadeira população da cidade do Rio de Janeiro* (Rio de Janeiro: Typ. do "Jornal do Commercio," 1901), p. 45.

65 Goulart, "Alguns dados," *RIHGB*, 34–35; Municipal Veterinarian to Camara Municipal, Rio de Janeiro, 28 November 1889, AGC-RJ, Commercio de Leite, 1856–1895, Cod. 59-1-7, fls. 57–58; President, Commissão Sanitaria . . . Santo

Antonio to President of the Junta Central de Hygiene Pública, Rio de Janeiro, 23 December 1879, AGC-RJ, Relatorios sobre assumptos de hygiene, Cod. 38-2-32, fl. 39v; Complaint lodged by the Sociedade Cosmopolita Protectora dos Empregados em Padarias, Rio de Janeiro, 22 December 1902, AGC-RJ, Commercio de pão, 1841–1907, Cod. 58-4-36, fls. 145–146; Junta Central de Hygiene Pública to Camara Municipal, Rio de Janeiro, 10 April 1864, Director do Matadouro Público to Camara Municipal, Rio de Janeiro, 30 November 1881, AGC-RJ, Carnes e matadouros . . . serviço sanitario, 1853–1909, Cod. 53-4-10, fls. 30–30v, 76.

66 Ewbank, *Life in Brazil*, p. 94; Everardo Backheuser, *Habitações populares* (Rio de Janeiro: Imprensa Nacional, 1906), p. 109; Kidder and Fletcher, *Brazil*, p. 174.

67 Kidder and Fletcher, *Brazil*, p. 174.

68 Chief of Police of Côrte to Minister of Justice, Rio de Janeiro, 3 January 1855, ANSPE, IJ6-219, Secção da Policia, Côrte, 1855, Case No. 16; José Marcellino Pereira de Vasconcellos, *Regimento dos Inspectores de Quarteirão ou Collecção dos actos e attribuições que competem a esta classe de funcionarios* (Rio de Janeiro: Typ. e Livraria de Bernardo Xavier Pinto de Souza, 1862), pp. 1–16.

69 Côrte de Apelação, Acção de Liberdade pela Belmira por seu curador, defendant, Francisco da Veiga Abreu, Rio de Janeiro, 1872, ANSPJ, Maço 216, N. 1740, fls. 41, 33v, 21.

70 Consulta, Conselho de Estado Secção do Imperio, Rio de Janeiro, 5 August 1889, AGC-RJ, Serviço Domestico; Projectos de posturas e pareceres do Conselho d'Estado sobre o serviço domestico no Rio de Janeiro, 1881–1889, Cod. 50-1-43; Louis Couty, *L'Esclavage au Brésil* (Paris: Guillaumen, 1881), pp. 44–45.

71 Adriano José de Figueiredo to Antonio Ferreira Vianna, 13 April 1859, Rio de Janeiro, AIHGB, L. 508, D. 14.

72 Arrolamento SC, 1870.

73 *JC*, 20 March 1875, 31 July 1884, 11 November 1896.

74 *JC*, 5 February 1882.

75 Federico Lisboa de Mara, *Histórico sobre o abastecimento de agua à Capital do Imperio desde 1861–1889* (Rio de Janeiro: Imprensa Nacional, 1889), pp. 3–19; Pimentel, *Subsidios*, pp. 261, 273–274; Inspector Geral to Camara Municipal, Rio de Janeiro, 16 March 1869, AGC-RJ, Abastecimento d'Agua; Inspecção Geral, 1860–1899, Cod. 51-1-30, fl. 7; *The British and American Mail*, 24 March 1878, p. 4; *Rio News*, 24 October 1879, p. 2.

76 Rego, *Esboço*, p. 206; Rio de Janeiro, Commissão do Saneamento, *Relatorios apresentados . . . 1896* (Rio de Janeiro: Imprensa Nacional, 1896), p. 36; *JC*, 11 November 1896, p. 2; Moradores de Villa Isabel to Camara Municipal, Rio de Janeiro, 7 January 1884, Director de Hygiene e Assistencia Pública to Prefeito, Rio de Janeiro, 5 September 1893, and Moradores de Copacabana to Prefeito, Rio de Janeiro, 2 December 1903, AGC-RJ, Abastecimento d'Agua; Canalização Geral, 1832–1903, Cod. 51-1-14, fls. 49, 50, 66. Tearing up streets to lay pipes generated further inconvenience and complaints. Director das Obras Municipaes to Camara Municipal, Rio de Janeiro, 21 December 1866, AGC-RJ, Abastecimento d'Agua; Canalização Geral, 1832–1903, Cod. 51-1-14, fl. 16.

77 Marc Ferrez, Photograph of the Largo da Carioca, AGC-RJ, SI, Coleção Emilio Brondi, 1, and his "Largo da Carioca, *c.* 1890," in Ferrez, *O Rio antigo do fotografo Marc Ferrez*, pp. 58–59, 190.

78 Cláudio Bardy, "O século XIX," in Fernando Nascimento Silva, ed., *Rio de Janeiro*

em seus quatrocentos anos: formação e desenvolvimento da cidade (Rio de Janeiro: Distribuidora Record, 1965), p. 117; Gilberto Ferrez, *A muito leal e heróica cidade de São Sebastião do Rio de Janeiro; quatro séculos de expansão e evolução* (Paris: Marcel Mouillot, 1965), p. 220; Shred of a letter from Camara Municipal, Rio de Janeiro, 16 May 1865, AGC-RJ, Documentação Avulsa; Lavanderias, 1863–1893, Cod. 45-4-34; Ministro de Agricultura to Inspector Geral, Rio de Janeiro, 26 November 1867, AGC-RJ, Abastecimento d'Agua; Chafarizes, 1832–1879, Cod. 51-1-11, fl. 53.

79 Delegacia de Policia da 9ª Circumscripção Urbana, defendant, Salvador Barbará, Rio de Janeiro, 1899, ANSPJ, Caixa 1069, N. 50, fls. 3, 8.

80 Miguel de Piero Machado and Francisco Pinto de Santa Valle to Camara Municipal, Rio de Janeiro, 5 November 1890, AGC-RJ, Diversos Mercados, 1843–1902, Cod. 61-1-24, fl. 14.

81 "Rua Carneirino," *c.* 1890, AGC-RJ, SI, Fotos do Rio de Janeiro; Decreto 1476, 15 January 1913, Art. 5, 6 quoted in Agenor Francisco Noronha Santos, *Meios de transporte no Rio de Janeiro. História e legislação,* 2 vols. in 1 (Rio de Janeiro: Typ. do "Jornal do Commercio," Rodriques & C., 1934), II, 167.

82 *The British and American Mail,* 24 September 1877, p. 3; João Vicente Torres Homem, *Annuario de observações colhidas nas enfermarias de clinica medica da Faculdade de Medicina em 1868* (Rio de Janeiro: Alves, 1869), Case N. 30, p. 288.

3 Private lives in public places

1 Delegacia de Policia da 9ª Circumscripção Urbana, defendant, Salvador Barbará, Rio de Janeiro, 1899, ANSPJ, Caixa 1069, N. 50, fls. 2–4, 6, 7v, 8–9v.

2 *Cidade do Rio,* 15 February 1889; Proposal from Olegario Pinto Ferreira Morado to Camara Municipal, Rio de Janeiro, 26 March 1885, AGC-RJ, Casas para classes pobres . . . 1885, Cod. 46-4-55, fl. 4; Delegacia de Policia da 9ª Circumscripção Urbana, defendant, Salvador Barbará, Rio de Janeiro, 1899, ANSPJ, Caixa 1069, N. 50, fl. 8.

3 Delegacia de Policia da 9ª Circumscripção Urbana, defendant, Salvador Barbará, Rio de Janeiro, 1899, ANSPJ, Caixa 1069, N. 50, fl. 6. Another case where having a lover provided legitimacy against the charge of vagabondage is Juizo da 3ª Pretoria, defendant, Amelia Francisca Alves, Rio de Janeiro, 1903, ANSPJ, Caixa 1080, N. 3950.

4 Delegacia de Policia da 9ª Circumscripção Urbana, defendant, Salvador Barbará, Rio de Janeiro, 1899, ANSPJ, Caixa 1069, N. 50, fls. 7v–8.

5 Officio do Chefe de Policia e projecto do subdelegado, Rio de Janeiro, 16 January 1890, AGC-RJ, Serviço domestico na freguezia da Lagôa, Cod. 50-1-46; Projecto de postura da Camara Municipal, Rio de Janeiro, 29 August 1885, AGC-RJ, Serviços domesticos; Projectos de posturas sobre a locação de serviços domesticos no Municipio Neutro, 1884, 1885, 1888, 1891 e 1896, Cod. 50-1-47, Art. 44, fl. 3.

6 Consulta, Conselho do Estado, Secções Reunidas de Justiça e Imperio, Rio de Janeiro, 5 August 1889, AGC-RJ, Cod. 50-1-43.

7 The actual number was 459 or 47 percent. Arrolamento SC, 1870.

8 Arrolamento SC, 1870; Juizo do Supremo Tribunal de Justiça, Revista Civel, defendant, Maria Dias de Abreu, Rio de Janeiro, 1887, ANSPJ, Maço 30, N. 676, fls. 4v–5.

9 Secretaria de Policia da Côrte to Camara Municipal, Rio de Janeiro, 19 March 1860, AGC-RJ, Escravidão e escravos ao ganho, 1860, Cod. 61-1-37, fl. 1; Agostinho Marques Perdigão Malheiro, *A escravidão no Brasil: ensaio histórico-jurídico-social*, 3 parts in 1 vol. (Rio de Janeiro: Typ. Nacional, 1866–1867), III, Tit. II, Cap. III, p. 115.

10 President, Commissão Sanitaria . . . Santo Antonio to the President, Junta Central de Hygiene Pública, Rio de Janeiro, 23 December 1879, AGC-RJ, Relatorios sobre assumptos de hygiene, Cod. 38-2-32, fl. 31v; Thomas Ewbank, *Life in Brazil: or a Journal of a Visit to the Land of the Cocoa and the Palm* (1856; rpt Detroit: Blaine Ethridge Books, 1971), p. 116; Juizo da 2ª Vara Criminal, Injurias Verbaes, defendant, Francisco Barbosa, Rio de Janeiro, 1870, ANSPJ, Maço 872, N. 4630.

11 Luiz Edmundo da Costa, *O Rio de Janeiro do meu tempo*, 3 vols. (Rio de Janeiro: Imprensa Nacional, 1938), II, 418.

12 Request by tavern owner to stay open beyond ten o'clock and Reply from the secretary of police, Rio de Janeiro, 1874, AGC-RJ, Casas de Negocios; Licenças commerciaes, 1843–1894, Cod. 53-3-54, fls. 42, 45; Guarda Urbana, Rio de Janeiro, 8 September 1877, AGC-RJ, Infracção de posturas, Sacramento, 1870–1879, Cod. 9-2-35, fls. 50–51; Secretaria de Policia da Côrte to Camara Municipal, Rio de Janeiro, 22 February 1876, AGC-RJ, Estalagem con casa de commercio, 1876, Cod. 43-1-24, fl. 2; Fiscal to Camara Municipal, Rio de Janeiro, 1 April 1876, AGC-RJ, Estalagens e cortiços, 1834–1880, Cod. 43-1-25, fls. 60–62.

13 Luiz Dormitzer to Camara Municipal, Rio de Janeiro, 13 July 1877, AGC-RJ, Infracção de posturas, Sacramento, 1870–1879, Cod. 9-2-35, fl. 50; Secretaria de Policia da Côrte to Camara Municipal, Rio de Janeiro, 22 February 1876, AGC-RJ, Estalagem com casa de commercio, 1876, Cod. 43-1-24, fl. 2.

14 Antonio Martins de Azevedo Pimentel, *Quaes os melhoramentos hygienicos que devem ser introduzidos no Rio de Janeiro, para tornar esta cidade mais saudavel* . . . (Rio de Janeiro: Moreira Maximino, 1884), pp. 132–133.

15 President, Commissão Sanitaria . . . Santo Antonio to President of the Junta Central de Hygiene Pública, Rio de Janeiro, 23 December 1879, AGC-RJ, Relatorios sobre assumptos de hygiene, Cod. 38-2-32, fl. 32; Fiscal to Camara Municipal, Rio de Janeiro, 11 February 1865, AGC-RJ, Habitações collectivas, estalagens ou "cortiços," 1855, 1864–1866 e 1868, Cod. 44-2-7, fl. 8.

16 AGC-RJ, Kiosques, 1880–1889, Cod. 45-4-21; Augusto César Malta, Photograph of workingmen in front of kiosk at the Arcos, 1911, in Herculano Gomes Mathias, *História ilustrada do Rio de Janeiro* (Rio de Janeiro: Edições de Ouro, 1965), p. 270.

17 Juizo do 23º Districto Federal, Defloramento, defendant, Manuel Afonso, Rio de Janeiro, 1909, ANSPJ, Caixa 778, N. 1001, fl. 5; Juizo da 3ª Pretoria Criminal, Inquerito sobre defloramento da menor, defendant [sic], Maria dos Anjos Almeida, Rio de Janeiro, 1900, ANSPJ, Maço 958, N. 6012, fl. 10.

18 Charles Expilly, *Mulheres e costumes do Brasil*, trans. Gastão Penalva, Série 5ª, Brasiliana, 56, 2nd edn., first published 1863 (São Paulo: Companhia Editôra Nacional, 1977), pp. 84–85, 87.

19 Requests for licenses, Rio de Janeiro, 10 October 1878, 4 February 1890; Police Commissioner, Rio de Janeiro, [1879], AGC-RJ, Diversões publicas, 1870–1891, Cod. 42-3-19, fls. 46, 54, 107; Fiscal to Camara Municipal, Rio de Janeiro, 16

February 1861, AGC-RJ, Diversões publicas, 1860–1864, Cod. 42-3-13, fl. 198v.

20 Delegacia de Policia da 3ª Circumscrição Suburbana, Inquerito sobre desaparecimento de um recemnascido, defendant, Etelvina de Aguila, Rio de Janeiro, 1906, ANSPJ, Caixa 741, N, 354, fls. 3–4, 5, 7–7v; R. W. Malcolmson, "Infanticide in the eighteenth century," in J. S. Cockburn, *Crime in England, 1550–1800* (Princeton University Press, 1977), pp. 187–209, argues that domestic servants, in desperate attempts to retain their positions in households that would not tolerate their having children, were among those who more frequently committed infanticide in England.

21 Juizo do Supremo Tribunal de Justiça, defendant, Maria Elenteria de Albuquerque, Rio de Janeiro, 1876, ANSPJ, Maço 23, N. 472, fls. 67v, 71v, 73–74v.

22 Juizo de Direito do 7° Districto Criminal, Ofensas fisicas, defendant, Elisa Benedita de Almeida, Rio de Janeiro, 1876, ANSPJ, Caixa 404, N. 1310, fl. 10.

23 Delegacia de Policia da 9ª Circumscripção Urbana, defendant, Salvador Barbará, Rio de Janeiro, 1899, ANSPJ, Caixa 1069, N. 50, fls. 4, 8; Juizo da 2ª Vara Criminal, defendant, Francisco Barbosa, Rio de Janeiro, 1870, ANSPJ, Maço 872, N. 4630, fl. 39.

24 Juizo da 2ª Vara Civel, Divorcio, defendant, Rufino Maria Baleta, Rio de Janeiro, 1857, ANSPJ, Caixa 877, N. 686; Louis Agassiz and Elizabeth Cary Agassiz, *A Journey in Brazil*, 2nd edn. (Boston: Ticknor and Fields, 1868), pp. 82–83; Expilly, *Mulheres*, p. 84; Ina von Binzer (pseud. Ulla Von Eck?), *Alegrias e tristezas de uma educadora alemã no Brasil*, trans. Alice Rossi and Luisita da Gama Cerqueira (São Paulo: Anhembí, 1956), p. 34; Adele Toussaint-Samson, *Une Parisienne au Brésil avec photographies originales* (Paris: Paul Ollendorff, 1883), pp. 44–46.

25 *O Sexo Feminino*, 9 June 1889, p. 4; Juizo da 2ª Vara Civel, Divorcio, defendant, Rufino Maria Baleta, Rio de Janeiro, 1857, ANSPJ, Caixa 877, N. 686.

26 Jean Baptiste Debret, *Voyage pittoresque et historique au Brésil, ou Séjour d'un artiste français au Brésil*, 3 vols. (Paris: Firmin Didot Frères, Imprimeurs de L'Institut de France, 1834–1839), II, Planche 33; *Revista Illustrada*, 1, no. 9 (1876), cover; ibid., 17, no. 640 (1892), pp. 4–5; Carlos Delgado de Carvalho, *História da cidade do Rio de Janeiro* (Rio de Janeiro: F. Alves, 1926), p. 98.

27 Adolfo Morales de los Rios Filho, *O Rio de Janeiro imperial* (Rio de Janeiro: Editôra, "A Noite," 1946), pp. 330–331; *Revista Illustrada*, 17, no. 640 (1892), pp. 4–5; for a rare photograph of a group of slaves at carnaval dressed as royalty, see [?] Christianoff, "Slaves at Carnival, Quitanda Street, Rio de Janeiro, Brazil, circa 1868," in H. L. Hoffenberg, *Nineteenth-century South America in Photographs* (New York: Dover Publications, 1982), plate 153; Eneida de Moraes, *História do carnaval carioca* (Rio de Janeiro: Civilização Brasileira, 1958), p. 106.

28 Juizo do Supremo Tribunal de Justiça, Revista Civel, defendant, Maria Elenteria de Albuquerque, Rio de Janeiro, 1872, ANSPJ, Maço 23, N. 472, fl. 71v.

29 Ancient Portuguese law had assigned appropriate dress to each occupation or social position and made punishable the sale or exchange of certain items of apparel. Similarly, a man or a woman who dressed as his or her sexual opposite committed serious offense. By 1689 in Portugal, all masks had been banned, even at festivals. Although among Brazilians by 1870 disguise no longer counted as punishable offense, it could recall past seriousness. Even in 1870, to commit a crime while disguised so as not to be recognized was considered by law to aggravate the crime and brought a stiffer penalty. *Código Philippino, 1870*, Liv. 5, Tit. XXXIV, n. 4; *Código Criminal do Imperio, 1876*, Art. 16, par. 16. Clothes not only

identified sex, but visibly indicated social rank and were "necessary to their service" and could not, therefore, be pawned, *Código Philippino, 1870*, Liv. 3, Tit. LXXXVI, par. 23, implying that the clothes might fall into unsuitable hands, enabling common people to imitate the nobility.

30 *Revista Illustrada*, 9, n. 373 (1884), pp. 4–5; J. F. de Mello Barreto and Hermeto Lima, *História de polícia do Rio de Janeiro: aspectos da cidade e da vida carioca, 1831–1870*, 3 vols. (Rio de Janeiro: Editôra "A Noite," 1942), II, 197, 305; *Rio News*, 24 January 1883, p. 2; Requests to Camara Municipal, [1875?], AGC-RJ, Carnaval, Cod. 40-3-86, fls. 2–3. That carnaval was for Rio's poor an affirmation and a legitimation of their dominance over street life and an expression of protest more than a reversal of roles or a letting off of steam – although carnaval was all that too – suggests both similarities and differences with other interpretations of other festivities. Compare: Natalie Zemon Davis, "Women on top," in *Society and Culture in Early Modern France* (Stanford University Press, 1979), pp. 124–151; Barbara A. Babcock, "Introduction," pp. 14–27, and Roger D. Abrahams and Richard Bauman, "Ranges of festival behavior," pp. 193–208, and James L. Peacock, "Symbolic reversal and social history: transvestites and clowns of Java," pp. 209–224, all in Barbara A. Babcock, ed. and intro., *The Reversible World: Symbolic Inversions in Art and Society* (Ithaca: Cornell University Press, 1978); Octavio Paz, "The Day of the Dead," in *The Labyrinth of Solitude*, trans. Lysander Kemp (London: Allen Lane, 1967), pp. 39–56.

31 *Revista Illustrada*, 9, no. 373 (1884), pp. 4–5; Alexandre José Melo Morais Filho, *Festas e tradições populares do Brasil*, 3rd edn. rev., notes by Luis da Camara Cascudo, first published 1888 (Rio de Janeiro: Briguiet, 1946), pp. 31–32.

32 Rios Filho, *O Rio de Janeiro*, p. 330. That the rich held balls indoors was consistent with the other celebrations they conducted in the exclusive settings of fine churches. Those who attended might include members of the royal family, ministers, or diplomats. Such was the feast in honor of Nossa Senhora da Glória. Carvalho, *História da cidade*, p. 93. The opulent church decorations at Easter – red curtains fringed in gold, hundreds of candles, pyramids of flowers – made a rich background for the re-enactment of the climb up Calvary led by officers of the National Guard. Georges Raeders, comp. and trans., *O conde de Gobineau no Brasil* (São Paulo: Secretaria da Cultura, Ciência e Tecnologia. Conselho Estadual de Cultura, 1976), pp. 59–60. Solemn high mass celebrated the emperor's birthday each December in the cathedral before a congregation of elite Rio de Janeiro society while troops in parade dress outside kept the curious away. Ida Pfeiffer, *A Woman's Journey Round the World, from Vienna to Brazil, Chili, Tahiti, China, Hindostan, Persia and Asia Minor*, 2nd edn. (London: [Office of the National Illustrated Library, 1852]), pp. 21–24. See also Toussaint-Samson's description of women in "grande toilette," attended by their children and servants, watching from their windows the procession of the Corpo de Deus and São Jorge, *Une Parisienne*, p. 77.

33 *Rio News*, 15 January 1883, p. 4, and 24 January 1883, pp. 2, 4.

34 Pedro Maria de Lacerda, Bishop of São Sebastião do Rio de Janeiro, *Pastoral*, no. 23 (14 March 1877) (Rio de Janeiro: Typ. do Apostolo, 1877), in Cartas Pastorais de D. Pedro Maria de Lacerda, 1870–1879, Arquivo da Cúria Metropolitana, Rio de Janeiro, Caixa 1 (hereafter cited as ACM-RJ), p. 3.

35 José Maria de Medeiros (1849–1925), "Cena de Carnaval," *c.* 1895 and "Cena de Carnaval," 1898, shown at Exposição "Universo do Carnaval: imagens e

reflexões; pinturas, desenhos, fotografias e máscaras," organized by Roberto Da Matta, Acervo Galeria de Arte, Rio de Janeiro, 24 February–31 March 1981.

36 *Código de Posturas, 1870,* Secção Segunda, Policia, Tit. VIII, Art. 2, first promulgated 1838; Américo Fluminense [pseud.], "O carnaval no Rio," *Kosmos* 4, no. 2 (February 1907), n.p.; Notice posted by Fiscal, parish of Candelaria, 4 February 1853, quoted in Melo Morais Filho, *Festas,* p. 30, and in Moraes, *História do carnaval,* p. 23; Chief of Police of Côrte to Minister of Justice, Rio de Janeiro, 3 February 1854, ANSPE, Indice de correspondencia recebida, 1854, IJ1-80.

37 President, Camara Municipal to Parish Inspectors, Rio de Janeiro, 14 February 1887, AGC-RJ, Carnaval, Cod. 40-3-87; *Código de Posturas, 1894,* Decreto 4, 14 January 1893, Art. 1; Circulars from Directoria Geral de Policia Administrativa, Archivo e Estatística to Inspectors, Rio de Janeiro, AGC-RJ, Repressão do jogo de entrudo, circulares de 1906 e 1907, Cod. 49-4-45; Postura, Rio de Janeiro, 9 March 1875, AGC-RJ, Carnaval, Cod. 40-3-86; Moraes, *História do carnaval,* pp. 25–26.

38 Writing about masks, costumes, and figurines, Victor Turner, *The Forest of Symbols: Aspects of Ndembu Ritual* (Ithaca: Cornell University Press, 1967), p. 103 argues that exaggeration is a form of abstraction; that which is exaggerated "is made into an object of reflection."

39 Melo Morais Filho, *Festas,* p. 27.

40 Sebastião Monteiro da Vide, *Constituições primeiras do Arcebispado da Bahia. Feitas e ordenadas pelo . . . Sebastião Monteiro da Vide, 5° Arcebispo do dito Arcebispado e do Conselho de Sua Magestade: Propostas e aceitas em o synodo diocesano que o dito Senhor celebrou em 12 de junho do anno de 1707. Impressas em Lisboa no anno de 1719 e em Coimbra em 1720. . . .* (São Paulo: Typ. "2 de Dezembro," 1853), Liv. 1, Tit. 68, n. 293 (hereafter cited as *Constituiações primeiras, 1853*). The authority of the *Constituiações primeiras* and of Canon Law was extended to independent Brazil by Decreto e Resolução, 3 November 1827 and recommended by Aviso, 25 June 1828, quoted in M. J. de Campos Porto, *Repertorio de legislação ecclesiastica desde 1500 até 1874* (Rio de Janeiro: Garnier, 1875), p. 191. That marriage must be performed in church was substantiated in civil law, see *Código Philippino,* 1870, Liv. 4, Tit. XLVI, n. 3. Until 1890, Canon Law established the qualifications and procedures to marry as set out in *Constituições primeiras, 1853,* Liv. 1, Tit. 64, no. 269, 270, 272; the qualifications are also summarized in Manoel do Monte Rodrigues d'Araujo, *Elementos de direito ecclesiastico em relação á disciplina geral da igreja e com applicação aos usos da igreja do Brasil,* 3 vols. (Rio de Janeiro: Livraria de Antonio Gonçalves Guimarães, 1857–1859), II, 195. Civil marriage entailed equivalent proofs, see *Leis do Brasil,* Decreto 181, 24 January 1890, Cap. 1, Art. 1–5, Cap. IV, Art. 24, 25; *Civil Code, 1916,* Special Part, Book 1, Title 1, Art. 180–188.

41 With origins remote in Iberian tradition, Portuguese law compiled in 1603 as the *Ordenações Philippinas* or Philippine Code, remained in effect in Brazil until 1916 when a civil code was promulgated that consolidated family law as practiced in Brazil. Until then an unwieldy corpus of laws and subsequent revisions protected dowry property, governed the rights and administrative duties each spouse exercised over conjugal property, established the line of succession, or specified the claims to property that legitimate and natural heirs could make, see *Código Philippino, 1870,* Liv. 4, Tit. LXXII; Tit. XCVI; *Civil Code, 1916,* Special Part, Book IV, Tit. I, art. 1576; Tit. II, art. 1603. Only if no blood kin survived, or, from 1916,

if no children, grandchildren, parents or grandparents survived, could a spouse inherit the full share of the deceased's property; that the 1916 civil code increased the disposable amount of property from one third to one half measured the cautious loosening of that enduring tradition, *Código Philippino, 1870*, Liv. 4, Tit. XCIV; *Civil Code, 1916*, Special Part, Book IV, Tit. II, art. 1611.

42 A couple's property could be owned communally (*comunhão de bens*) in halves, separately with each partner in exclusive control over his or her portion (*separação de bens*), or in some specified combination (*separação parcial*), *Código Philippino*, 1870, Liv. 4, Tit. XLVI–XLVII; *Civil Code, 1916*, Special Part, Book I, Tit. III, art. 256–277. Alida Metcalf demonstrates how marriage, property, and inheritance were played out in family economies, "The families of planters, peasants, and slaves: strategies for survival in Santana de Parnaíba, Brazil, 1720–1820," (Ph.D. diss., University of Texas at Austin, 1983); for an insightful unraveling of those concerns and the special place of women, see Eleanor Searle, "Seigneurial control of women's marriage: the antecedents and function of merchet in England," *Past and Present*, no. 82 (February 1979), pp. 3–43.

43 *Código Philippino, 1870*, Liv. 5, Tit. XXI–XXIII.

44 Ibid., Liv. 4, Tit. LXXXVIII.

45 The percentage of married heads of households in São Cristovão was 56, Arrolamento SC, 1870. The *Recenseamento, 1872* presented occupation by marital status only for free women, not for slave women, and the *Recenseamento do Rio de Janeiro, 1906* did not provide information on occupation by marital status at all.

46 Brazil, *Decisões do Governo do Imperio do Brasil*, Aviso 138, 15 April 1851. At least some high-ranking churchmen argued that the fees charged for performing the sacraments ought to be uniform across all parishes, and, if regulated by civil law, all abuses by local clerics would end. One bishop felt, however, that the sacraments ought to be available without charge, the faithful offering only what they could or wished to give, "Annexo C: Relatorios dos Reverendos Prelados Diocesanos, Officio do Reverendo Bispo de Marianna," in Ministerio do Imperio, *Relatorio*, 1867, p. 11, and *Relatorio*, 1868, pp. 39–40.

47 Papal Bull, 26 January 1790, quoted in Antônio Manuel de Melo Castro e Mondonça, "Memória economica-política da capitania de São Paulo . . . 1800," rpt. *Anais do Museu Paulista* 15 (1961), Cap. 2., par. 13; ACM-RJ, Visitas Pastorais, 1845–1892, contains proofs and dispensations regarding marriage, see, for example, 1855, Liv. 35, fls. 1, 2v. In 1870, one illiterate father permitted his 15-year-old daughter to marry José Ferraz, "being a person of good habits and a worker," in Habilitação matrimonial, José Ferraz and Maria Candida da Silva, Rio de Janeiro, 11 January 1870, ACM-RJ, Visitas Pastorais, 1845–1892, fl. 9.

48 *Código Criminal do Imperio, 1876*, Art. 247–248, n. 187; just as under Portuguese rule the royal treasury could confiscate the offender's property or inheritance right, Porto, *Repertorio*, p. 190.

49 *Constituições primeiras*, 1853, Liv. 1, Tit. 71, no. 34.

50 *Leis do Brasil*, Lei 1144, 11 September 1861, Art. 1, 2; *Constituições primeiras, 1853*, Liv. 1, Tit. 71, no. 304.

51 Ibid., no. 303.

52 When the Republic was established and church and state were separated, civil unions received full legal sanction, *Leis do Brasil*, Decreto 181, 24 January 1890.

53 Juizo da 2ª Vara Civel, Divorcio, defendant, Rufino Maria Baleta, Rio de Janeiro, 1857, ANSPJ, Caixa 877, N. 686.

54 Perfilhação, Rio de Janeiro, 1880, ANSPJ, Cartório do Segundo Ofício, Escrituras, Liv. 245, fls. 50v–55 (hereafter cited as ANSPJ, CSO); Perfilhação, Rio de Janeiro, 1864, ANSPJ, CPO, Escrituras, Liv. 291, fl. 25; Perfilhação, Rio de Janeiro, 1871, ANSPJ, CPO, Escrituras, Liv. 317, fls. 27–27v; Perfilhação, Rio de Janeiro, 1880, ANSPJ, CSO, Escrituras, Liv. 245, fl. 42.

55 *Código Philippino, 1870*, Liv. 5, Tit. xxii, n. 2. Nor were deflowerings infrequent. For the year 1885, Dr. Manoel Thomaz Coelho, *Annuario Medico Brasileiro*, 1886, p. 32, in charge of the medical division of the Rio de Janeiro police, reported that police doctors had conducted 55 examinations for deflowering. Presumably those cases represented only the women who sought court intervention, while other women arrived at solutions privately or did not try.

56 A fine was first decreed in 1860, Brazil, *Decisões do Governo do Imperio do Brazil*, Aviso N. 464, 23 October 1860; *Código Criminal, 1876*, Art. 219, 222, 226–227; Antonio Bento de Faria, *Annotações theorico-practicas ao Código Penal do Brasil de accordo com a doutrina e legislação e a jurisprudencia, nacionaes e estrangeiras, seguido de um appendice contendo as leis em vigor e que lhe são referentes.* . . . 4th edn., 2 vols. (Rio de Janeiro: Jacintho Ribeiro dos Santos, 1929), Art. 267, 168 (hereafter cited as *Código Penal, 1890*).

57 Juizo da 3ª Circumscrição, Defloramento, defendant, Antonio Cespedes Barbosa Sobrinho, Rio de Janeiro, 1901, ANSPJ, Caixa 745, N. 358, fls. 4, 8.

58 Juizo do 25° Districto Policial, Defloramento, defendant, João Cardoso de Albuquerque, Rio de Janeiro, 1910, ANSPJ, Caixa 756, N. 534, fils. 2, 4–4v, 14.

59 Juizo da 11ª Pretoria, 16° Districto Policial, Inquerito Policial, defendant, Laura da Cruz Almeida, Rio de Janeiro, 1909, ANSPJ, Caixa 1156, N. 4895, fls. 2–2v, 5–5v, 15.

60 Juizo do 23° Districto Federal, Defloramento, defendant, Manoel Afonso, Rio de Janeiro, 1909, ANSPJ, Caixa 778, N. 1001, fls. 2, 4, 5–5v, 17.

61 Juizo da 2ª Vara Civel, Divorcio, defendant, Rufino Maria Baleta, Rio de Janeiro, 1857, ANSPJ, Caixa 877, N. 686.

62 Juizo Municipal da 2ª Vara Civel, Injurias Verbaes, defendant, Emilia Julia da Conceição, Rio de Janeiro, 1870, ANSPJ, Maço 885, N. 833, fl. 16v.

63 Historians have begun to examine evidence that challenges the once accepted view that most Brazilians lived in extended families. See Elizabeth Kuznesof, "Household composition and headship as related to changes in modes of production: São Paulo 1765 to 1836," *Comparative Studies in Society and History* 22 (January 1980), 100–101; Donald Ramos, "Marriage and the family in colonial Vila Rica," *HAHR* 55 (May 1975), 200–225;Iraci del Nero da Costa, "A estrutura familial e domiciliária em Vila Rica no alvorecer do século xix," *Revista do Instituto de Estudos Brasileiros* 19 (1977), 25, 27, 31. Long ignored was the estimate recorded by John Luccock, *Notes on Rio de Janeiro, and the Southern Parts of Brazil; Taken During a Residence of Ten Years in that Country, from 1808 to 1818* (London: Samuel Leigh, 1820), p. 41, that in Rio de Janeiro some 4,000 women headed households.

64 In an attempt to correct the view that American slaves did not form or maintain stable two-parent families, Herbert G. Gutman, *The Black Family in Slavery and Freedom, 1750–1925* (New York: Pantheon Books, 1976), errs in another direction. By locating and celebrating nuclear and extended slave families, Gutman implicitly discredits single parent families or any other grouping of kin who might think of themselves as family. The point is not to judge some families as

more truly families than others, but rather to discover what bonds of kinship were possible, which could be and were maintained, and, at best, to know the meanings assigned them.

65 Antonio do Espirito Santo, household head, [n. ?] Estalagem, Praça de D. Pedro I, 6° quarteirão, and Bernardo José da Costa, household head, casa n. L, rua São Luiz Gonzaga, 11° quarteirão, and Bemvindo, household head, casa n. 24A, rua de José Clemente, 5° quarteirão, and Pedro Antonio Lino, household head, casa n. 1, rua da Imperial Quinta, 8° quarteirão, Arrolamento SC, 1870; Brazilian naming practices can confound the social historian, see Maria Luiza Marcílio, *A cidade de São Paulo: povoamento e população, 1750–1850* (Universidade de São Paulo, 1974), pp. 70–73.

66 José da Silva Vieira, household head, casa n. 40, Estalagem Mauá, rua dos Lazaros, 2° quarteirão, and Carlos Rodrigues Coelho, household head, casa n. 17, rua de Aurora, 7° quarteirão, Arrolamento SC, 1870.

67 Joze Antonio Pinto da Costa, household head, casa n. 22, Praça das Mangueiras, 9° quarteirão, Arrolamento SC, 1870.

68 Brazil, Secretaria d'Estado dos Negocios do Imperio, Diretoria, Secção de Estatística, *Trabalhos da secção de estatística . . . 1886* (Rio de Janeiro: Imprensa Nacional, 1887), p. 87. The total number of children baptized was 7,729, and of those 2,568 were illegitimate. Mappa demonstrativo do movimento de partos na maternidade, Rio de Janeiro, April–December 1881, AGC-RJ, Casas de Maternidade, Cod. 46-2-32, fls. 14–15.

69 Candida Roza da Silva, household head, casa n. 12, rua do Bomfim, 5° quarteirão, and Guilhermina d'Souza Machado, household head, casa n. 95 B, rua de D. Pedro I, 7° quarteirão, and Paula Maria Barreto, Household head, casa n. 5, rua da Imperial Quinta, 8° quarteirão, and Maria Jacintha de [N?]azaret, household head, casa n. 4, Estalagem Mauá, rua dos Lazaros, 2° quarteirão, and Engracia Maria da [Conceição?], household head, casa n. 31, Estalagem Mauá, rua dos Lazaros, 2° quarteirão, Arrolamento, SC, 1870. Because even upperclass families often gave different last names to their children the inference cannot always be confidently made.

70 Agassiz and Agassiz, *A Journey*, p. 84.

71 Juizo de Direito da 1ª Vara Civel, defendant, Serafina (preta), Rio de Janeiro, 1882, ANSPJ, Maço 555, N. 3498, fls. 4v, 15, 22, 71–74; João Antonio de Barros, household head, casa n. E [C?], rua de Bemfica, 11° quarteirão, Arrolamento SC, 1870; *JC*, 16 October 1909; Locação de Serviço e Carta de Liberdade, Rio de Janeiro, 1881, ANSPJ, CPO, Escrituras, Liv. 375, fl. 91. Compare the situation of domestics, able to keep children with them, to French factory women who were forced to give their children out to wet-nurses, in George D. Sussman, "The wet-nursing business in nineteenth-century France," *French Historical Studies* 9 (1975), 304–328.

72 Henrique Mangeon, household head, casa n. 3 A, rua de Vianna, 7° quarteirão, and José Emilio Pinto Leite Braga, household head, casa n. B, rua da Feira, 2° quarteirão, and Francisco Severiano Machado, household head, casa 1 A, rua de Bemfica, 11° quarteirão, and D. Antonia Maria dos Santos [Farrucho?], household head, casa n. 111, Campo de São Cristovão, 6° quarteirão, and João Fernandes de Mattos Lima, household head, casa n. 54, rua dos Lazaros, 2° quarteirão, Arrolamento SC, 1870.

73 Izabel Maria, household head, casa n. 23, Estalagem Mauá, rua dos Lazaros, 2°

quarteirão, Arrolamento SC, 1870; Inventory, Anna Maria da Conceição, Rio de Janeiro, 1863, ANSPJ, Caixa 3617, N. 55, fls. 16, 23v, 88v.

74 Compare this interpretation for Rio de Janeiro with Theresa M. McBride, *The Domestic Revolution: The Modernization of Household Service in England and France, 1820–1920* (New York: Holmes & Meier, 1976), pp. 56, 84, and with David M. Katzman, *Seven Days a Week: Women and Domestic Service in Industrializing America, 1870–1920* (New York: Oxford University Press, 1978), p. 115, where, they argue, servant women found themselves isolated from family or friends.

75 Florença da Silva to Balbina da Silva, Cidade do Grão Mogol, 14 April 1862, AN, Werneck Papers, Cod. 112, vol. 8, Cartas Avulsas fl. 13-q.

76 Maria Lourindo, living in the province of Rio Grande do Sul, placed a notice in a Pernambuco newspaper near where they had lived as a family, slaves of Sr. Jeronymo Ignacio de Albuquerque Maranhão, asking for information about Victoriana, *Diario de Pernambuco*, 12 November 1860, p. 4.

77 Juizo de Direito da 2° Vara Civel, defendant Antonio Viêtas da Costa, Rio de Janeiro, 1870, ANSPJ, Maço 872, no. 4645, fls. 2, 4, 6–8v, 13v–15v, 17, 22v, 23v, 24v–25, 69, 71–71v, 73, 81, 109–109v, 110v–111.

78 Augusto José Pereira das Neves, Meu nascimento e factos mais notaveis da minha vida [1835–1909], MS, in the possession of Guilherme Paulo Castagnoli Pereira das Neves, Rio de Janeiro, fl. 116, described his daughter's delivery at home without a midwife, as there "had not been time to call one." José Vieira Fazenda, "A roda (casa dos expostos)," *RIHGB*, Tomo LXXI, Vol. 118, parte II (1908), 172; Madame Joanna Beau to Camara Municipal, Rio de Janeiro, 1847, AGC-RJ, Parteiras, 1820–1878, Cod. 47-1-47, fl. 12; Madame Cocural to Camara Municipal, Rio de Janeiro, 23 December 1879, AGC-RJ, Parteiras, 1879, Cod. 47-1-50; a total of 18 midwives were listed in the *Almanak Laemmert*, 1875, pp. 644–645.

79 Fazenda, "Roda," pp. 172–173; *Almanak Laemmert*, 1880, p. 700.

80 Neves, Meu nascimento, fl. 129; Mappa demonstrativo do movimento de partos na maternidade municipal, Rio de Janeiro, April–December 1881, AGC-RJ, Casas de Maternidade, Cod. 46-2-32, fl. 14; "Maternidade," *O Commentario*, ser. III, no. 6 (October 1905), p. 105.

81 Francisco Peixoto de Lacerda Werneck to João Baptista Leite Cia., Monte Alegre, 16 February 1861, AN, Werneck Papers, Cod. 112, vol. 3, fls. 245, 247, 256, 257, 262; João Vicente Torres Homem, *Elementos de clinica medica . . .* (Rio de Janeiro: Alves, 1870), p. 737.

82 "Palestra do medico," *A Mãe de Familia*, March 1881, pp. 33–34; Felippe Neri Collaço, *O conselheiro da familia brasileira* (Rio de Janeiro: Garnier, 1883), p. 199.

83 José Rodrigues dos Santos to Camara Municipal, Rio de Janeiro, 4 January 1877, AGC-RJ, Maternidade e casa de saude, 1877–1899, Cod. 46-2-32, fl. 4; José Rodrigues dos Santos to Camara Municipal, Rio de Janeiro, [c. 1883], AGC-RJ, Maternidade, Cod. 46-2-33, fl. 2; Report of the Commission of the Treasury of the Camara Municipal, 20 February 1883, AGC-RJ, Maternidade Municipal, 1883–1884, Cod. 46-2-34. By as late as 1898 the city council had not established a maternity hospital. When directed to do so by the federal government, the council again refused. See Minister of Justice and Interior to Prefect, Rio de Janeiro, 18 January 1898, and Prefect to Director de Obras e Transporte, 3 February 1898, AGC-RJ, Maternidade e casa de saude, 1877–1899, Cod. 46-2-32, fls. 55, 57.

84 Arthur Moncorvo Filho, *Da assistencia publica no Rio de Janeiro e particularmente da assistencia á infancia* . . . (Rio de Janeiro: Imprensa Nacional, 1907), pp. 8–11.

85 "Maternidade," pp. 101–107.

86 Luiz Corrêa de Azevedo, "Memoria lida na Academia Imperial de Medicina . . . as causas da mortalidade das crianças," *Annaes Brazilienses de Medicina* 21 (1869), 120.

87 Juizo da 3ª Pretoria Criminal, Inquerito sobre defloramento da menor, defendant [sic], Maria dos Anjos Almeida, Rio de Janeiro, 1900, ANSPJ, Maço 958, N. 6012, fls. 8–8v, 10, 11.

88 The *roda* or wheel was a shelf, the base of a rotating cylinder. From the street, goods or an infant could be placed on the shelf, the cylinder turned and received by someone inside, neither party ever visible to the other. Common at the convents of cloistered orders, the wheel became in Brazil a social institution. See Fazenda, "A roda," p. 155; Ubaldo Soares, *O passado heróico da Casa dos Expostos* (Rio de Janeiro: Fundação Romão de Matos Duarte, 1959), p. 228; Perfilhação, Rio de Janeiro, 1860, ANSPJ, CPO, Escrituras, Liv. 281, fls. 22–22v.

89 A. J. R. Russell-Wood, *Fidalgos and Philanthropists, The Santa Casa da Misericórdia of Bahia, 1550–1755* (Berkeley: University of California Press, 1968), p. 316; Soares, *O passado*, p. 48, lists the salaries paid to women who worked as wet-nurses at the Santa Casa.

90 At a time when middle class women repeatedly lost their young children, how much more often did early death claim the infants of the poor. Of the five daughters in the family of a military physician who had each married and borne children, three had children who died either within the first days after birth or before reaching age six. One, Alice, alone suffered the deaths of four of her seven children, while her sister Josefina had lost two, and both women were then young enough to expect further pregnancies. Neves, Meu nascimento, fls. 121–122, referring to the period 1887–1908.

91 José Pereira Rego, *Apontamentos sobre a mortalidade da cidade do Rio de Janeiro particularmente das crianças e sobre o movimento de sua população no primeiro quatriennio depois do recenseamento feito em 1872* (Rio de Janeiro: Typ. Nacional, 1878), pp. 20–21, 67.

92 Quoted in Francisco Agenor de Noronha Santos, *Chorographia do Districto Federal (cidade do Rio de Janeiro)*, 3rd edn. (Rio de Janeiro: Benjamin de Aguila, 1913), pp. 156–159; *Relatorio, 1870*, p. 23; Rego, *Apontamentos*, pp. 20–21.

93 Arthur Moncorvo Filho, "A tuberculose e as collectividades infantis," *A Ordem Social*, no. 3 (1911), pp. 67–70.

94 J. C. Oakenfull, *Brazil in 1912* (London: Atkinson, 1913), p. 132; Inventory, Aguida Maria da Conceição, Rio de Janeiro, 1859, ANSPJ, Caixa 78, N. 332, fl. 242; *The Empire of Brazil at the Universal Exhibition of 1876 in Philadelphia* (Rio de Janeiro Imperial Instituto Artistico, 1876), p. 476; "No. 10: Mappa dos obitos de escravos sepultados nos Cemeterios da Santa Casa da Misericordia, . . ." *Relatorio, 1870*.

95 Although catholicism remained the state religion until 1890, persons could worship privately as they chose as long as the places of worship bore no outward form of a temple and no objects were displayed offensive to the religion of the state, to morality, or to proper conduct. See *Código Criminal, 1876*, Art. 276–279; *Código Penal, 1890*, Art. 185–186. No wholly satisfactory history has yet been written that reconstructs and interprets not only the belief systems but also the

actions, practices, rituals, and ceremonies that comprised *macumba, candomblé, espiritismo,* and *feiticeirismo.* The historical record that would enable reconstruction is not easy to come by. The most acceptable account of black, African influences in Brazilian religious experience remains Roger Bastide, *The African Religions of Brazil: Toward a Sociology of the Interpenetration of Civilizations,* trans. Helen Sebba (Baltimore: The Johns Hopkins University Press, 1978), based on research initiated in 1938. The enduring presence of African culture brought by slaves to Rio de Janeiro in the first half of the nineteenth century is one of the principal themes examined by Mary C. Karasch, *Slave Life in Rio de Janeiro, 1808–1850* (Princeton University Press, 1987), see especially pp. 261–272, 284–287.

96 "A Mãe escrava," *A Mãe de Familia,* May 1880, p. 77, and November 1879, p. 174; Paulo Barreto (pseud. João do Rio), *As religiões do Rio* (1906; rpt. Rio de Janeiro: Organização Simões, 1951), pp. 36, 200–201.

97 Museu da Fundação Carlos Costa Pinto, Salvador, Bahia; homemade amulets were collected by Moncorvo Filho from children brought to his clinic and described in Arthur Moncorvo Filho, "Amuletos e abusões," in Arthur Moncorvo Filho, *et al, Assistencia á infancia, hygiene infantil; ás mães pobres; conferencias realizadas no Dispensario Moncorvo, 1901–1907* (Rio de Janeiro: Imprensa Nacional, 1907), p. 55; Expilly, *Mulheres,* pp. 85–86.

98 Adela Neval to Camara Municipal, Rio de Janeiro, 12 December 1876; Junta Central de Hygiene Pública to Camara Municipal, Rio de Janeiro, 20 December 1876, AGC-RJ, Espiritismo e sonambulismo, 1876–1883, Cod. 43-1-6, fls. 1–2; Barreto, *As religiões,* p. 200.

4 Protection and obedience

1 For accounts of paternalistic relations in other places which helped shape and clarify my understanding of the Brazilian case, see Howard Newby, "The deferential dialectic," *Comparative Studies in Society and History* 17 (April 1975), 139–164; Patrick Joyce, *Work, Society and Politics: The Culture of the Factory in Later Victorian England* (New Brunswick NJ: Rutgers University press, 1980). Eugene Genovese, *Roll, Jordan, Roll: The World the Slaves Made* (New York: Pantheon, 1974), examines paternalism in the context of slavery in the United States' South; James Oakes, *The Ruling Race: A History of American Slaveholders* (New York: Alfred A. Knopf, 1982), challenges Genovese. On matters of culture and class, I draw from Clifford Geertz, *The Interpretation of Cultures, Selected Essays* (New York: Basic Books, 1973); E. P. Thompson, "Patrician Society, Plebeian Culture," *Journal of Social History* 7 (Summer 1974), 382–405; Maurice Godelier, in "Economic structures of pre-capitalist societies," Lecture, 19 March 1979, University of Texas at Austin, developed the notion of an "idiom of interpretation," that is, the meanings people assign to events. These, he argued, are part of the process of realizing social life, not structures but ways of acting and understanding; for his discussion of dominance, see Maurice Godelier, "Infra-structures, societies and history," *Current Anthropology* 19 (December 1978), 763–771.

2 *JC,* 1852, quoted in Daniel P. Kidder and James C. Fletcher, *Brazil and the Brazilians Portrayed in Historical and Descriptive Sketches,* 9th edn. rev. (London: Sampson Low, Marston, Searle, and Rivington, 1879), p. 255; Júlia Lopes de

Notes to pages 91–94

Almeida, *Livro das noivas*, 3rd edn. (Rio de Janeiro: Companhia Nacional Editora, 1896), pp. 94; *A Mãe de Familia*, January 1881, p. 12; Ina von Binzer (pseud.? Ulla Von Eck), *Alegrias e tristezas de uma educadora alemã no Brasil*, trans. Alice Rossi and Luisita da Gama Cerqueira (São Paulo: Anhembí, 1956), p. 99.

3 Almeida, *Livro das noivas*, pp. 92, 121.

4 José Joaquim França Junior, "Visitas," and "Visinhos," in *Folhetins* (Rio de Janeiro: Typ. da "Gazeta de Noticias," 1878), pp. 45, 113; for a consideration of França Junior as a mediocre dramatist but an apt source for the historian, see Roderick J. Barman, "Politics on the stage: the late Brazilian empire as dramatized by França Junior," *Luso-Brazilian Review* 13 (Winter 1976), 244–260.

5 Agostinho Marques Perdigão Malheiro, *A escravidão no Brasil: ensaio histórico-jurídico-social*, 3 parts in 1 vol. (Rio de Janeiro: Typ. Nacional, 1866–67), 1, Secção v, Art. 1, par. 146, pp. 183–185, 187; III, Tit. II, Cap. III, p. 119.

6 Juizo da 1ª Vara de Orphãos, Inventory, Antonia Luiza dos Santos Albuquerque, Rio de Janeiro, 1880, ANSPJ, Caixa 4003, N. 237, fl. 36.

7 Luiz Francisco da Silva, household head, casa 105 A, Praça de Dom Pedro I, 6° quarteirão, Arrolamento SC, 1870; "A educação da mulher," *A Mãe de Familia*, January 1881, p. 20.

8 Almeida, *Livro das noivas*, pp. 163–164; Antonio Corrêa de Souza Costa, *Alimentação de que usa a classe pobre do Rio de Janeiro e sua influência sôbre a mesma classe* (Rio de Janeiro: Perseverança, 1865), p. 31.

9 *JC*, 31 July 1884, 11 November 1896, Juizo da 5ª Pretoria Civel, defendant, Eva de tal, Rio de Janeiro, 1892, ANSPJ, Maço 1334, N. 6852.

10 *Código de Posturas, 1870*, Secção Segunda, Policia, Tit. IV, art. 6; Kidder and Fletcher, *Brazil*, p. 133.

11 Juizo do Supremo Tribunal de Justiça, defendant, Maria Elenteria de Albuquerque, Rio de Janeiro, 1872, ANSPJ, Maço 23, N. 472, fl. 65; Inventory, Anna Maria da Conceição, ANSPJ, Caixa 3617, N. 55, fl. 24; Ida Pfeiffer, *A Woman's Journey Round the World, from Vienna to Brazil, Chili, Tahiti, China, Hindostan, Persia, and Asia Minor*, 2nd edn. (London: [Office of the National Illustrated Library, 1852]), p. 17; advertisement for a runaway slave women, *JC*, 20 March 1875; Juizo da 3ª Circumscrição, Inquerito policial, defendant, Maria Luiza da Conceição, Rio de Janeiro, 1899, ANSPJ, Caixa 732, N. 20, fl. 3.

12 Boris Kossoy, *Origens e expansão da fotografia no Brasil, século XIX* (Rio de Janeiro: Edição FUNARTE, 1980), p. 45. The clothes of the two amas contrast with the African style – white turban, beads, loose cotton blouse – worn by the street vendor pictured on the same page; for the date, see also Pedro Vasquez, *Dom Pedro II e a fotografia no Brasil* (Rio de Janeiro: Fundação Roberto Marinho and Companhia Internacional de Seguros, [1986]), p. 24; Juizo do Supremo Tribunal de Justiça, Revista Civel, defendant, Maria Elenteria de Albuquerque, Rio de Janeiro, 1872, ANSPJ, Maço 23, N. 472, fls. 65, 88, 92.

13 Costa, *Alimentação*, pp. 33–36.

14 Francisco Fernandes Padilha, *Qual o regimen alimentar das classes pobres do Rio de Janeiro? Quaes as molestias que mais commummente grassão entre ellas? Que relações de causalidade se encontrão entre esse regimen e molestias?* (Rio de Janeiro: Laemmert, 1853), p. 14; Costa, *Alimentação*, pp. 12–13.

15 João Baptista A. Imbert, *Guia medico das mães de familia, ou a infancia considerada na sua hygiene, suas molestias e tratamentos* (Rio de Janeiro: Typ. Franceza, 1843), pp. 55–56; Thomaz Eboli, *Dissertação sobre a hygiene: os prejuizos que causam uma má alimentação* (Rio de Janeiro: Popular, 1880), pp. 9–10.

16 Francisco Peixoto de Lacerda Werneck, *Memoria sobre a fundação de uma fazenda na provincia do Rio de Janeiro, sua administração, e épochas em que devem fazer as plantações, suas colheitas, etc., etc.* (Rio de Janeiro: Laemmert, 1847), p. 181.

17 Dr. Antonio Joaquim Fortes Bustamante, household head casa n. 21 a 25, rua do Retiro Saudoso, 14° quarteirão, Arrolamento SC, 1870.

18 Ubaldo Soares, *Um século no roteiro da caridade: o hospital da Misericórdia, 1852–1952. Subsídios históricos* (Rio de Janeiro: "Jornal do Comercio," 1952), p. 195; Mappa demonstrativo do movimento de partos na maternidade municipal, Rio de Janeiro, April to December 1881, AGC-RJ, Casas de maternidade, Cod. 46-2-32, fls. 14–15.

19 Inventory, Aguida Maria da Conceição, Rio de Janeiro, 1859, ANSPJ, Caixa 78, N. 332, fl. 240; Inventory, Anna Maria da Conceição, Rio de Janeiro, 1863, ANSPJ, Caixa 3617, N. 55, fls. 90v, 28.

20 João Vicente Torres Homem, *Annuario de observações colhidas nas enfermarias de clinica medica da Faculdade de Medicina em 1868* (Rio de Janeiro: Alves, 1869), Case n. 30, pp. 288–291.

21 Ibid., Case n. 33, pp. 307–313; Case n. 35, pp. 326–329.

22 Werneck, *Memoria*, pp. 179–180.

23 Richard Burton, *Explorations of the Highlands of the Brazil; with a Full Account of the Gold and Diamond Mines. Also, Canoeing Down 1500 Miles of the Great River São Francisco from Sabará to the Sea*, 2 vols. (London: Tinsley Brothers, 1869), 1, 237–239, recorded the muster of some 1,100 slaves at the Morro Velho mine in Minas Gerais that ended with the full company attending mass; Juizo do Supremo Tribunal de Justiça, Revista Civel, defendant, Maria Elenteria de Albuquerque, Rio de Janeiro, 1872, ANSPJ, Maço 23, N. 472, fls. 63v–64.

24 Carta de liberdade, Rio de Janeiro, 1875, ANSPJ, CSO, Escrituras, Liv. 114, fl. 62v.

25 Manoel Jacintho Carneiro Nogueira da Gama, *Testamento* (Freguezia de Santa Thereza [Valença, Rio de Janeiro]: Typ. de Santa Rosa, 1883), pp. 3, 10; Juizo do Tesouro Nacional, Maria Bernarda Esteves, Rio de Janeiro, 1864, ANSPJ, Inscrição Verba Testamentaria, Liv. 4, N. 203, fl. 228.

26 For examples see, Carta de liberdade, Rio de Janeiro, 1880, ANSPJ, CSO, Escrituras, Liv. 245, fls. 5v–6; Carta de Liberdade, Rio de Janeiro, 1871, ANSPJ, CPO, Escrituras, Liv. 317, fls. 30–30v; Juizo da Provedoria, Francisca Joaquina de Souza Ramos, 1886, ANSPJ, Conta Testamentaria, Caixa 361, N 307, fls. 4v, 12.

27 Augusto José Pereira das Neves, Meu nascimento e factos mais notaveis da minha vida [1835–1909], MS, in the possession of Guilherme Paulo Castagnoli Pereira das Neves, Rio de Janeiro, fls. 123–124.

28 Juizo do Tesouro Nacional, João Martins Vianna, Rio de Janeiro, 1861, ANSPJ, Inscrição Verba Testamentaria, Liv. 2, N. 118, fl. 136; Juizo do Tesouro Nacional, José Pinto Ferreira, Rio de Janeiro, 1865, ANSPJ, Inscrição Verba Testamentaria, Liv. 5, N. 124, fl. 141.

29 Inventory, Lourenço Souza Meirelles, Rio de Janeiro, 1870, ANSPJ, Caixa 1418, N. 520, fls. 153, 155v–156v, 162v.

30 Eduardo von Lyvel, Rio de Janeiro, 1909, ANSPJ, Inscrição Verba Testamentaria, Vol. 92, N. 61, fl. 63v; Severino Antonio Correa, Rio de Janeiro, 1909, ANSPJ, Inscrição Verba Testamentaria, vol. 92, N. 50, fl. 51v; [?], Rio de Janeiro, 1911, ANSPJ, Inscrição Verba Testamentaria, vol. 95, N. 217, fl. 2v.

31 *Correio Mercantil,* 16 May 1864, p. 1.

32 "O festival da Praça da Republica, 8 setembro 1903," *Archivo de Assistencia á Infancia,* 2, nos. 7–9 (July–September 1903), p. 147.

33 Malheiro, *A escravidão no Brasil,* III, Cap. III, Tit. II, pp. 115–116, 118.

34 *JC,* 2 July 1890, 2 September 1905, 5 October 1909, 4 and 11 July 1877.

35 The servant women referred to here include the 516 live-in servants who could be identified as members of specific households, Arrolamento SC, 1870; João Gomes d'Campos Luzano Freitas, household head, casa n. 23, rua da Aurora, 6° quarteirão, and João Antonio Alves Botelho, casa n. 10 A, rua do Bomfim, 6° quarteirão, and D. Isabel Maria d'Almeida, casa n. 2 A, rua de Maruhy, 6° quarteirão, Arrolamento SC, 1870; Neves, Meu nascimento, 7 February 1892, fl. 168.

36 *JC,* 2 July 1851, 26 January 1850, 18 July 1877, 14 August 1872, 18 July 1855.

37 James McFadden Gaston, *Hunting a Home in Brazil. The Agricultural Resources and other Characteristics of the Country; also, the Manners and Customs of the Inhabitants* (Philadelphia: King and Baird Printers, 1867), p. 225; *JC,* 1 July 1882, 2 July 1890.

38 Juizo da Provedoria, Antonio Hernandes, Rio de Janeiro, 1863, ANSPJ, Conta de Thesouro, Caixa 386, N. 1247, fls. 3, 4v–5, 7–7v; Juizo do Tesouro Nacional, Antonio Hernandes, Rio de Janeiro, 1861, ANSPJ, Inscrição Verba Testamentaria, Liv. 3, N. 61, fls. 77–78.

39 Arrolamento SC, 1870.

40 Juizo da Provedoria e Residuos, Inventory, Joaquim Maria Machado de Assis, Rio de Janeiro, 1908, ANSPJ, Caixa 3892, N. 1, fls. 3–4.

41 Juizo do Supremo Tribunal de Justiça, Revista Civel, defendant, Maria Elenteria de Albuquerque, Rio de Janeiro, 1872, ANSPJ, Maço 23, N. 472, fl. 63.

42 *JC,* 16 July and 23 July 1890, 5 May 1900, 8 June 1900; *Codigo Philippino, 1870,* Liv. 4, Tit. XXIX, par. 1, n. 1.

43 Louis Couty, *L'Esclavage au Brésil* (Paris: Guillaumen, 1881), p. 44; *A Mãe de Familia,* May 1879, p. 73.

44 Locação de Serviço e Carta de Liberdade, Rio de Janeiro, 1878 and 1874, ANSPJ, CPO, Escrituras, Liv. 353, fl. 35 and Liv. 337, fl. 23v.

45 Maria Joaquina, household head, casa n. A do cortiço, rua São Luiz Gonzaga, 11° quarteirão, Arrolamento SC, 1870; Juizo de Direito do 7° Districto Criminal, Ofensas fisicas, defendant, Elisa Benedita de Almeida, Rio de Janeiro, 1876, ANSPJ, Caixa 404, N. 1310, fl. 23.

46 Juizo Municipal da 1ª Vara, Injurias Verbaes, defendant, Josefina das Dores, Rio de Janeiro, 1865, AGC-RJ, Maço 791, N. 16027, fl. 2–2v, 6v; Habeas Corpus, defendant, Amelia Francisca Alves, Rio de Janeiro, 1906, ANSPJ, Maço 932, N. 4224, fls. 2v–3, 5–5v.

47 Almeida, *Livro das noivas,* p. 79; Consulta, Conselho de Estado, Secções Reunidas de Justiça e Imperio, Rio de Janeiro, 5 August 1889, AGC-RJ, Serviço Domestico; Projectos de posturas e pareceres do Conselho d'Estado sobre o serviço domestico no Rio de Janeiro, 1881–1889, Cod. 50-1-43.

48 *JC,* 20 March 1875, 1 February 1882.

49 Florença da Silva to Balbina da Silva, Cidade de Grão Mogol, 14 April 1862, AN, Werneck Papers, Cod. 112, vol. 8, Cartas Avulsas, fl. 13–q; Manoel Esteves Ottoni to João Vieira Machado da Cunha, Philadelphia, Minas Gerais, 9 January 1863, AN, Werneck Papers, Cod. 112, vol. 8, Doc. 47.

50 Juizo do Supremo Tribunal de Justiça, Revista Civel, defendant, Maria Elenteria de Albuquerque, Rio de Janeiro, 1872, ANSPJ, Maço 23, N. 472, fl. 87v; Juizo de Direito da 1ª Vara Civel, defendant, Serafina (preta), Rio de Janeiro, 1882, ANSPJ, Maço 555, N. 3498, fls. 58–59v.

51 João [Branho?] Muniz to Conselho de Intendencia da Capital Federal, Rio de Janeiro, [c. 1892], AGC-RJ, Documentação Avulsa; Serviço Domestico, 1882–1904; Serrarias, 1875–1911, Cod. 50-1-41; João Alfredo Correia de Oliveira, Minority Report, 18 October 1889, in Consulta, Conselho de Estado, Secções Reunidas de Justiça e Imperio, Rio de Janeiro, 5 August 1889, AGC-RJ, Serviço Domestico; Projectos de posturas e pareceres do Conselho d'Estado sobre o serviço domestico no Rio de Janeiro, 1881–1889, Cod. 50-1-43; "Educação da mulher," *A Mãe de Familia*, January 1881, p. 19; Consulta, Conselho de Estado, Secções Reunidas de Justiça e Imperio, Rio de Janeiro, 5 August 1889, AGC-RJ, Serviço Domestico; Projectos de posturas e pareceres do Conselho d'Estado sobre o serviço domestico no Rio de Janeiro, 1881–1889, Cod. 50-1-43; "Serviço domestico," *O Commentario*, pp. 148–151.

52 Ministerio da Justiça, *Relatorio*, 1882, p. 197.

53 *JC*, 4 July 1877, 26 July 1882, 23 July 1884, 2 July 1890.

54 *JC*, 4 July 1877, 28 August 1872, 2 and 9 July 1890, 5 May 1900, 2 July 1890.

55 Consulta, Conselho do Estado, Secções Reunidas de Justiça e Imperio, Rio de Janeiro, 5 August 1889, AGC-RJ, Minority Report of João Alfredo Correia de Oliveira, 18 October 1889, Cod. 51-1-43.

56 *JC*, 5 May 1900, 22 May 1900, 2 September 1905, 2 July 1890.

57 *JC*, 5 October 1909.

58 *Leis do Brasil*, Decreto 2433, 15 June 1859, Cap. IV, Art. 85; although the court eventually refused Deolinda her freedom, her case, running to 180 pages, was seen as serious enough to reach an appellate court, Supremo Tribunal de Justiça, Revista Civel, defendant, Deolinda por seu curador, Rio de Janeiro, 1883, ANSPJ, Maço 410, N. 4763, fls. 1, 6.

59 Juizo do Supremo Tribunal de Justiça, Revista Civel, defendant, Maria Elenteria de Albuquerque, Rio de Janeiro, 1872, ANSPJ, Maço 23, N. 472, fls. 14–14v, 17, 106v, 133; regarding the charge of "illicit and immoral" use of a slave, see Malheiro, *Escravidão no Brasil*, 1, Sec. 3ª, Art. III, par. 95, no. 8 and n. 507.

60 Juizo da 5ª Circumscripção, Inquerito, defendant, Stella Bandeira, Rio de Janeiro, 1896, ANSPJ, Maço 2279, N. 1334, fls. 2v–4, 10v–11, 18.

61 Marcellina's stiffly posed photograph shows her richly dressed in a long dark silk gown with a slight bustle, a bead-trimmed jacket closed at the throat with a cameo, in her hand a fan. Her full bust and slender waist suggest a tightly laced corset beneath. She conveys a somber image that perhaps discloses the conflictive world she had entered: no longer a house servant, she would never comfortably belong to her master's world. Juizo Municipal, Comarca de Vassouras, Embargo, defendant, Antonio Alves de Azevedo Nogueira, 1887, Cartório do Primeiro Ofício, Vassouras, Rio de Janeiro, Processos Diversos, fls. 2–2v, 18–21, 24, 28, 29–32v, 38, 46. Robert W. Slenes kindly shared this case with me.

62 Juizo Ecclesiastico, defendant, João Rodrigues Pereira d'Almeida, Rio de Janeiro, 1874, ACM-RJ, Libelos de Divorcio, 1870–1879, Caixa 3A, fls. 2, 4v, 10, 21, 68v.

63 Among the paradoxes that paternalistic relations produced, I would argue, the issue of legitimacy was central. By depriving servants of any sustainable claim to

an independent existence, those who dominated ironically denied themselves the possibility of receiving from them any voluntary or convincing confirmation of their authority. Without legitimacy thus conferred, masters were left to justify their very real power through a show, at least, of benevolent gestures that masked the fundamental conflict between master and servant.

64 Delegacia da Policia da 3ª Circumscrição Suburbana, Inquerito sobre desaparecimento de um recemnascido, defendant, Etelvina de Aguia, Campo Grande, 1906, Caixa 741, N. 354, fls. 5, 7.

5 Contagion and control

1 Robert Conrad, *The Destruction of Brazilian Slavery, 1850–1888* (Berkeley: University of California Press, 1972), pp. 20–46; Sessão 3 August 1870, Brazil, Congresso, Camara dos Deputados, *Anais*, 1870, IV, 21; *Leis do Brasil*, Lei 2040, 28 September 1871, Art. 1, which further permitted masters the option of ending responsibility toward slave children when they reached age eight, although few apparently did so.

2 Agostinho Marques Perdigão Malheiro, *A escravidão no Brasil: ensaio histórico-jurídico-social*, 3 parts in 1 vol. (Rio de Janeiro: Typ. Nacional, 1866–1867), III, Tit. I, Cap. VII, pp. 208–210; Joaquim Norberto Souza e Silva, *Investigações sobre os recenseamentos da populaçao geral do Imperio e de cada provincia de per si tentados desde os tempos coloniais até hoje feitas em virtude do aviso de 15 de março de 1870* . . . (Rio de Janeiro: Perseverança, 1870), p. 166; Brazil, Ministerio da Agricultura, Commercio e Obras Publicas, *Relatorio*, 1886, p. 34; ibid., 1888, p. 24. Higher taxes levied on slaves in the capital somewhat encouraged owners to sell or free them, *Leis do Brasil*, Lei 1507, 26 September 1867, Art. 18.

3 Supremo Tribunal de Justiça, Habeas Corpus, defendant [*sic*], Albano (escravo), Rio de Janeiro, 1873, ANSPJ, Maço 1718, N. 2312; *JC*, 21 July 1851, 7 August 1872.

4 *Código de Posturas, 1870*, Secção Segunda, Policia, Tit. VII, par. 5–6.

5 Pedro João Mauger, household head, casa n. 29 A 1, rua Retiro Saudoso, 14° quarteirão, Arrolamento SC, 1870; Registro de Casamento, 1876, Parish Records of Santa Rita, Rio de Janeiro, Liv. 7, fl. 114v; *Leis do Brasil*, Lei 1695, 15 September 1869, Art. 2.

6 Francisco Luíz da Gama Roza, *Hygiene do casamento* (Rio de Janeiro: Leuzinger, 1876), p. 87; Thomaz Eboli, *Dissertação sobre a hygiene: os prejuizos que causam uma má alimentação* (Rio de Janeiro: Popular, 1880), p. 7; Thiago Jose dos Passos, household head, casa no. 102, rua de São Luiz Gonzaga, 9° quarteirão, and Guilhermina Pereira Dias da Silva, household head, casa n. 8–D, rua São Januario, 8° quarteirão, Arrolamento SC, 1870.

7 AGC-RJ, Africanos livres ao ganho, 1855–1880, Cod. 39-1-30, fls. 6, 11; AGC-RJ, Ganhadores livres, 1837–1873, Cod. 44-1-27, fl. 15; *JC*, 5 July, 1884.

8 José Pereira Rego, *Esboço historico das epidemias que tem grassado na cidade do Rio de Janeiro desde 1830 a 1870* (Rio de Janeiro: Typ. Nacional, 1872), pp. 170–175; Francisco Agenor de Noronha Santos, *Chorographia do Districto Federal (cidade do Rio de Janeiro)*, 3rd edn. (Rio de Janeiro: Benjamin de Aguila, 1913), pp. 162, 164; Rio de Janeiro, Commissão do Saneamento, *Relatorios apresentados ao Exm. Sr. Dr. Prefeito Municipal pelos Drs. Manoel Victorino Pereira, presidente da commissão e Nuno de Andrade, relator em 31 de agosto de 1896* (Rio de Janeiro: Imprensa Nacional,

1896), pp. 6–7; Donald Cooper, "Oswaldo Cruz and the impact of yellow fever on Brazilian history," *The Bulletin of the Tulane University Medical Faculty* 26 (February 1967), 49–52.

9 Placido Barbosa and Cassio Barbosa de Rezende, *Os serviços de saude publica no Brasil, especialmente na cidade do Rio de Janeiro, 1808–1907*, 2 vols. (Rio de Janeiro: Imprensa Nacional, 1909), 1, 79; "Report of the cholera," 15 October 1855, Great Britain, Foreign Office, FO13/331, 198v, quoted in Donald Cooper, "The 'New Black Death': Cholera in Brazil, 1855–1856," *Social Science History* 10 (Winter 1986), 480, 479–481.

10 Santos, *Chorographia*, pp. 162–163; Rego, *Esboço*, p. 170.

11 Aureliano Gonçalves de Souza Portugal, *Primeiro annuario de estatistica demographo-sanitaria da cidade do Rio de Janeiro* (Rio de Janeiro: Imprensa Nacional, 1890), pp. 66, 78, 82, 88, 157; "Mappa 1: Mappa da mortalidade do Rio de Janeiro durante o ano de 1868," in Annexo F: Oficio do medico encarregado da estatistica pathologica e mortuaria, Brazil, Ministerio do Imperio, *Relatorio*, 1869, p. 2; Annexo E, Relatorio sobre os trabalhos da Inspectoria Geral de Hygiene, Brazil, Ministerio do Imperio, *Relatorio*, 1888, p. 11; J. P. Favilla Nunes, *Estatistica do Rio de Janeiro e serviços concernentes á salubridade publica da cidade do Rio de Janeiro* (Rio de Janeiro: Imprensa Nacional, 1885), p. 8. Basic statistics on fatal diseases are also found in: José Pereira Rego, *Memoria historica das epidemias da febre amarella e cholera-morbo que têm reinado no Brazil* (Rio de Janeiro: Typ. Nacional, 1873); Barbosa and Rezende, *Serviços de saude*, 1, 449.

12 Rio de Janeiro, Commissão do Saneamento, *Relatorios*, pp. 14–43, summarizes an earlier 1856 report. Not until 1903 did medical experiments in Brazil confirm the somewhat earlier hypothesis that the *Aedes* mosquito was the carrier of yellow fever. Nancy Stepan, *Beginnings of Brazilian Science: Oswaldo Cruz, Medical Research and Policy, 1890–1920* (New York: Science History Publications, 1981), pp. 59, 143.

13 *Leis do Brasil*, Decreto 598, 14 September 1850, created the Junta Central de Hygiene Pública to advise the government on necessary measures to improve public health; Barbosa and Rezende, *Serviços de saude*, 1, 61–63, 66. See also Santos, *Chorographia*, p. 166, for a useful list of principal public health institutions and their founding dates; Geraldo F. Sampaio, "Saneamento das cidades brasileiras," in Leonidio Ribeiro, organizer, *Medicina no Brasil* (Rio de Janeiro: Imprensa Nacional, 1940), pp. 191–192, briefly describes early English sewerage inventions that would eventually be adopted in Brazil. To compare Rio with São Paulo, see John Allen Blount, "The public health movement in São Paulo, Brazil: A history of the sanitary service, 1892–1918" (Ph.D. diss., Tulane University, 1971).

14 Edital, 24 March 1863, *Código de Posturas, 1870*, p. 114; *Leis do Brasil*, Decreto 1929, 16 April 1857.

15 Nunes, *Estatistica*, p. 5; *Revista Illustrada*, 1, n. 10 (4 March 1876), back cover.

16 Rio de Janeiro, Commisão de Melhoramentos, *Primeiro relatorio da Commissão de Melhoramentos da cidade do Rio de Janeiro*, 2 vols. in 1 (Rio de Janeiro: Typ. Nacional, 1875–1876); Torquato Xavier Monteiro Tapajós, . . . *Estudos de hygiene; a cidade do Rio de Janeiro; primeira parte: terras, aguas e ares; idéias finaes* (Rio de Janeiro: Imprensa Nacional, 1895), p. 233. Regarding clogged drains as a cause of yellow fever see the discussion on the 1860–1864 period, in Portugal, *Primeiro annuario de estatistica*, p. 16.

17 Rego, *Esboço*, p. 175; José Pereira Rego, *Apontamentos sobre a mortalidade da cidade do Rio de Janeiro particularmente das crianças e sobre o movimento de sua população no*

primeiro quatriennio depois do recenseamento feito em 1872 (Rio de Janeiro: Typ. Nacional, 1878), p. 59n.

18 Tapajós, *Estudos de hygiene*, pp. 46, 235; Rio de Janeiro, Commissão do Saneamento, *Relatorios*, pp. 29, 73; José Ricardo Pires de Almeida, Informações . . . Junta Central de Hygiene Pública . . . 1879, AGC-RJ, Relatorios sobre assumptos de hygiene, Cod. 38-2-32, fl. 16; José Felix da Cunha Menezes, *Hygiene relativa ao saneamento da cidade do Rio de Janeiro* (Rio de Janeiro: Villeneuve, 1890).

19 Consulta, Conselho de Estado, Secções Reunidas de Justiça e Imperio, Rio de Janeiro, 5 August 1889, AGC-RJ, Serviço Domestico; Projectos de posturas e pareceres do Conselho d'Estado sobre o serviço domestico no Rio de Janeiro, 1881–1889, Cod. 50-1-43.

20 Brazil, Ministerio da Justiça, *Relatorio*, 1882, pp. 195–196.

21 Consulta, Conselho de Estado, Secções Reunidas de Justiça e Imperio, Rio de Janeiro, 5 August 1889, AGC-RJ, Serviço Domestico; Projectos de posturas e pareceres do Conselho d'Estado sobre o serviço domestico no Rio de Janeiro, 1881–1889, Cod. 50-1-43.

22 José Modesto de Souza Junior, *Do regimen alimentar dos recemnascidos* . . . (Rio de Janeiro: Imprensa Gutenberg, 1895), p. 44; *A Mã de Familia*, May 1879, p. 73.

23 Projecto de postura sobre a locação de serviços domesticos no Municipio Neutro, Camara Municipal to Ministerio do Imperio, 29 August 1885, AGC-RJ, Serviço Domestico; Projectos de posturas e pareceres do Conselho d'Estado sobre o serviço domestico no Rio de Janeiro, 1881–1889, Cod. 50-1-43; "A educação da mulher," *A Mãe de Familia*, January 1881, pp. 19–20.

24 Brazil, Ministerio da Justiça *Relatorio*, 1882, p. 197.

25 Evaristo de Moraes to Intendencia Municipal, Rio de Janeiro, 19 March 1892, AGC-RJ, Serviço Domestico; Propostas, . . . 1884–1906, Cod. 48-4-56, fl. 18.

26 Brazil, Ministerio da Justiça, *Relatorio*, 1882, p. 197. This view was also expressed by those who urged government protections for industry. They argued that industrial work would "moralize" Brazilians and eradicate the presence of shiftless vagabonds: "In the factories, which are in miniature the representation of the states, the worker is subject to a rigorous discipline that will inculcate in his spirit respect toward superiors. . . . Trained in these principles, the worker transmits them to his children, implanting in the bosom of the family the same order and regularity that he learned at the workshop. . . . The citizen respects constituted authorities as the worker respects [his] patrão. . . . Citizens educated in respect and obedience to superiors . . . [do not] perturb the public order." Associação Industrial, Rio de Janeiro, *O trabalho nacional e seus adversarios* (Rio de Janeiro: Leuzinger, 1881), pp. 165–166.

27 Fiscal of Santa Rita parish to Camara Municipal, Rio de Janeiro, 1 August 1855, AGC-RJ, Habitações collectivas, estalagens, ou cortiços, 1855, 1864–1866, 1868, Cod. 44-2-7, fl. 1; Rego, *Apontamentos*, pp. 22, 71.

28 Sociedade de Hygiene do Brasil, *Relatorio apresentado na sessão anniversaria de 23 de junho 1893 pelo secretario geral interino Dr. Carlos Augusto de Brito e Silva* (Rio de Janeiro: Barreiros, 1893), p. 10; Relatorio do Chefe de Policia da Côrte, in Annexo B, Relatorios de Diversas Autoridades, Brazil, Ministerio da Justiça, *Relatorio*, 1867, p. 55.

29 Rio de Janeiro, Commissão do Saneamento, *Relatorios*, p. 38; Everardo Backheuser, "Onde moram os pobres," *Renascença* 2, no. 13 (March 1905), 89. Immigrants, as an easily identified group, took their share of blame. By one

account the more than 400 Germans in the parish of Gloria "convert to their own use the worst accommodations in a large cortiço . . . true center of miasmas . . . [and] pernicious disease." Infected with yellow fever, they posed a public danger, Companhia praça da Gloria to Camara Municipal, Rio de Janeiro, 31 October 1878, AGC-RJ, Mercado da Gloria, 1844–1904, Cod. 61-2-4, fl. 31; Fiscal of Gloria to Camara Municipal, Rio de Janeiro, 17 April 1874, AGC-RJ, Mercado da Gloria, 1844–1904, Cod. 61-2-4, fl. 23; Augusto Stahl, photographer, shows the main square in Gloria in 1865 and the large square market building that was transformed into a cortiço, in *Fotografie Lateinamerika von 1860 bis heute*, Konsept und Realisation von Ausstellung und Katalog, Erika Billeter und Ubersetzung der spanischen Texte, Bert Sommer, Kunsthaus Zurich, 20 August–15 November 1981 (Bern: Benteli, 1981), p. 49.

30 In São Cristovão in 1870, 55 percent of the 106 laundresses who lived independently lived in rented cortiço rooms. Arrolamento SC, 1870.

31 Antonio Martins de Azevedo Pimentel, *Subsidios para o estudo da hygiene do Rio de Janeiro* (Rio de Janeiro: Gaspar da Silva, 1890), p. 193; Rio de Janeiro, Prefeitura do Districto Federal, *Album da cidade do Rio de Janeiro: commemorativo do primeiro centenario da independencia do Brasil, 1822–1922* (Rio de Janeiro; Paulo Witte, 1922), n.p., and Luiz Edmundo da Costa, *O Rio de Janeiro do meu tempo*, 3 vols. (Rio de Janeiro: Imprensa Nacional, 1938), III, 859 both contain photographs of laundry drying in cortiço patios; Edital, 17 April 1866, *Código de Posturas, 1870*; shred of a letter, Sala das Sessões [Camara Municipal?], Rio de Janeiro, 16 May 1865, AGC-RJ Documentação Avulsa, Lavanderias, 1863–1893, Cod. 45-4-34.

32 Commissão Sanitaria da Gloria to Junta Central de Hygiene Pública, Rio de Janeiro, 8 May 1880, AGC-RJ, Salubridade do Rio de Janeiro e commissões sanitarias, freguezias de Gloria, Lagôa e Gavea, 1864–1899, Cod. 8-4-25, fl. 6; Proposal to Prefeito do Districto Federal, Rio de Janeiro, 12 July 1893, AGC-RJ, Documentação Avulsa, Lavanderias, 1863–1893.

33 Francisco Soares de Andrea to [?], Rio de Janeiro, 1 August 1872, AGC-RJ, Documentação Avulsa, Lavanderias, 1863–1893, Cod. 45-4-34; Projecto de postura sobre lavagem de roupa, Rio de Janeiro, 13 October 1881, approved 1 December 1881, AGC-RJ, Lavagem de roupa; cópia do projecto de postura, 1881, Cod. 46-1-1; Júlia Lopes de Almeida, *Livro das noivas* (Rio de Janeiro: Typ. da Companhia Nacional, 1896), p. 20; *Rio News*, 24 October 1881, p. 2; Edital, 28 July 1891, Art. 2, *Código de Posturas, 1894*, pp. 320–321.

34 Untitled report on public health, c. 1893, AGC-RJ, Relatorios sobre assumptos de hygiene, Cod. 38-2-32, fl. 107; Rego, *Apontamentos*, p. 34; José Jayme de Almeida Pires, *Nutrizas mercenarias especialmente no Brasil* (Niteroi, RJ: Amerino, 1906), p. 32.

35 *JC*, 2 July 1890, 28 August 1872; Candida Maria da Silva, household head, casa n. 8 F, rua de São Januario, 8° quarteirão, Arrolamento SC, 1870; Peçanha da Silva, "Memoria ou observações . . . sobre a amamentação e as amas de leite," *Annaes Brasilienses de Medicina* 21 (1869), 256; José Jayme de Almeida Pires, *Amas de leite* (Rio de Janeiro: Imprensa Nacional, 1909), p. 7; *A Mãe de Familia*, June 1879, p. 82.

36 José Pereira Rego, Barão Lavradio, Speech to the Brazilian Medical Academy, 1873, quoted in Arthur Moncorvo Filho, *Histórico da protecção á infancia no Brasil, 1500–1922* (Rio de Janeiro: Paulo, Pongetti e Cia., 1926), pp. 61, 69, 97. Theresa M. McBride, *The Domestic Revolution: The Modernization of Household Service in*

England and France, 1820–1920 (New York: Holmes & Meier, 1976), p. 26, describes similar concern in France and England over entrusting children to wet-nurses who might pass on tuberculosis and syphilis.

37 Medical study had shown that, received from wet-nurses, the "germs of disease remain, as if incubated in the organism to develop after many years have passed." Peçanha da Silva, "Memoria ou observações . . . sobre a amamentação e as amas de leite," p. 253.

38 João Baptista A. Imbert, *Guia medico das mães de familia, ou a infancia considerada na sua hygiene, suas molestias e tratamentos* (Rio de Janeiro: Typ. Franceza, 1843), pp. 51–52; Eboli, *Dissertação*, pp. 6–7; Carlos Vasconcellos, "Amas de leite," *Revista de Hygiene* 1, no. 2 (June 1886), 60, 63.

39 Vasconcellos, "Amas de leite," 59; Rego, Speech, 1873, quoted in Moncorvo Filho, *Histórico*, p. 69; Antonio Nunes de Gouvêa Portugal, *Influencia da educação physica do homem* . . . (Rio de Janeiro: Laemmert, 1853), p. 18; Maria Graham, *Journal of a Voyage to Brazil and Residence There, During Part of the Years 1821, 1822, 1823* (1824; rpt. New York: Praeger, 1969), p. 273.

40 "Palestra do medico sobre amas de leite," *A Mãe de Familia*, July 1879, p. 89; Untitled report on amas de leite, *c.* 1893, AGC-RJ, Relatorios sobre assumptos de hygiene, Cod. 38-2-32, fl. 107; Rego, Speech, 1873, quoted in Moncorvo Filho, *Histórico*, p. 69.

41 President, Commissão Sanitaria . . . Santo Antonio to President of the Junta Central de Hygiene pública, Rio de Janeiro, 23 December 1879, AGC-RJ, Relatorios sobre assumptos de hygiene, Cod. 38-2-32, fls. 29v–31; Junta Central de Hygiene Pública to Camara Municipal, Rio de Janeiro, 5 November 1875, AGC-RJ, Estalagens e cortiços; Requerimentos e outros papeis relativos á existencia e á fiscalização sanitaria e de costumes dessas habitações collectivas, 1834–1880, Cod. 43-1-25, fl. 51.

42 I borrow the phrase from Emmanuel Le Roy Ladurie, *Montaillou: the Promised Land of Error*, trans. Barbara Bray (New York: G. Braziller, 1978), p. 221, who attributes a dread of contagion in Montaillou to the wave of plagues after 1348.

43 President, Commissão Sanitaria . . . Santo Antonio to President of the Junta Central de Hygiene Pública, Rio de Janeiro, 23 December 1879, AGC-RJ, Relatorios sobre assumptos de hygiene, Cod. 38-2-32, fls. 30, 28, 56. For city-wide figures, see: "Mappa 7: Mappa demonstrativo do numero de cortiços e moradores dos mesmos, existentes nas freguezias da Côrte," in Relatorio do Chefe de Policia da Côrte, Annexo B, Relatorios de Diversas Autoridades, in Brazil, Ministerio da Justiça, *Relatorio*, 1867, p. 69; Pimentel, *Subsidios*, pp. 187–188. Because census figures do not correspond exactly to the years in which the cortiços were counted, I have derived percentages using the following base population figures or estimate: "N. 1: Mappa da população do Municipio da Côrte, no mez de abril de 1870," in *Relatorio, 1870*, n.p.; *Recenseamento, 1872*, Municipio Neutro, pp. 1–33; J. P. Favilla Nunes, "A população do Municipio Neutro," *Revista da Sociedade de Geographia*, 1886, pp. 27–29; Brazil, Directoria Geral de Estatística, *Recenseamento geral da República dos Estados Unidos do Brazil em 31 dezembro 1890: Districto Federal (cidade do Rio de Janeiro)* (Rio de Janeiro: Leuzinger, 1895), pp. 424–425.

44 Pimentel, *Subsidios*, pp. 187–188; Ministerio da Justiça, *Relatorio*, 1867, p. 69.

45 President, Commissão Sanctaria . . . Santo Antonio to President of the Junta Central de Hygiene Pública, Rio de Janeiro, 23 December 1879, AGC-RJ,

Relatorios sobre assumptos de hygiene, Cod. 38-2-32, fl. 49; Fiscal of Santo Antonio to Camara Municipal, Rio de Janeiro, AGC-RJ, Estalagens e cortiços; Requerimentos e outros papeis relativos á existencia e á fiscalização sanitaria e de costumes dessas habitações collectivas, 1834–1880, Cod. 43-1-25, fl. 88v.

46 Relação das casas de commodos e estalagem, Rio de Janeiro, 1896, AGC-RJ, Documentação Avulsa; Habitações collectivas, 1901–1906, Cod. 44-2-11; Mappa [São José], AGC-RJ, Habitações collectivas; Notas estatisticas, 1–10 September 1895, Cod. 44-2-10, fl. 1; President, Commissão Sanitaria . . . Santo Antonio to President of the Junta Central de Hygiene Pública, Rio de Janeiro, 23 December 1879, AGC-RJ, Relatorios sobre assumptos de hygiene, Cod. 38-2-32, fls. 30–31; Pimentel, *Subsidios*, p. 186.

47 "Mappa 7: Mappa demonstrativo do numero de cortiços e moradores dos mesmos, existentes nas freguezias da Côrte," in Relatorio do Chefe de Policia da Côrte, Annexo B, Relatorios de Diversas Autoridades, Brazil, Ministerio da Justiça, *Relatorio*, 1867, p. 69; Pimentel, *Subsidios*, pp. 187–188.

48 President, Commissão Sanitaria . . . Santo Antonio to President of the Junta Central de Hygiene Pública, Rio de Janeiro, 23 December 1879, AGC-RJ, Relatorios sobre assumptos de hygiene, Cod. 38-2-32, fl. 49; Commissão Sanitaria of Santa Anna, 6 February 1880, AGC-RJ, Habitações collectivas, estalagens ou cortiços, 1875–1881, 1883–1885, Cod. 44-2-8, fl. 105; Luiz Raphael Vieira Souto and Antonio Domingues dos Santos Silva, Memorial, Rio de Janeiro, 24 January 1885, AGC-RJ, Casas para operarios e classes pobres, 1885, Cod. 46-4-56.

49 Junta Central de Hygiene Pública to Camara Municipal, Rio de Janeiro, 6 March 1874, AGC-RJ, Febre amarella, medidas hygienicas, 1873–1874, Cod. 43-3-28; Jorge Mirandola Filho, Parecer aprovado pela Junta Central de Hygiene Pública, Rio de Janeiro, 2 May 1883, AGC-RJ, Casas para operarios e classes pobres, Cod. 46-4-48; *Revista Illustrada*, 1, no. 5 (29 January 1876), pp. 3, 8. For examples see: Commissão Sanitaria of Santo Antonio to Junta Central de Hygiene Pública, Rio de Janeiro, 9 January 1880, AGC-RJ, Estalagens e cortiços; Requerimentos e outros papeis relativos á existencia e á fiscalização sanitaria e de costumes dessas habitações collectivas, 1834–1880, Cod. 43-1-25, fl. 90; Commissão Sanitaria of São Cristovão, Rio de Janeiro, 22 January 1880, AGC-RJ, Salubridade do Rio de Janeiro e commissões sanitarias . . . 1865–1900, fls. 27–29; Letters from the Santa Casa, parish inspectors, police, and the Junta Central de Hygiene Pública to Camara Municipal notifying the council of yellow fever deaths, January–March 1880, AGC-RJ, Febre amarella; Varios papeis sobre providencias adoptados contra a epidemia da febre amarella e meios prophylacticos, 1873–1881, Cod. 43-3-29.

50 Secretaria de Policia da Côrte to Junta Central de Hygiene Pública, Rio de Janeiro, 3 March 1880, AGC-RJ, Estalagens e cortiços; Requerimentos e outros papeis relativos á existencia e á fiscalização sanitaria e de costumes dessas habitações collectivas, estalagens, ou cortiços, 1875–1881, 1883–1885, Cod. 44-2-8, fl. 1; ibid., 1890, 1892, 1893, Cod. 44-2-9.

51 *Revista Illustrada*, 1, no. 12 (18 March 1876), back cover; Luiz da Silva Brandão, Oficio do medico encarregado da estatistica pathologica e mortuaria, Annexo F, in Brazil, Ministerio do Imperio, *Relatorio*, 1869, p. 2; Manoel Thomaz Coelho to Secretaria de Policia da Côrte, Rio de Janeiro, 28 January 1868, AGC-RJ, Habitações collectivas, estalagens, ou cortiços, 1855, 1864–1866, 1868, Cod. 44-

2-7, fls. 15–16; Luiz Raphael Vieira Souto and Antonio Domingues dos Santos Silva, Rio de Janeiro, 24 January 1885, AGC-RJ, Casas para operarios e classes pobres, 1885, Cod. 46-4-56.

52 The notion of a sponsor was widely used; the precise phrase used here to express that notion comes from *Código de Posturas, 1870*, Secção Segunda, Policia, Tit. IX, par. 16. The device of a legal contract was hardly innovative. Patrões who sought to assure order in new and troubling times turned to old ways for solutions. Portuguese law, which had applied to the hiring and firing of agricultural labor in Brazil, guided the proposals that would regulate urban domestic labor. Even the precise terms that fixed servants' broad obligations or narrowed patrons' responsibility were modifications of feudal Portuguese traditions. See *Código Philippino, 1870*, Liv. 4, Tit. XXIX–XXXV, especially XXXI. Both the institution of slavery and forms of control in Brazil after slavery derived, at least to some extent, from medieval Portuguese law, providing further continuity to the transition from slavery to post-abolition society. Nor were nineteenth-century Brazilians the only masters who proposed such measures. See McBride, *The Domestic Revolution*, p. 22, where she refers to a "system of work permits" and "later schemes for placement agencies" in late nineteenth-century France.

53 For examples, see AGC-RJ, Serviço Domestico; Propostas . . . 1884–1906, Cod. 48-4-56; and AGC-RJ, Serviço Domestico; Projectos de posturas . . . 1884, 1885, 1888, 1891, e 1896, Col. 50-1-47.

54 Proposed regulation adopted, Camara Municipal, Rio de Janeiro, 22 November 1888 and remitted to Ministerio do Imperio, 17 December 1888, AGC-RJ, Serviços Domesticos . . . Cod. 50-1-45, fls. 2, 3; Jeronymo de Assis Pinto Freitas e Companhia to Camara Municipal, Rio de Janeiro, 29 August 1887, AGC-RJ, Documentação Avulsa; Serviço Domestico, 1882–1904; Serrarias, 1875–1911, Cod. 50-1-41; Projecto to Camara Municipal, 29 August 1885, AGC-RJ, Serviço Domestico; Projectos de posturas . . . 1884, 1885, 1888, 1891 e 1896, Cod. 50-1-47, fl. 3.

55 Brazil, Ministerio da Justiça, *Relatorio*, 1882, p. 197; Consulta, Conselho de Estado, Sessões Reunidas de Justiça e Imperio, Rio de Janeiro, 5 August 1889, AGC-RJ, Serviço Domestico; Projectos de posturas e pareceres do Conselho d'Estado sobre o serviço domestico no Rio de Janeiro, 1881–1889, Cod. 50-1-43.

56 Rego, Speech, 1873, quoted in Moncorvo Filho, *Histórico*, pp. 68–70, and on establishing the first clinic pp. 88–89; Pires, *Amas de leite*, p. 1; Carlos Arthur Moncorvo de Figueiredo, "Projecto de Regulamento das Amas de Leite," *Gazeta Medica da Bahia*, 1876, pp. 498–504.

57 Reported in *A Mãe de Familia*, January 1880, pp. 2–3.

58 José Guilherme Lisboa to Camara Municipal, Rio de Janeiro, 30 April 1885, AGC-RJ, Documentação Avulsa, 1885–1912; Instituto de amas de leite, 1885, Cod. 44-2-60; Francisco Rebello de Carvalho to Camara Municipal, Rio de Janeiro, 31 July 1884, AGC-RJ, Instituto municipal de amas de leite, 1884–1885, Cod. 41-1-40, fls. 3–5; Rio de Janeiro, Camara Municipal, Sessão, 17 July 1884, *Boletim*, 1884, p. 19; ibid., Sessão, 19 August 1884, *Boletim*, 1884, p. 60; AGC-RJ, Projecto de organização do pessoal medico da Camara Municipal; exame de carnes-verdes, estabulos de vaccas e serviço de amas de leite, 1884, Cod. 48-4-3.

59 Pires, *Amas de leite*, pp. 7–10; Arthur Moncorvo Filho, *Da assistencia publica no Rio de Janeiro e particularmente da assistencia á infancia*. . . . (Rio de Janeiro: Imprensa

Nacional, 1907), p. 22; João Branho Muniz to Conselho da Intendencia da Capital Federal, Rio de Janeiro [*c.* 1892], AGC-RJ, Documentação Avulsa; Serviço domestico, 1882–1904; Serrarias, 1875–1911, Cod. 50-1-41.

60 Imbert, *Guia medico*, pp. 49–50; J. A. C. Nabuco de Araújo, quoted in Moncorvo Filho, *Histórico*, p. 60; Rego, Speech, 1873, quoted in Moncorvo Filho, *Histórico*, p. 68; Nicolao Joaquim Moreira, "Duas palavras sobre a educação moral da mulher, . . ." *Annaes Brasilienses de Medicina* 20 (1868), 103.

61 Moncorvo Filho, *Histórico*, pp. 109–111; see *A Mãe de Familia*, March, May, and November 1879; *O Quinze de Novembro do Sexo Feminino*, Rio de Janeiro, 3–6, no. 5–7, 9, 12 (August 1892–March 1896). Portuguese law instructed that women were obliged to raise and care for a child, including nursing, until age three, although Brazilians understood that that obligation lasted only through the child's first year. Certain women were exempt from having to breast-feed: those too ill or weak or those without enough milk, aristocratic women, and women so poor that they had to work to keep themselves. *Código Philippino, 1870*, Liv. 4, Tit. xcix, par. 1, p. 986n. A similar emphasis on maternal breast-feeding in preference to using hired wet-nurses, but for different reasons, occurred in eighteenth- and nineteenth-century France and England. See: Lawrence Stone, *The Family, Sex and Marriage in England, 1500–1800* (London: Weidenfeld and Nicolson, 1977), pp. 426–432; Edward Shorter, *The Making of the Modern Family* (New York: Basic Books, 1975), pp. 191–199.

62 Rui Barbosa to Maria Luiza Vianna Ferreira Bandeira, Rio de Janeiro, 25 June 1880, Casa de Rui Barbosa, unnumbered; Augusto José Pereira das Neves, Meu nascimento e factos mais notaveis da minha vida [1835–1909], MS, in the possession of Guilherme Paulo Castagnoli Pereira das Neves, Rio de Janeiro, fl. 139.

63 Attempts to remove or clean up cortiços and the public commentary the attempts provoked are exemplified in the following: Projecto de Posturas sobre cortiços, accepted September 1881 by Camara Municipal, Rio de Janeiro, AGC-RJ, Habitações collectivas, estalagens ou cortiços, 1875–1881, 1883–1885, Cod. 44-2-8, fls. 52–54v; *Rio News*, 24 December 1879, p. 2; *Gazeta de Notícias*, 9 January 1884, p. 2; Summons from the Commissão Vaccinico-Sanitario da Gloria, Rio de Janeiro, 8 October 1885, AGC-RJ, Commissão Vacina da Gloria, 1884, Cod. 8-3-19; AGC-RJ, Habitações collectivas, 1906; papeis, plantas . . . Morro do Castello, Cod. 44-2-12, fls. 8–14. Calls for repairs, clean-up, modifications, or demolition appear in AGC-RJ, Habitações collectivas, estalagens, ou cortiços, 1875–1881, 1883–1885, Cod. 44-2-8; ibid., 1890, 1892, 1893, Cod. 44-2-9; Estalagens e cortiços; Requerimentos e outros papeis relativos á existencia e á fiscalização sanitaria e de costumes dessas habitações collectivas, 1834–1880, Cod. 43-1-25, especially fls. 25–121.

64 *Gazeta da Tarde*, 16 February 1884, p. 1; 20 February 1884, p. 1; Commissão Sanitaria de Santa Anna to Junta Central de Hygiene Pública, Rio de Janeiro, 24 January 1880, AGC-RJ, Estalagens e cortiços; Requerimentos e outros papeis relativos á existencia e á fiscalização sanitaria e de costumes dessas habitações collectivas, 1834–1880, Cod. 43-1-25, fls. 99–99v; *Gazeta de Notícias*, 7 January 1884, p. 2.

65 Roberto Macedo, *Barata Ribeiro, administração do primeiro prefeito do Distrito Federal* (Rio de Janeiro: Departamento Administrativo do Serviço Publico, 1955), pp. 20–29; idem, *Efemérides cariocas* (Rio de Janeiro: Companhia Brasileira

de Artes Gráficas, 1943), pp. 25–26; AGC-RJ, Cortiços e estalagens; papeis relativos a demolição de cortiços e estalagens existentes no Rio de Janeiro, 1892–1899, Cod. 41-4-5; "A cidade do Rio de Janeiro nos meados do século XIX, baseada na Planta Garnier, 1852," in Eduardo Canabrava Barreiros, *Atlas da evolução urbana da cidade do Rio de Janeiro; ensaio, 1565–1965* (Rio de Janeiro: Instituto Histórico e Geográfico Brasileiro, 1965), Prancha 16, p. 21; *JC*, 27 January 1893, p. 1; *Rio News*, 31 January 1893, p. 4; The mayor inspired a jingle that played on his name, *barata*, meaning cockroach, and one magazine published as its cover a huge pig's head on a platter, a tear in its eye and on its forehead a large, ugly cockroach, *Revista Illustrada*, 18, no. 656 (1893), p. 1.

66 Fernando Francisco da Costa Ferraz, "A salubridade da Capital do Imperio e os cortiços," *Annaes Brazilienses de Medicina* 35 (1884), 445, 451, 458, 464–465.

67 President, Commissão Sanitaria . . . Santo Antonio to President of the Junta Central de Hygiene Pública, Rio de Janeiro, 23 December 1879, AGC-RJ, Relatorios sobre assumptos de hygiene, Cod. 38-2-32, fl. 31; Rio de Janeiro, Commissão do Saneamento, *Relatorios*, p. 10; Ferraz, "A salubridade," p. 446.

68 Sérgio Buarque de Holanda, ed., *História geral da civilização brasileira*, Tomo II; *O Brasil monárquico*, vol. III; *Reações e transações*, 2nd edn. (São Paulo: Difusão Européia do Livro, 1969), 15–16, 23, 53; ibid., vol. V; *Do império à república* (São Paulo: Difusão Européia do Livro, 1972), 151; see also the photograph of Cariocas disembarking the ferry to board the train at the head of the bay where the ascent to Petrópolis began, in *Nosso Século, 1900–1910*, I, 30–31; *JC*, 1 January 1896, p. 15 carried, for example, an advertisement for a governess to accompany a family to Petrópolis for the summer.

69 Proposals to Camara Municipal, Rio de Janeiro, 5 May 1881 and 23 March 1884; Secretaria de Policia to Ministro do Imperio, Rio de Janeiro, 8 February 1889, AGC-RJ, Serviço Domestico; Projectos de posturas e pareceres do Conselho d'Estado sobre o serviço domestico no Rio de Janeiro, 1881–1889, Cod. 50-1-43.

70 *Rio News*, 5 February 1888, p. 2; Proposed regulation adopted, Camara Municipal, Rio de Janeiro, 22 November 1888 and remitted to Ministerio do Imperio, 17 December 1888, AGC-RJ, Serviços Domesticos . . . Cod. 50-1-45, fl. 3.

71 Consulta, Conselho de Estado, Secções Reunidas de Justiça e Imperio, Rio de Janeiro, 5 August 1889, AGC-RJ, Serviço Domestico; Projectos de posturas e pareceres do Conselho d'Estado sobre o serviço domestico no Rio de Janeiro, 1881–1889, Cod. 50-1-43. The tantalizing report from a Recife newspaper that ". . . the registration of wet-nurses and other private servants has caused some inconvenience by the ill will of servants who through ignorance refuse to observe the law, alleging it to be a new form of slavery" is a puzzle. Apparently Recife authorities succeeded initially in obtaining a law for registering domestics. In Rio where actual registration never began, the opportunity for publicly demonstrated opposition by servants never presented itself. *O Binóculo*, 14 January 1888, p. 2, quoted in Gilberto Freyre, *Ordem e progresso*, 2 vols. (Rio de Janeiro: José Olympio, 1959), I, 224.

72 Consulta, Conselho de Estado, Secção do Imperio, Rio de Janeiro, 10 January 1882, AGC-RJ, Serviço Domestico; Projectos de posturas e pareceres do Conselho d'Estado sobre o serviço domestico no Rio de Janeiro, 1881–1889, Cod. 50-1-43.

73 Tristão de Alencar Araripe Junior to Ministro do Interior, marginal comment in

Intendencia Municipal to Ministro do Interior, Rio de Janeiro, 18 May 1891, AGC-RJ, Serviço Domestico; Propostas, . . . 1884–1906, Cod. 48-4-56, fl. 14; Miguel Lemos, *A liberdade de profissão e o regulamento para o serviço domestico* (Rio de Janeiro: Tip. Central, 1890), p. 1.

74 Secretaria de Policia da Capital Federal to President da Intendencia Municipal, Rio de Janeiro, 7 May 1891, AGC-RJ, Documentação Avulsa, Serviço Domestico, 1882–1904; Serrarias, 1875–1911, Cod. 50-1-41.

75 Regarding the 1896 regulation, see Rio de Janeiro, Intendencia Municipal da Capital Federal, Sessão 15 June 1896, *Boletim*, April to September 1896, p. 38; ibid., Sessão 24 October 1896, Decreto 45, 24 October 1896, *Boletim*, October to December 1896, p. 15; Regulamento para o serviço domestico no Districto Federal, Decreto 284, 15 June 1896, AGC-RJ, Documentação Avulsa, Serviço Domestico, 1882–1904; Serrarias 1875–1911, Cod. 50-1-41; João Branho Muniz to President da Intendencia da Capital Federal, Rio de Janeiro, 30 January 1903, AGR-RJ, Documentação Avulsa, Serviço Domestico, 1882–1904; Serrarias 1875–1911, Cod. 50-1-41. Subsequent law did specify contractual terms for hiring servants: *Civil Code, 1916*, Book III, Tit. v, ch. IV, Sec. II, art. 1216–1236; *Leis do Brasil*, Decreto 16,107, 30 July 1923 and Decreto 3078, 27 February 1941. The latter two laws went unenforced and the 1941 law was revoked two years later, see Emílio Gonçalves, *Empregados domésticos: doutrina, legislação e jurisprudência* (São Paulo: Edições LTr., 1973), pp. 18–22, 89–91.

76 *JC*, 4 July 1895, 2 September 1905, 22 May 1900.

77 Arthur Moncorvo Filho, "Exames de amas de leite do 'Dispensario Moncorvo,'" *Archivos de Assistencia á Infancia* 2, no. 10–12 (October–December 1903), 167; *Leis do Brasil*, Decreto 5117, 18 January 1904, Art. 1; ibid., Decreto 5154, 3 March 1904, Art. 1.

78 Moncorvo Filho, *Da assistencia publica*, pp. 8–11; idem, *Histórico*, p. 140; *Arquivos de Assistencia á infancia*, 2, no. 7–9 (July–September 1903), cover page; Arthur Moncorvo Filho, *Hygiene publica. Da alimentação pelo leite, Communicação apresentada á sociedade scientifica protectora da infancia em novembro de 1902* (São Paulo: Espindola, Siqueira, 1903), pp. 5, 7, 17, 20–23.

79 Pires, *Amas de leite*, pp. 3–5.

80 Ibid., p. 3.

81 Untitled report on amas de leite, *c.* 1893, AGC-RJ, Relatorios sobre assumptos de hygiene, Cod. 38-2-32, fls. 107–108.

82 *JC*, 5 October 1909, 3 September 1909. The antiseptic and well equipped examination room at the dispensary and the white-coated, professional-looking staff may have increased women's willingness and confidence to undergo the examinations. See photographs, "Noticiário," *Archivos de Assistencia á Infancia* 2, no. 10–12 (October–December 1903), 191.

83 Speech of Alvaro Caminha, 5 September 1887, Brazil, Congresso, Câmara dos Deputados, *Anais*, 1887, v, 19; *Cidade do Rio*, January–February 1889, especially 7 and 16 February 1889; Conselho Municipal to Ministerio do Interior, Rio de Janeiro, 5 July 1894, AGC-RJ, Feiras e pequenos mercados, 1848–1916, Cod. 61-2-5, fl. 23. For a failed attempt by the Spanish to recast social life by remaking the landscape, see Inga Clendinnen, "Landscape and world view: The survival of Yucatec Maya culture under Spanish conquest," *Comparative Studies in Society and History* 22 (July 1980), 374–393. I borrow the phrase "remaking the landscape" from Renato I. Rosaldo, "The rhetoric of control: Ilongots viewed as natural

bandits and wild indians," in Barbara A. Babcock, ed. and intro., *The Reversible World: Symbolic Inversion in Art and Society* (Ithaca: Cornell University Press, 1978), pp. 240–257.

84 Delegacia de Policia da 20ª Circumscrição Urbana, defendant, Balbina Miguel Domingos Alfredo, Rio de Janeiro, 1905, ANSPJ, Maço 1565, N. 9156; Juizo da 3ª Pretoria, defendant, Amelia Francisca Alves, Rio de Janeiro, 1903, ANSPJ, Caixa 1080, N. 3950.

85 Francisco Pereira Passos, "Relatorio do Prefeito do Districto Federal ao Conselho Municipal, 1 setembro 1903," in *Annaes do Conselho Municipal e Synopse de seus Trabalhos* (Rio de Janeiro: Typ. do "Jornal do Commercio," 1904) p. 25; for a full list of city ordinances that aimed to make Rio a sanitary place, see Rio de Janeiro, Prefeitura do Districto Federal, *Codificação Sanitária, 1884–1913* (Rio de Janeiro: Officina do "Paiz," 1913), pp. 21–43.

86 Stepan, *Beginnings of Brazilian Science*, pp. 59, 143.

87 J. C. Oakenfull, *Brazil in 1912* (London: Atkinson, 1913), p. 23; the campaign against yellow fever involved inspections and disinfection of private homes and the isolating or hospitalization of any persons already ill, see Barbosa and Rezende, *Serviços de saude*, 1, 144–151.

88 *Leis do Brasil*, Lei 1261, 31 October 1904. For account of the earlier rounds of smallpox vaccinations, see Moncorvo Filho, *Histórico*, pp. 46–48; Relatorio do Inspector Geral do Instituto Vaccinico, in Annexo F, Relatorio do Presidente da Junta Central de Hygiene Pública, in Brazil, Ministerio do Imperio, *Relatorio*, 1884; ibid., 1885; Barbosa and Rezende, *Serviços de saude*, 1, 442; Nunes, *Estatistica*, pp. 31–32, gives figures for those who voluntarily received vaccinations between 1872 and 1885; Cooper, "Oswaldo Cruz and the impact of yellow fever," pp. 49–52.

89 *Correio da Manhã*, 6 November 1904, p. 1; 12 November, 1904, p. 2.

90 The standard interpretation at the time put it that rabble rousers had exploited the "credulity of the people," taking advantage of uncertainty about the law and calling it "an attack on individual liberty" solely to "disturb public order." See Raymundo Austregesilo de Athayde, *Pereira Passos, o reformador do Rio de Janeiro: biografia e história* (Rio de Janeiro: Editôra "A Noite," [1944]), pp. 255–278, especially 257, 260, 267–269; Barbosa and Rezende, *Serviços de saude*, 1, 442; among Rio newspapers only the *Correio da Manhà* reported the protests in detail, 1–18 November 1904. Some saw in the events an anti-republican conspiracy to discredit the government and restore the monarchy, see A. A. Cardoso Castro, *Relatorio sobre os crimes de novembro . . .* (Rio de Janeiro: Imprensa Nacional, 1904). While Robert Nachman, "Positivism and revolution in Brazil's First Republic: the 1904 Revolt," *The Americas* 34, no. 1 (July 1977), 30–39, hints that the riots were, as well, popular protest; Teresa Meade, "'Civilizing Rio de Janeiro:' the public health campaign and riot of 1904," *Journal of Social History* 20 (Winter 1986), 301–322, joins the issues of slum clearance and rioting.

91 *Correio da Manhã*, 2 November 1904, p. 1; 5 November 1904, p. 1.

92 Rio de Janeiro, Prefeitura Municipal, Planta da cidade do Rio de Janeiro, indicando os melhoramentos em execução, 1905, Benson Latin American Collection, University of Texas at Austin; Marc Ferrez, "Canal do Mangue, *c.* 1905," in Gilberto Ferrez, ed., *O Rio antigo do fotografo Marc Ferrez: Paisagens e tipos humanos do Rio de Janeiro, 1865–1918* (São Paulo: Ex Libris Ltda., 1984), pp. 158–159; Alured Gray Bell, *The Beautiful Rio de Janeiro* (London: Heinemann,

[1914]), p. 28, 54; Max Fleiuss, *História da cidade do Rio de Janeiro (Distrito Federal); resumo didáctico* (São Paulo: Melhoramentos, [1928]), p. 225.

93 Moradores da rua Frei Caneca to Prefeito, Conselho Municipal, Rio de Janeiro, 8 February 1905, AGC-RJ, Documentação Avulsa, vol. II, Limpeza publica, 1881–1909, Cod. 31-1-32; Fleiuss, *História da cidade*, p. 225; Santos, *Chorographia*, pp. 46–47, summarized the major physical renovations executed by the Passos administration; Rio de Janeiro, Prefeitura da cidade do Rio de Janeiro, *O Rio de Janeiro e seus prefeitos*, vol. 3, *Evolução urbanista da cidade* (Rio de Janeiro: Prefeitura da Cidade do Rio de Janeiro, 1977), 26–27.

94 Brazil, Conselho Superior de Saude Publica, *Pareceres sobre os meios de melhorar as condições das habitações destinadas ás classes pobres* (Rio de Janeiro: Imprensa Nacional, 1886), p. 25; Luiz Raphael Vieira Souto and Antonio Domingues dos Santos Silva, Memorial, Rio de Janeiro, 24 January 1885, AGC-RJ, Casas para operarios e classes pobres, 1885, Cod. 46-4-56; Laemmert e Cia., *Planta da cidade do Rio de Janeiro e suburbios* (Rio de Janeiro: Laemmert [1889]; Internal memorandum, Ministerio do Interior, Rio de Janeiro, 20 June 1891, AGC-RJ, Casas para operarios e classes pobres, 1891, Cod. 46-4-61, fls. 20–21. The cortiço issue was also a political issue in that private interests vied with city and national governments for newly generated powers. An 1882 law granted tax exemptions and the right to disappropriate private land in exchange for demolishing cortiços, indemnifying owners, and building popular housing in their place, while in 1893 city government assumed direct responsibility. *Leis do Brasil*, Lei 3151, 9 December 1882; ibid., Decreto 32, 29 March 1893. For a different interpretation of the housing issue, see Lia de Aquino Carvalho, "Contribuição ao estudo das habitações populares, Rio de Janeiro: 1886–1906," (M.A. thesis, Universidade Federal Fluminense, 1980).

95 Rio de Janeiro, Prefeitura, *Rio de Janeiro*, vol. 3: *Evolução urbanista*, 9.

96 Bell, *Beautiful Rio*, pp. 21; Rio de Janeiro, Prefeitura, *Rio de Janeiro*, vol. 3, *Evolução urbanista*, 18, 21; Carlos Delgado de Carvalho, *História da cidade do Rio de Janeiro* (Rio de Janeiro: F. Alves, 1926), pp. 120–121; Fotos de Rio de Janeiro, AGC-RJ, SI; for an extraordinary photographic history of the construction of the Avenida Central, see Marc Ferrez, *O Álbum da Avenida Central: Um documento fotográfico da construção da Avenida Rio Branco, Rio de Janeiro, 1903–1906*, introduction by Gilberto Ferrez and essay by Paulo S. Santos (São Paulo: Ex Libris Ltda., 1983), especially pp. 16–17, 50–53; Marc Ferrez, "Avenida Beira Mar, *c.* 1906," in Ferrez, *O Rio antigo do fotografo Marc Ferrez*, pp. 195, 198–199, 202–203; Augusto César Malta, "Avenida Central, circa 1906," in H. L. Hoffenberg, *Nineteenth-Century South America in Photographs* (New York: Dover Publications, 1982), frontispiece.

97 For photographs, see Rio de Janeiro, Prefeitura, *Rio de Janeiro*, vol. 3: *Evolução urbanista*, 31–48; "O Teatro Municipal, numa vista para o norte da Avenida Central," in Ferrez, *O Álbum da Avenida Central*, p. 35, and in the right foreground notice the black woman with a load of laundry balanced on her head as she walks along the street.

Tables

1 Working women as a percentage of women of working age, Rio de Janeiro, 1870–1906

	1870[a]		1872[b]		1906[c]
	Free	Slave	Free	Slave	
Working	63	88	58	89	49
No declared occupation	37	12	42	11	51
Total	100	100	100	100	100
	(45,018)	(16,217)	(58,667)	(16,501)	(208,879)

Sources:

[a]Brazil, Directoria Geral de Estatística, *Relatorio apresentado ao Ministro e Secretário d'Estado dos Negocios do Imperio pela Commissão encarregada da direcção dos trabalhos do arrolamento da população do Municipio da Côrte a que se procedeu em abril de 1870* (Rio de Janeiro: Typ. Perseverança, 1871), Mappas A-K, n.p.

[b]Brazil, Directoria Geral de Estatística, *Recenseamento da população do Imperio do Brazil a que se procedeu no dia 1º de agosto de 1872* (Rio de Janeiro: Typ. de G. Leuzinger & Filhos, 1873–1876), Municipio Neutro, pp. 1–33.

[c]Brazil, [Directoria Geral de Estatística], *Recenseamento do Rio de Janeiro (Districto Federal) realizado em 20 de setembro de 1906* (Rio de Janeiro: Officina da Estatística, 1907), pp. 174–317.

Notes: Throughout this book the city of Rio de Janeiro refers to the urban parishes of the Municipio Neutro or Federal District. In 1870 and 1872 they were Sacramento, São José, Candelaria, Santa Rita, Santo Antonio, Espirito Santo, Engenho Velho, São Cristovão, Gloria, Lagôa; by 1906 the urban parishes further included Gavea, Engenho Novo, Santa Tereza, Gambôa, Andarahy, Tijuca, and Meyer.

Because the published census figures for 1870, 1872, and 1906 were either not consistent in the age groupings used or not complete enough that I could re-order their figures, I have had to define somewhat arbitrarily the working age population. With respect to the 1870 population, I set working age for slave girls and women at eight years or older, and for free women at fifteen years or older. For 1872 and 1906, with figures available for each year of age, I considered all women aged eleven years or older as potentially part of the working population.

Absolute figures are enclosed in parentheses.

2 *Occupations of working women, Rio de Janeiro, 1870–1906, in percentages*

	1870[a]			1872[b]			1906[c]
	Free	Slave	Total	Free	Slave	Total	
Domestic service	61	90	71	65	87	72	76
Seamstress				26	8	20	
Day laborer				3	5	4	
Manufacturing	31	9	24				19
Commerce	3		2	1		1	1
Professional	2		1	2		1	3
Property owning	2		2	3		2	1
Agriculture	1						
Odd jobs							
Totals	100	99	100	100	100	100	100
	(28,537)	(14,347)	(42,884)	(33,886)	(14,672)	(48,558)	(101,496)

Sources:

[a] Brazil, Directoria Geral de Estatística, *Relatorio apresentado ao Ministro e Secretario d'Estado dos Negocios do Imperio pela Commissão encarregada da direção dos trabalhos do arrolamento da população do Municipio da Côrte a que se procedeu em abril de 1870* (Rio de Janeiro: Typ. Perseverança, 1871), Mappas A-K, n.p.

[b] Brazil, Directoria Geral de Estatística, *Recenseamento da população do Imperio do Brazil a que se procedeu no dia 1º de agosto de 1872* (Rio de Janeiro: Typ. de G. Leuzinger & Filhos, 1873–1876), Municipio Neutro, pp. 1–33.

[c] Brazil [Directoria Geral de Estatística], *Recenseamento do Rio de Janeiro (Districto Federal) realizado em 20 de setembro de 1906* (Rio de Janeiro: Officina da Estatística, 1907), pp. 174–317.

Note: Absolute numbers are enclosed in parentheses.

3 *Legal condition of servant women, Rio de Janeiro
1870 and 1872, in percentages*

	1870[a]	1872[b]
Free	57	63
Slave	43	37
Total	100	100
	(30,329)	(34,821)

Sources:
[a]"N. 1, Mappa da população do Municipio da Côrte," in Brazil, Directoria Geral de Estatística, *Relatorio apresentado ao Ministro e Secretário d'Estado dos Negocios do Imperio pela Commissão encarregada da direcção dos trabalhos do arrolamento da população do Municipio da Côrte a que se procedeu em abril de 1870* (Rio de Janeiro: Typ. Perseverança, 1871), n.p.
[b]Brazil, Directoria Geral de Estatística, *Recenseamento da população do Imperio do Brazil a que se procedeu no dia 1º de agosto de 1872* (Rio de Janeiro: Typ. de G. Leuzinger & Filhos, 1873–1876), Municipio Neutro, pp. 1–32.
Note: Absolute numbers are enclosed in parentheses.

4 *Legal condition of servant women, São Cristovão, 1870, in percentages*

	Live-in servants	Independent servants	Total %
Free	26	86	55
Ex-slave	8	13	10
Slave	66	1	35
Total	100	100	100
	(516)	(459)	(975)

Source: Brazil, Directoria Geral de Estatística, Arrolamento da população do Municipio da Côrte (São Cristovão) 1870, MS, Instituto Brasileiro de Geografia e Estatística, Rio de Janeiro, Departamento de Documentação e Referência.
Note: The number of cases is enclosed in parentheses.

5 *São Cristovão households with declared servants, 1870*

No. of servants in household	No. of households	Percentage of households with servants	Cumulative percentage	Percentage of all households in parish
1	110	44	44	8
2	55	22	66	4
3, 4, 5	48	19	85	3.4
6, 7, 8	25	10	95	
9, 10, 11	9	4	99	2.5
12, 13	2	1	100	0.1
Total	249	100	100	18

Source: Brazil, Directoria Geral de Estatística, Arrolamento da população do Municipio da Côrte (São Cristovão) 1870, MS, Instituto Brasileiro de Geografia e Estatística, Rio de Janeiro, Departmento de Documentação e Referência.

6 Birthplace of Rio de Janeiro women, 1870–1906, in percentages

	1870[a]			1872[b]			1890[c]	1906[d]
	Slave	Free	Total	Slave	Free	Total		
Brazil	19	60	79				80	80
Rio de Janeiro (city)				13*	57*	70	45	
Rio de Janeiro (province)				3	6	9	17	
All other provinces							15	
Sub-total	19	60	79	16	63	79	77	80
Foreign	5	16	21					
Africa				4	3	7		
Portugal					11	11	14	11
All other					3	3	9	9
Sub-total	5	16	21	4	17	21	23	20
Total	24	76	100	20	80	100	100	100
	(24,573)	(77,488)	(102,061)	(18,726)	(75,364)	(94,090)	(184,089)	(266,432)

Sources:

[a]"N. 1, Mappa da população do Municipio da Côrte," in Brazil, Directoria Geral de Estatística, *Relatorio apresentado ao Ministro e Secretário d'Estado dos Negocios do Imperio pela Commisão encarregada da direção dos trabalhos do arrolamento da população do Municipio da Côrte a que se procedeu em abril de 1870* (Rio de Janeiro: Typ. Perseverança, 1871), n.p.

[b]Brazil, Directoria Geral de Estatística, *Recenseamento da população do Imperio do Brazil a que se procedeu no dia 1° de agosto de 1872* (Rio de Janeiro: Typ. de G. Leuzinger & Filhos, 1873–1876), Municipio Neutro, pp. 1–32.

[c]Brazil, Directoria Geral de Estatística, *Recenseamento Geral da República dos Estados Unidos do Brazil em 31 dezembro 1890: Districto Federal (cidade do Rio de Janeiro)* (Rio de Janeiro: Typ. Leuzinger, 1895), pp. 44, 165, 169, 175, 177.

[d]Brazil [Directoria Geral de Estatística], *Recenseamento do Rio de Janeiro (Districto Federal) realizado em 20 de setembro de 1906* (Rio de Janeiro: Officina da Estatística, 1907), pp. 178–314.

Note: *Figures include the city of Rio de Janeiro. Absolute numbers are enclosed in parentheses.

7 *Birthplace of São Cristovão servant women, 1870, in percentages*

| | Live-in servants | | Independent servants | | Total % |
	Slave	Free	Slave	Free	
Brazil	29	10	[0.3]	37	76
Africa	10	2		4	16
Portugal		2		5	7
Other Europe				1	1
Total	39	14	[0.3]	47	100
	(374)	(136)	(3)	(454)	(967)

Source: Brazil, Directoria Geral de Estatística, Arrolamento da população do Municipio da Côrte (São Cristovão) 1870, MS, Instituto Brasileiro de Geografia e Estatística, Rio de Janeiro, Departamento de Documentação e Referência.
Note: The number of cases is enclosed in parentheses.

8 *Nationality of free servant women, Rio de Janeiro, 1870–1906, in percentages*

	1870[a]	1872[b]	1906[c]
Brazilian	77	67	78
Foreign-born		33	22
African	10		
Portuguese, other	13		
Total	100	100	100
	(590)	(22,094)	(77,294)

Sources:
[a]Brazil, Directoria Geral de Estatística, Arrolamento da população do Municipio da Côrte (São Cristovão) 1870, MS, Instituto Brasileiro de Geografia e Estatística, Rio de Janeiro, Departamento de Documentação e Referência.
[b]Brazil, Directoria Geral de Estatística, *Recenseamento da população do Imperio do Brazil a que se procedeu no dia 1° de agosto de 1872* (Rio de Janeiro: Typ. de G. Leuzinger & Filhos, 1873–1876), Municipio Neutro, pp. 3–33.
[c]Brazil Directoria Geral de Estatística, *Recenseamento do Rio de Janeiro (Districto Federal) realizado em 20 de setembro de 1906* (Rio de Janeiro: Officina de Estatística, 1907), pp. 181–317.
Note: Figures for 1870 refer to those in São Cristovão parish only; figures for 1872 and 1906 refer to all urban parishes in the city. Absolute numbers are enclosed in parentheses.

9 *Marital status of servant women, Rio de Janeiro, 1870 and 1872, in percentages*

| | São Cristovão, 1870[a] | | | All urban parishes, 1872[b] |
	Live-in	Independent	Total	
Single	88	32	65	68
Single with children	7	21	9	
Sub-total	95	53	74	68
Married or widowed	4	37	21	32
Consensual unions	1	10	5	
Total	100	100	100	100
	(471)	(457)	(928)	(31,860)

Sources:
[a]Brazil, Directoria Geral de Estatística, Arrolamento da população do Municipio da Côrte (São Cristovão) 1870, MS, Instituto Brasileiro de Geografia e Estatística, Rio de Janeiro, Departamento de Documentação e Referência.
[b]Brazil, Directoria Geral de Estatística, *Recenseamento da população do Imperio do Brazil a que se procedeu no dia 1° de agosto de 1872* (Rio de Janeiro: Typ. de G. Leuzinger & Filhos, 1873–1876), Municipio Neutro, pp. 1–33.
Notes: Totals for 1870 include slave and free women. Marital status for slaves was not provided in the 1872 census, thus totals for 1872 include only free women.

10 *Marital status of all persons of marriageable age, Rio de Janeiro,
1872–1906, in percentages*

	1872[a]	1890[b]	1906[c]
Single	71	60.3	50
Married	23	31.3	40
Widowed	6	8.4	10
Total	100	100.0	100
	(168,404)	(303,047)	(424,843)

Sources:
[a]Brazil, Directoria Geral de Estatística, *Recenseamento da população do Imperio do Brazil a que se procedeu no dia 1° de agosto de 1872* (Rio de Janeiro: Typ. de G. Leuzinger & Filhos, 1873–1876), Municipio Neutro, pp. 1–32, 58–59.
[b]Brazil, Directoria Geral de Estatística, *Recenseamento Geral da Republica dos Estados Unidos do Brazil em 31 dezembro 1890: Districto Federal (cidade do Rio de Janeiro)* (Rio de Janeiro: Typ. Leuzinger, 1895), 49–87.
[c]Brazil [Directoria Geral de Estatística], *Recenseamento do Rio de Janeiro (Districto Federal) realizado em 20 de setembro de 1906* (Rio de Janeiro: Officina de Estatística, 1907), pp. 90–91.

Notes: The legal age of marriage varied during this period. In 1872, with permission of parent or legal guardian, women could marry at age 12, men at 14; by 1890, the legal age had been raised to 14 for women and 16 for men; in 1916 it was raised again to 16 for women and 18 for men, reflecting practices that presumably were visible if not commonplace by 1906. For age of marriage, see Sebastião Monteiro da Vide, *Constituições primeiras do Arcebispado da Bahia. Feitas e ordenadas pelo . . . Sebastião Monteiro da Vide, 5° Arcebispo do dito Arcebispado e do Conselho de Sua Magestade: Propostas e aceitas em o synodo Diocesano que o dito Senhor celebrou em 12 de junho do anno de 1707. Impressas em Lisboa no anno de 1719 e em Coimbra em 1720. . . .* (São Paulo: Typ. "2 de Dezembro," 1853), Liv. I, Tit. 64, no. 267; Brazil, Laws, statutes, etc., *Collecção das leis do Brasil* (Rio de Janeiro: Imprensa Nacional, 1808–), Decreto 181, 24 January 1890, Cap. II, Art. 8; Joseph Wheless, trans., *The Civil Code of Brazil [1916]* (St. Louis: Thomas Law Book Co., 1920), Special Part, Book I, Tit. I, art. 183, par. 12.

The 1872 figures combine slave and free populations. The 1872 census does not present marital status by age. Therefore, I have estimated the single population by subtracting from it all those under age 16. This further assumes that all married or widowed persons were 16 or older, when, in fact, some almost certainly were not. Only the 1890 census, however, presents marital status by precise age. The 1872 census divides the population into 5-year age groups, and the 1906 one into those older or younger than age 15. For these two censuses, I have considered as marriageable those 16 or older of either sex. My decision seems justified by the fact that in 1890 only 18 men and 34 women, younger than 16 or 14 respectively, were listed as married, and in 1906 only 47 persons younger than 16 were listed as married.

Absolute numbers are enclosed in parentheses.

Glossary of Portuguese words

agregado, agregada dependent household member; could be a family member, a former slave, or someone wholly unrelated

ama de leite wet-nurse

amo master or owner, head of house or family who provided for his servants

aparadeira midwife without formal training

benção blessing

bondes mule-drawn street cars, named for British bonds that first financed them

cabeça de casal head of a couple, and therefore head of the household or family

caderneta passbook

cafuné massage of the head or scalp

candomblé African religion, especially of Yoruba influence

carnaval pre-Lenten celebrations

casa house

chefe chief or head of family

comadre midwife without formal training

companheira, companheiro common-law spouse

conto Brazilian unit of currency, equal to one thousand *mil-réis*

copeira pantry servant or one who waited table

cortiço beehive and in Rio de Janeiro came to mean slum dwelling

curiosa midwife without formal training

diligencia public coach

dona da casa mistress of the house

entrudo a time to mock or poke fun at

fâmulo those who serve the family; servants or dependents

fantasia fantasy, imagination, extravagance, in Brazil, the fancy dress or masquerade worn at carnaval

feijoada dish made of black beans and pork

feiticeiro sorcerer, someone who can summon the forces of white or black magic

figa amulet in the form of a hand in which the thumb extends between the index and middle fingers; worn against illness or accident

fogo hearth or household

goiabada paste made from guavas and sugar

gôndola public coach

jornal daily wage earned by slaves and turned over to their masters

mil-réis Brazilian unit of currency, equal to one thousand *réis*

moringue small, double-spouted clay water jug

mucama   slave woman who served principally her mistress, even accompanying her on errands or social outings

onibus   public coach

parda   mulatto, brown-skinned

patrão, patroa, patrões   master or mistress, connoting protector

pelourinho   whipping post

pilão   over-sized mortar and pestle for grinding coffee, salt, corn

preta   black, often meaning African or slave

quitanda   produce or other foods sold by street vendors

quitandeira   street or market vendor

réis   Brazilian unit of currency

rua   street

senhor, senhora   master or mistress

talha   clay water jug, wide-mouthed and holding ten to fifteen gallons

tamancos   wooden sandals worn by the poor

tigre   barrel for transporting night soil

tuyanté   French pleating

Bibliography

Archives and manuscript materials

Arquivo da Cúria Metropolitana. Rio de Janeiro.
Arquivo do Instituto Histórico e Geográfico Brasileiro. Rio de Janeiro.
Arquivo Geral da Cidade do Rio de Janeiro. Rio de Janeiro.
Arquivo Nacional. Rio de Janeiro.
Benson Latin American Collection, University of Texas at Austin. Austin, Texas.
Cartório do Primeiro Ofício. Vassouras, Rio de Janeiro.
Instituto Brasileiro de Geografia e Estatística, Departamento de Documentação e Referência. Rio de Janeiro.
Neves, Augusto José Pereira das. Meu nascimento e factos mais notaveis da minha vida [1835–1909], MS, in the possession of Guilherme Paulo Castagnoli Pereira das Neves, Rio de Janeiro.

Exhibitions

Exposição "A cozinha no Rio antigo," Museu Histórico da Cidade, Rio de Janeiro, 4 July–3 August 1980.
Exposição "Universo do Carnaval: imagens e reflexões; pinturas, desenhos, fotografias e Máscaras." Organized by Roberto Da Matta. Acervo Galeria de Arte, Rio de Janeiro, 24 February–31 March 1981.
Museu da Fundação Carlos Costa Pinto. Salvador, Bahia.

Government publications

Brazil. Congresso. Câmara dos Deputados. *Anais.*
Congresso. Câmara dos Deputados. *Manual parlamentar, regimento interno da Camara dos Deputados* . . . Rio de Janeiro: Imprensa Nacional, 1887.
Conselho Nacional de Estatística. *Anuário estatístico do Brasil. 1908–1912.* 2 vols. Rio de Janeiro: Typ. da Estatística, 1916–1917.
Conselho Superior de Saude Publica. *Pareceres sobre os meios de melhorar as condições das habitações destinadas ás classes pobres.* Rio de Janeiro: Imprensa Nacional, 1886.
Decisões do Governo do Imperio do Brazil.
Directoria Geral de Estatística. *Recenseamento da população do Imperio do Brazil a que se procedeu no dia 1º de agosto de 1872.* Rio de Janeiro: Leuzinger, 1873–1876.
[Directoria Geral de Estatística.] *Recenseamento do Rio de Janeiro (Districto Federal) realizado em 20 de setembro de 1906.* Rio de Janeiro: Officina de Estatística, 1907.

Directoria Geral de Estatística. *Recenseamento Geral da Republica dos Estados Unidos do Brazil em 31 dezembro 1890: Districto Federal (cidade do Rio de Janeiro).* Rio de Janeiro: Leuzinger, 1895.

Directoria Geral de Estatística. *Relatorio apresentado ao Ministro e Secretário d'Estado dos Negocios do Imperio pela Commissão encarregada da direcção dos trabalhos do arrolamento da população do Municipio da Côrte a que se procedeu em abril de 1870.* Rio de Janeiro: Typ. Perseverança, 1871.

Instituto Brasileiro de Geografia e Estatística. Conselho Nacional de Estatística. Serviço Nacional de Recenseamento. Divisão de Geografia. *A área central da cidade do Rio de Janeiro.* Rio de Janeiro: Instituto Brasileiro de Geografia e Estatística, 1967.

Laws, statutes, etc. *Coleção das Leis do Brasil.*

Ministerio da Agricultura, Commercio e Obras Publicas. *Relatorio*, 1883–1886.

Ministerio da Justiça. *Notícia histórica dos serviços, instituições e estabelecimentos pertencentes a esta repartição, elaborada por ordem do respectivo ministro, Dr. Amaro Cavalcanti.* Rio de Janeiro: Imprensa Nacional, 1898.

Ministerio da Justiça. *Relatorio*, 1856–1882.

Ministerio do Imperio. *Relatorio*, 1869–1888.

Secretaria d'Estado dos Negocios do Imperio. Directoria, Secção da Estatística. *Trabalhos da secção de estatística . . . 1886.* Rio de Janeiro: Imprensa Nacional, 1887.

Rio de Janeiro. Biblioteca Nacional. *Album Cartográfico do Rio de Janeiro, séculos XVIII e XIX.* Organized by Lygia de Fonseca Fernandes da Cunha. Rio de Janeiro: Biblioteca Nacional, 1971.

Camara Municipal. *Boletim da Illma. Camara Municipal da Côrte*, 1879.

Camara Municipal. *Codigo de posturas da Illma. Camara Municipal do Rio de Janeiro e editaes da mesma Camara.* Rio de Janeiro: Laemmert, 1870.

Commissão de Melhoramentos. *Primeiro relatorio da Commissão de Melhoramentos da cidade do Rio de Janeiro.* 2 vols. in 1. Rio de Janeiro: Typ. Nacional, 1875–1876.

Commissão do Saneamento. *Relatorios apresentados ao Exm. Sr. Dr. Prefeito Municipal pelos Drs. Manoel Victorino Pereira, presidente da commissão e Nuno de Andrade, relator em 31 de agosto de 1896.* Rio de Janeiro: Imprensa Nacional, 1896.

Inspectoria geral da illuminação da Côrte. *Tabela das horas de acender e apagar os combustadores publicos.* Rio de Janeiro: Imprensa Nacional, 1889.

Intendencia Municipal da Capital Federal. *Boletim*, 1896.

Intendencia Municipal do Districto Federal. *Código de Posturas, Leis, Decretos, Editaes e Resoluções da Intendencia Municipal do Districto Federal.* Rio de Janeiro: Mont'Averne, 1894.

Prefeitura da Cidade do Rio de Janeiro. *O Rio de Janeiro e seus prefeitos.* 4 vols. Rio de Janeiro: Prefeitura da Cidade do Rio de Janeiro, 1977.

Prefeitura do Districto Federal. *Album da cidade do Rio de Janeiro: commemorativo do primeiro centenario da independencia do Brasil, 1822–1922.* Rio de Janeiro: Paulo Witte, 1922.

Prefeitura do Districto Federal. *Codificação Sanitária, 1884–1913.* Rio de Janeiro: Officina do "Paiz," 1913.

Other published materials and theses

Abrahams, Roger D. and Richard Bauman, "Ranges of festival behavior." In *The Reversible World: Symbolic Inversion in Art and Society.* Ed. and intro. Barbara A. Babcock. Ithaca: Cornell University Press, 1978, pp. 193–208.

Affonseca Junior, Léo de. *O custo da vida na cidade do Rio de Janeiro*. Rio de Janeiro: Imprensa Nacional, 1920.

Agassiz, Louis and Elizabeth Cary Agassiz. *A Journey in Brazil*. 2nd edn. Boston: Ticknor and Fields, 1868.

Almanak administrativo, mercantil e industrial . . . do Rio de Janeiro. Rio de Janeiro: Laemmert, 1860–1910.

Almeida, Candido Mendes de, comp. and ed. *Código Philippino; ou Ordenações e leis do reino do Portugal, recopiladas por mandado d'el-rey D. Philippe I. 14 ed. segundo a primeira de 1603 e a nona de Coimbra de 1824. Addicionada com diversas notas . . .* Rio de Janeiro: Typ. do Instituto Philomathico, 1870.

Almeida, Júlia Lopes de. *Livro das noivas*. 3rd edn. Rio de Janeiro: Typ. da Companhia Nacional Editora, 1896.

Andrews, Christopher Columbus. *Brazil: Its Condition and Prospects*. 3rd edn. New York: D. Appleton & Co., 1891.

Araújo, Manoel do Monte Rodrigues d'. *Elementos de direito ecclesiastico em relação á disciplina geral da igreja e com applicação aos usos da igreja do Brasil*. 3 vols. Rio de Janeiro: Livraria de Antonio Gonçalves Guimarães, 1857–1859.

A. S. Q. *O cozinheiro e doceiro popular*. Rio de Janeiro: Editôra Quaresma, 1927.

Associação Industrial, Rio de Janeiro. *O trabalho nacional e seus adversarios*. Rio de Janeiro: Leuzinger, 1881.

Athayde, Raymundo Austregesilo de. *Pereira Passos, o reformador do Rio de Janeiro: biografia e história*. Rio de Janeiro: Editôra "A Noite," [1944].

O Auxiliador da Industria Nacional 9 (February 1881), 328.

Azevedo, Luiz Corrêa de. "Memoria lida na Academia Imperial de Medicina . . . as causas da mortalidade das crianças." *Annaes Brazilienses de Medicina* 21 (1869), 112–122.

Babcock, Barbara A., ed. and intro. *The Reversible World: Symbolic Inversion in Art and Society*. Ithaca: Cornell University Press, 1978.

Backheuser, Everardo. *Habitações populares*. Rio de Janeiro: Imprensa Nacional, 1906.

"Onde moram os pobres." *Renascença*, 2, no. 13 (March 1905), 89–94.

Barbosa, Placido and Cassio Barbosa de Rezende. *Os serviços de saude publica no Brasil, especialmente na cidade do Rio de Janeiro, 1808–1907*. 2 vols. Rio de Janeiro: Imprensa Nacional, 1909.

Bardy, Cláudio. "O século XVI (da fundação até o fim)" and "O século XVII," and "O século XIX." In *Rio de Janeiro em seus quatrocentos anos; formação e desenvolvimento da cidade*. Ed. Fernando Nascimento Silva. Rio de Janeiro: Distribuidora Record, 1965, pp. 49–79, 102–124.

Barman, Roderick J. "Politics on the stage: the late Brazilian empire as dramatized by França Junior." *Luso-Brazilian Review* 13 (Winter 1976), 244–260.

Barreiros, Eduardo Canabrava. *Atlas da evolução urbana da cidade do Rio de Janeiro: ensaio, 1565–1965*. Rio de Janeiro: Instituto Histórico e Geográfico Brasileiro, 1965.

"Cartograma conjectural da cidade do Rio de Janeiro na época de sua fundação." In *Rio de Janeiro em seus quatrocentos anos: formação e desenvolvimento da cidade*. Ed. Fernando Nascimento Silva. Rio de Janeiro: Distribuidora Record, 1965 [p. 393].

Barreto, J. F. de Mello and Hermeto Lima. *História da polícia do Rio de Janeiro: aspectos da cidade e da vida carioca, 1831–1870*. 3 vols. Rio de Janeiro: Editôra "A Noite," 1942.

Barreto, Paulo, (pseud. João do Rio). *As religiões do Rio*. 1906; rpt. Rio de Janeiro: Organização Simões, 1951.

Bastide, Roger. *The African Religions of Brazil: Toward a Sociology of the Interpenetration of Civilizations.* Trans. Helen Sebba. Baltimore: The Johns Hopkins University Press, 1978.

Bell, Alured Gray. *The Beautiful Rio de Janeiro.* London: Heinemann [1914].

Bernardes, Lygia Maria Cavalcanti. "Posição geográfica do Rio de Janeiro." In *Rio de Janeiro em seus quatrocentos annos; formação e desenvolvimento da cidade.* Ed. Fernando Nascimento Silva. Rio de Janeiro: Distribuidora Record, 1965, pp. 19–28.

Bertichem, P. G. *O Rio de Janeiro e seus arrabaldes, 1856.* Intro. and notes by Gilberto Ferrez. Rio de Janeiro: Kosmos, 1976.

Blount, John Allen. "The public health movement in São Paulo, Brazil. A history of the sanitary service, 1892–1918." Ph.D. diss., Tulane University, 1971.

The British and American Mail. Rio de Janeiro, 1877–1879.

Burmeister, Karl Hermann Konrad. *Viagem ao Brasil através das províncias do Rio de Janeiro e Minas Gerais, visando especialmente a história natural dos distritos auridiamantíferos.* Trans. Manoel Salvaterra and Hubert Schoenfeldt. Biblioteca Histórica Brasileira, 19. First published 1853. São Paulo: Martins, 1952.

Burton, Richard F. *Explorations of the Highlands of the Brazil; with a Full Account of the Gold and Diamond Mines. Also, Canoeing Down 1500 Miles of the Great River São Francisco from Sabará to the Sea.* 2 vols. London: Tinsley Brothers, 1869.

Calmon, Pedro. *História social do Brasil.* Série 5ª, Brasiliana, 83. São Paulo: Companhia Editôra Nacional, 1940.

Carvalho, Carlos Delgado de. *História da cidade do Rio de Janeiro.* Rio de Janeiro: F. Alves, 1926.

Carvalho, José Luiz Sayão de Bulhões. *A verdadeira população da cidade do Rio de Janeiro.* Rio de Janeiro: Typ. do "Jornal do Commercio," 1901.

Carvalho, Lia de Aquino. "Contribuição ao estudo das habitaçães populares, Rio de Janeiro: 1886–1906." M.A. thesis, Universidade Federal Fluminense, 1980.

Cascudo, Luis da Camara, ed. *Antologia da alimentação no Brasil.* Rio de Janeiro: Livros Técnicos e Científicos Editôra, 1977.

Castro, A. A. Cardoso. *Relatorio sobre os crimes de novembro . . .* Rio de Janeiro: Imprensa Nacional, 1904.

Centro Industrial do Brasil. *Le Brésil. Ses richesses naturelles, ses industries.* 3 vols. Rio de Janeiro: Imprimerie M. Orosco, 1909.

Cidade do Rio. Rio de Janeiro, 1889.

Clendinnen, Inga. "Landscape and world view: the survival of Yucatec Maya culture under Spanish conquest." *Comparative Studies in Society and History* 22 (July 1980), 374–393.

Coelho, Manoel Thomaz. [Untitled report.] *Annuario Medico Brasileiro,* 1886, p. 32.

Collaço, Felippe Neri. *O conselheiro da familia brasileira.* Rio de Janeiro: Garnier, 1883.

Companhia Brasil Industrial. *Relatorio . . . 1878.* Rio de Janeiro: Moreira, Maximino, 1878.

Relatorio . . . 1882. Rio de Janeiro: Moreira, Maximino, 1882.

Companhia de Fiação e Tecelagem Brazil Industrial. *Relatorio . . . 1891.* Rio de Janeiro: Leuzinger, 1891.

Conrad, Robert. *The Destruction of Brazilian Slavery, 1850–1888.* Berkeley: University of California Press, 1972.

Cooper, Donald. "Oswaldo Cruz and the impact of yellow fever on Brazilian history." *The Bulletin of the Tulane University Medical Faculty* 26 (February 1967), 49–52.

"The New 'Black Death': Cholera in Brazil, 1855–1856." *Social Science History* 10 (Winter 1986), 467–488.

Correio da Manhã. Rio de Janeiro, 1904, 1964.

Correio Mercantil. Rio de Janeiro, 1851, 1857–1868.

Costa, Antonio Corrêa de Souza. *Alimentação de que usa a classe pobre do Rio de Janeiro e sua influência sôbre a mesma classe.* Rio de Janeiro: Typ. Perseverança, 1865.

Costa, Emília Viotti da. *Da senzala à colônia.* Corpo e Alma do Brasil, 19. São Paulo: Difusão Européia do Livro, 1966.

The Brazilian Empire. University of Chicago Press, 1985.

Costa, Iraci del Nero da. "A estructura familial e domiciliária em Vila Rica no alvorecer do século XIX." *Revista do Instituto de Estudos Brasileiros* 19 (1977), 17–34.

Costa, Luiz Edmundo da. *O Rio de Janeiro do meu tempo.* 3 vols. Rio de Janeiro: Imprensa Nacional, 1938.

Couty, Louis. *L'Esclavage au Brésil.* Paris: Guillaumen, 1881.

Cruls, L. *O clima do Rio de Janeiro.* Rio de Janeiro: H. Lombaerts & Comp., Impressores do Observatorio, 1892.

Da Matta, Roberto. *Carnavais, malandros e heróis: para uma sociologia do dilema brasileiro.* 2nd edn. Rio de Janeiro: Zahar, 1981.

Davis, Natalie Zemon. *Society and Culture in Early Modern France.* Stanford University Press, 1979.

Dean, Warren. *Rio Claro: A Brazilian Plantation System, 1820–1920.* Stanford University Press. 1976.

Debret, Jean Baptiste. *Voyage pittoresque et historique au Brésil, ou Séjour d'un artiste français au Brésil.* 3 vols. Paris: Firmin Didot Frères, Imprimeurs de L'Institut de France, 1834–1839.

Dent, Charles Hastings. *A Year in Brazil, with Notes on Abolition of Slavery, the Finances of the Empire, Religion, Meteorology, Natural History, Etc.* London: K. Paul, Trench, 1886.

Diario de Pernambuco. Recife, 1860.

di Cavalcanti, Emiliano. *Viagem da minha vida.* Rio de Janeiro: Civilização Brasileira, 1955.

Dias, Maria Odila Leite da Silva. *Quotidiano e poder em São Paulo no século XIX–Ana Gertrudes de Jesus.* São Paulo: Brasiliense, 1984.

Duncan, Julian Smith. *Public and Private Operation of the Railways in Brazil.* Studies in History, Economics, and Public Law, 367. New York: Columbia University Press, 1932.

Dunlop, Charles Julius. *Os meios de transporte do Rio antigo.* Rio de Janeiro: Grupo de Planejamento Gráfico, 1973.

Subsídios para a história do Rio de Janeiro. Rio de Janeiro: Editôra Rio Antigo, 1957.

Eboli, Thomaz. *Dissertação sobre a hygiene: os prejuizos que causam uma má alimentação.* Rio de Janeiro: Popular, 1880.

"A educação da mulher." *A Mãe de Familia,* January–February 1881, pp. 5–29.

Ellis, Myriam. *A baléia no Brasil colonial.* São Paulo: Melhoramentos, 1969.

The Empire of Brazil at the Universal Exhibition of 1876 in Philadelphia. Rio de Janeiro: Imperial Instituto Artistico, 1876.

A Estação. Rio de Janeiro, 1879.

O Estado de São Paulo. São Paulo, 1961.

Ewbank, Thomas. *Life in Brazil: or a Journal of a Visit to the Land of the Cocoa and the Palm.* 1856; rpt. Detroit: Blaine Ethridge Books, 1971.

Expilly, Charles. *Le Brésil tel qu'il est.* 3rd edn. Paris: Charlieu et Huillery, 1864.
Mulheres e costumes do Brasil. Trans. Gastão Penalva. 2nd edn. Série 5ª, Brasiliana, 56. First published 1863. São Paulo: Companhia Editôra Nacional, 1977.

Fairchilds, Cissie. *Domestic Enemies: Servants and Their Masters in Old Regime France.* Baltimore: The Johns Hopkins University Press, 1983.

Faoro, Raymundo. *Os donos do poder: Formação do patronato político brasileiro.* 2 vols., 2nd edn. Porto Alegre: Globo, and São Paulo: Editôra da Universidade de São Paulo, 1975.

Faria, Antonio Bento de. *Annotações theorico-praticas ao Código Penal do Brasil de accordo com a doutrina e legislação e a jurisprudencia, nacionaes e estrangeiras, seguido de um appendice contendo as leis em vigor e que lhe são referentes.* . . . 2 vols. 4th edn. Rio de Janeiro: Jacintho Ribeiro dos Santos, 1929.

Fazenda, José Vieira. "A roda (casa dos expostos)." *Revista do Instituto Histórico e Geográfico Brasileiro* Tomo LXXI, vol. 118, parte II (1908), 153–181.

Fernandes, Florestan. *The Negro in Brazilian Society.* Trans. Jacqueline D. Skiles, A. Brunel, and Arthur Rothwell. Ed. Phyllis B. Eveleth. New York: Columbia University Press, 1969.

Ferraz, Fernando Francisco da Costa. "A salubridade da capital do Imperio e os cortiços." *Annaes Brazilienses de Medicina* 35 (1884), 443–469.

Ferrez, Gilberto. *A muito leal e heróica cidade de São Sebastião do Rio de Janeiro; quatro séculos de expansão e evolução.* Paris: Marcel Mouillot, 1965.

A Praça 15 de Novembro, antigo Largo do Carmo. Rio de Janeiro: Riotur Empresa de Turismo do Município do Rio de Janeiro, 1978.

ed. *O Rio antigo do fotografo Marc Ferrez: Paisagens e tipos humanos do Rio de Janeiro, 1865–1918.* São Paulo: Ex Libris Ltda., 1984.

and Weston J. Naef. *Pioneer Photographers of Brazil, 1840–1920.* New York: The Center for Inter-American Relations, 1976.

Ferrez, Marc. *O Álbum da Avenida Central: Um documento fotográfico da construção da Avenida Rio Branco, Rio de Janeiro, 1903–1906.* Intro. by Gilberto Ferrez and essay by Paulo S. Santos. São Paulo: Ex Libris Ltda., 1983.

"O festival da Praça da Republica, 8 setembro 1903." *Archivo de Assistencia á Infancia* 2, no. 7–9 (July–September 1903), 147–148.

Figueiredo, Carlos Arthur Moncorvo de. "Projecto de Regulamento das Amas de Leite." *Gazeta Medica da Bahia,* 1876, pp. 498–504.

Filgueiras Junior, [José Antonio de] Araújo, ed. *Código Criminal do Imperio do Brasil.* 2nd edn. Rio de Janeiro: Laemmert, 1876.

Fleiuss, Max. *História administrativa do Brasil.* 2nd edn. Rio de Janeiro: Melhoramentos [1925].

História da cidade do Rio de Janeiro (Distrito Federal) resumo didáctico. São Paulo: Melhoramentos, [1928].

Fluminense, Américo [pseud.]. "O carnaval no Rio." *Kosmos* 4, no. 2 (February 1907), n.p.

Fotografie lateinamerika von 1860 bis heute. Konsept und Realisation von Ausstellung und Katalog, Erika Billeter und Ubersetzung der spanischen Texte, Bert Sommer. Kunsthaus Zurich, 20 August–15 November 1981. Bern: Benteli, 1981.

França Junior, Joaquim José. *Folhetins.* Rio de Janeiro: Typ. da "Gazeta de Notícias," 1878.

Freitas, B. Ribeiro. "Hygiene da habitação: os corredores longos e as alcovas das casas do Rio de Janeiro." *Revista dos Constructores*, no. 7 (August 1886), pp. 110–112.

Freyre, Gilberto. *Ordem e progresso.* 2 vols. Rio de Janeiro: José Olympio, 1959.

——— *Sobrados e mucambos: decadência do patriarcado rural e desenvolvimento do urbano.* 3rd edn. 2 vols. Rio de Janeiro: José Olympio, 1961.

——— "Social life in Brazil in the middle of the nineteenth century." *Hispanic American Historical Review* 5 (1922), 597–630.

Gama, Manoel Jacintho Carneiro Nogueira da. *Testamento.* Freguezia da Santa Thereza [Valença, Rio de Janeiro]: Typ. de Santa Rosa, 1883.

Gaston, James McFadden. *Hunting a Home in Brazil. The Agricultural Resources and other Characteristics of the Country; also, the Manners and Customs of the Inhabitants.* Philadelphia: King and Baird Printers, 1867.

Gazeta da Tarde. Rio de Janeiro, 1881, 1884.

Gazeta de Notícias. Rio de Janeiro, 1884.

Geertz, Clifford. *The Interpretation of Cultures, Selected Essays.* New York: Basic Books, 1973.

Genovese, Eugene D. *Roll, Jordan, Roll: The World the Slaves Made.* New York: Pantheon, 1974.

Godelier, Maurice. "Economic structures of pre-capitalist societies." Lecture, 19 March 1979, University of Texas at Austin.

——— "Infrastructures, societies and history." *Current Anthropology* 19 (December 1978), 763–771.

Gonçalves, Emílio. *Empregados domésticos: doutrina, legislação e jurisprudência.* São Paulo: Edições LTr, 1973.

Gorender, Jacob. *O escravismo colonial.* São Paulo: Editôra Ática, 1978.

Goulart, José Alípio. "Alguns dados sôbre o comércio ambulante do leite no Rio de Janeiro do século XIX." *Revista do Instituto Histórico e Geográfico Brasileiro* 263 (April–June 1964), 31–54.

Graham, Maria. *Journal of a Voyage to Brazil and Residence There, During Part of the Years 1821, 1822, 1823.* 1824; rpt. New York: Praeger, 1969.

Graham, Richard. *Britain and on the Onset of Modernization in Brazil, 1850–1914.* Cambridge Latin American Studies, 4. Cambridge University Press, 1968.

——— "Causes for the abolition of negro slavery in Brazil: an interpretive essay." *Hispanic American Historical Review* 46 (May 1966), 123–137.

Guimarães, Bernardo. *A escrava Isaura.* First published 1875. Belo Horizonte: Itatiaia, 1977.

Gutman, Herbert G. *The Black Family in Slavery and Freedom, 1750–1925.* New York: Pantheon, 1976.

Hoffenberg, H. L. *Nineteenth-Century South America in Photographs.* New York: Dover Publications, 1982.

Holanda, Sérgio Buarque de, ed. *História geral da civilização brasileira,* tomo II: *O Brasil mónarquico,* vol. III; *Reações e transações,* 2nd edn. São Paulo: Difusão Européia do Livro, 1969.

——— ed. *História geral da civilização brasileira,* tomo II: *O Brasil mónarquico,* vol. V; *Do império à república.* São Paulo: Difusão Européia do Livro, 1972.

Homem, João Vicente Torres. *Annuario de observações colhidas nas enfermarias de clinica medica da Faculdade de Medicina em 1868 . . .* Rio de Janeiro: Alves, 1869.

——— *Elementos de clinica medica . . .* Rio de Janeiro: Alves, 1870.

Imbert, João Baptista A. *Guia medico das mães de familia, ou a infancia considerada na sua hygiene, suas molestias e tratamentos.* Rio de Janeiro: Typ. Franceza, 1843.

James, Preston. "Rio de Janeiro and São Paulo." *Geographical Review* 23 (1933), 271–298.

Jornal do Commercio. Rio de Janeiro, 1850–1910.

Joyce, Patrick. *Work, Society and Politics: The Culture of the Factory in Later Victorian England.* New Brunswick NJ: Rutgers University Press, 1980.

Judt, Tony. "A Clown in Royal Purple: Social History and the Historians," *History Workshop* 7 (Spring 1979), 66–94.

Karasch, Mary C. *Slave Life in Rio de Janeiro, 1808–1850.* Princeton University Press, 1987.

Katzman, David M. *Seven Days a Week: Women and Domestic Service in Industrializing America, 1870–1920.* New York: Oxford University Press, 1978.

Kidder, Daniel P. and James C. Fletcher. *Brazil and the Brazilians Portrayed in Historical and Descriptive Sketches.* 9th edn. rev. London: Sampson Low, Marston, Searle, and Rivington, 1879.

Kossoy, Boris. *Origens e expansão da fotografia no Brasil, século XIX.* Rio de Janeiro: Edição FUNARTE, 1980.

Koster, Henry. *Travels in Brazil.* Ed. and intro. C. Harvey Gardiner. First published 1817. Carbondale, Ill.: Southern Illinois University Press, 1966.

Kuznesof, Elizabeth. "Household composition and headship as related to changes in modes of production: São Paulo, 1765 to 1836." *Comparative Studies in Society and History* 22 (January 1980), 78–108.

Laemmert e Cia. *Planta da cidade do Rio de Janeiro e suburbios.* Rio de Janeiro: Laemmert [1889].

Lemos, Carlos A. C. *Cozinhas, etc. Um estudo sobre as zonas de serviço da casa paulista.* Debates, 94, São Paulo: Perspectiva, 1976.

Lemos, Miguel. *A liberdade de profissão e o regulamento para o serviço domestico.* Rio de Janeiro: Tip. Central, 1890.

Le Roy Ladurie, Emmanuel. *Montaillou: The Promised Land of Error.* Trans. Barbara Bray. New York: Braziller, 1978.

Linhares, Maria Yedda Leite. *História do abastecimento; uma problemática em questão (1530–1918).* Coleção Estudos sobre o Desenvolvimento Agrícola, vol. 5. Brasília: BINAGRI Edições, 1979.

Lobo, Eulália Maria Lahmeyer. *História do Rio de Janeiro: do capital comercial ao capital industrial e financeiro.* 2 vols. Rio de Janeiro: IBMEC, 1978.

Lombardi, John V. "Comparative Slave Systems in the Americas: A Critical Review." In *New Approaches to Latin American History.* Ed. Richard Graham and Peter H. Smith. Austin: University of Texas Press, 1974, pp. 156–174.

Luccock, John. *Notes on Rio de Janeiro and the Southern Parts of Brazil; Taken During A Residence of Ten Years in that Country, from 1808 to 1818.* London: Samuel Leigh, 1820.

Macedo, Roberto. *Barata Ribeiro, administração do primeiro prefeito do Distrito Federal.* Rio de Janeiro: Departamento Administrativo do Serviço Público, 1955.

Efemérides cariocas. Rio de Janeiro: Companhia Brasileira de Artes Gráficas, 1943.

A Mãe de Familia. Rio de Janeiro, 1879–1881.

"A mãe escrava." *A Mãe de Familia,* November 1879–May 1880, pp. 165–177.

Malcolmson, Patricia E. *English Laundresses: A Social History, 1850–1930.* Urbana and Chicago: University of Illinois Press, 1986.

Malcolmson, R. W. "Infanticide in the Eighteenth Century." In *Crime in England, 1550–1800.* Ed. J. S. Cockburn. Princeton University Press, 1977, pp. 187–209.

Malheiro, Agostinho Marques Perdigão. *A escravidão no Brasil: ensaio histórico-jurídico-social.* 3 parts in 1 vol. Rio de Janeiro: Typ. Nacional, 1866–1867.

Mara, Federico Lisboa de. *Histórico sobre o abastecimento de agua à Capital do Imperio desde 1861–1889.* Rio de Janeiro: Imprensa Nacional, 1889.

Marcílio, Maria Luiza. *A cidade de São Paulo: povoamento e população, 1750–1850.* Universidade de São Paulo, 1974.

"Maternidade." *O Commentario,* ser. III, no. 6 (October 1905), 101–107.

Mathias, Herculano Gomes. *História ilustrada do Rio de Janeiro.* Rio de Janeiro: Edições de Ouro, 1965.

Maza, Sarah C. *Servants and Masters in Eighteenth-Century France: The Uses of Loyalty.* Princeton University Press, 1983.

McBride, Theresa M. *The Domestic Revolution: The Modernization of Household Service in England and France, 1820–1920.* New York: Holmes & Meier, 1976.

Meade, Teresa. "'Civilizing Rio de Janeiro:' the public health campaign and riot of 1904." *Journal of Social History* 20 (Winter 1986), 301–322.

Mello, Pedro Carvalho de. "The economics of labor in Brazilian coffee plantations, 1850–1888." Ph.D. diss., University of Chicago, 1977.

Mendonça, Antônio Manuel de Melo Castro e. "Memória ecônomica-política da capitania de São Paulo . . . 1800." rpt. *Anais do Museu Paulista* 15 (1961), n.p.

Menezes, Adolpho Bezerra de. *O Governo e a Camara Municipal da Côrte. Artigos publicados na "Reforma."* Rio de Janeiro: Typ. da "Reforma," 1873.

Menezes, José Felix da Cunha. *Hygiene relativa ao saneamento da cidade do Rio de Janeiro.* Rio de Janeiro: Villeneuve, 1890.

Merrick, Thomas W. and Douglas H. Graham. *Population and Economic Development in Brazil, 1800 to the Present.* Baltimore: The Johns Hopkins University Press, 1979.

Metcalf, Alida. "The families of planters, peasants, and slaves: strategies for survival in Santana de Parnaíba, Brazil, 1720–1820." Ph.D. diss., University of Texas at Austin, 1983.

Moncorvo Filho, Arthur. *Da assistencia publica no Rio de Janeiro e paticularmente da assistencia á infancia.* . . . Rio de Janeiro: Imprensa Nacional, 1907.

"Exames de amas de leite do 'Dispensario Moncorvo.'" *Archivos de Assistencia á Infancia* 2, no. 10–12 (October–December 1903) 167–173.

Histórico da protecção á infancia no Brasil, 1500–1922. Rio de Janeiro: Paulo, Pongetti e Cia., 1926.

Hygiene publica. Da alimentação pelo leite, communicação apresentada á sociedade scientifica protectora da infancia em novembro de 1902. São Paulo: Espindola, Siqueira, 1903.

"A tuberculose e as collectividades infantis." *A Ordem Social,* no. 3 (1911), 67–70.

Moncorvo Filho, Arthur, et al. *Assistencia á infancia, hygiene infantil á mães pobres; conferencias realizadas no Dispensario Moncorvo, 1901–1907.* Rio de Janeiro: Imprensa Nacional, 1907.

Moraes, Eneida de. *História do carnaval carioca.* Rio de Janeiro. Civilização Brasileira, 1958.

Morais Filho, Alexandre José Melo. *Festas e tradições populares do Brasil.* 3rd edn. rev. Notes by Luis da Camara Cascudo. First published 1888. Rio de Janeiro: Briguiet, 1946.

Moreira, Nicolao Joaquim. "Duas palavras sobre a educação moral da mulher, . . ." *Annaes Brasilienses de Medicina* 20 (1868), 96–107.

Nabuco, Carolina. *The Life of Joaquim Nabuco.* Trans. and ed. Ronald Hilton. First published 1928. Stanford University Press, 1950.

Meu livro de cozinha. Rio de Janeiro: Editôra Nova Fronteira, 1977.

Nachman, Robert. "Positivism and revolution in Brazil's First Republic: the 1904 Revolt." *The Americas* 34 (July 1977), 30–39.

Newby, Howard. "The deferential dialectic." *Comparative Studies in Society and History*, 17 (April 1975), 139–164.

Nosso Século, 1900–1910, 1.

"Noticiário." *Archivos de Assistencia á Infancia* 2, no. 10–12 (October–December 1903), 191–195.

Nunes, J. P. Favilla. *Estatistica do Rio de Janeiro e serviços concernentes á salubridade publica da cidade do Rio de Janeiro*. Rio de Janeiro: Imprensa Nacional, 1885.

"A população do Municipio Neutro." *Revista da Sociedade de Geographia*, 1886, pp. 27–29.

Oakenfull, J. C. *Brazil in 1912*. London: Atkinson, 1913.

Oakes, James. *The Ruling Race: A History of American Slaveholders*. New York: Alfred A. Knopf, 1982.

Padilha, Francisco Fernandes. *Qual o regimen alimentar das classes pobres do Rio de Janeiro? Quaes as molestias que mais commummente grassão entre ellas? Que relações de causalidade se encontrão entre esse regimen e molestias?* Rio de Janeiro: Laemmert, 1853.

"Palestra do Medico." *A Mãe de Familia*, March 1881, pp. 33–34.

"Palestra do Medico sobre Amas de Leite." *A Mãe de Familia*, July 1879, p. 89.

Passos, Francisco Pereira. "Relatorio do Prefeito do Districto Federal ao Conselho Municipal, 1 setembro 1903." In *Annaes do Conselho Municipal e Synopse de seus Trabalhos*. Rio de Janeiro: Typ. do "Jornal do Commercio," 1904, 24–82.

Paz, Octavio. *The Labyrinth of Solitude*. Trans. Lysander Kemp. London: Allen Lane, 1967.

Peacock, James L. "Symbolic reversal and social history: transvestites and clowns of Java." In *The Reversible World: Symbolic Inversion in Art and Society*. Ed. and intro. Barbara A. Babcock. Ithaca: Cornell University Press, 1978, pp. 209–224.

Pfeiffer, Ida. *A Woman's Journey Round the World, from Vienna to Brazil, Chili, Tahiti, China, Hindostan, Persia, and Asia Minor*. 2nd edn. London: [Office of the National Illustrated Library, 1852].

Pimentel, Antonio Martins de Azevedo. *Quaes os melhoramentos hygienicos que devem ser introduzidos no Rio de Janeiro, para tornar esta cidade mais saudavel . . .* Rio de Janeiro: Moreira Maximino, 1884.

Subsidios para o estudo da hygiene do Rio de Janeiro. Rio de Janeiro: Gaspar da Silva, 1890.

Pires, José Jayme de Almeida. *Amas de leite*. Rio de Janeiro: Imprensa Nacional, 1909.

Nutrizas mercenarias especialmente no Brasil. Niteroi: Typ. Amerino, 1906.

Porto, M. J. de Campos. *Repertorio de legislação ecclesiastica desde 1500 até 1874*. Rio de Janeiro: Garnier, 1875.

Portugal, Antonio Nunes de Gouvêa. *Influencia da educação physica do homem . . .* Rio de Janeiro: Laemmert, 1853.

Portugal, Aureliano Gonçalves de Souza. *Primeiro annuario de estatistica demographo-sanitaria da cidade do Rio de Janeiro*. Rio de Janeiro: Imprensa Nacional, 1890.

O Quinze de Novembro do Sexo Feminino. Rio de Janeiro, 1892–1896.

Raeders, Georges, comp. and trans. *O conde de Gobineau no Brasil*. São Paulo: Secretaria da Cultura, Ciência e Tecnologia. Conselho Estadual de Cultura, 1976.

Ramos, Donald. "Marriage and the family in colonial Vila Rica." *Hispanic American Historical Review* 55 (May 1975), 200–225.

Rebello, Eugenio. "Da vida sedentaria e de seus inconvenientes anti-hygienicos." *Revista de Hygiene*, September 1886, 184–188.

Rego, José Pereira. *Apontamentos sobre a mortalidade da cidade do Rio de Janeiro particularmente das crianças e sobre o movimento de sua população no primeiro quatriennio depois do recenseamento feito em 1872.* Rio de Janeiro: Typ. Nacional, 1878.

———. *Esboço historico das epidemias que tem grassado na cidade do Rio de Janeiro desde 1830 a 1870.* Rio de Janeiro: Typ. Nacional, 1872.

———. *Memoria historica das epidemias da febre amarella e cholera-morbo que têm reinado no Brasil.* Rio de Janeiro: Typ. Nacional, 1873.

Reis, João José. "Slave rebellion in Brazil: the African Muslim uprising in Bahia, 1835." Ph.D. diss., University of Minnesota, 1983.

Revista dos Constructores, July 1886.

Revista Illustrada. Rio de Janeiro, 1876–1893.

Ribeiro, Leonidio, organizer. *Medicina no Brazil*. Rio de Janeiro: Imprensa Nacional, 1940.

The Rio News. Rio de Janeiro, 1879–1893.

Rios Filho, Adolfo Morales de los. *O Rio de Janeiro imperial*. Rio de Janeiro: Editôra "A Noite," 1946.

Roberts, David. *Paternalism in Early Victorian England*. New Brunswick, NJ: Rutgers University Press, 1979.

Rodrigues, J. Wasth. *Mobiliário do Brasil antigo (Evolução de cadeiras luso-brasileiras)*. São Paulo: Companhia Editôra Nacional, 1958.

Rosaldo, Renato I. "The rhetoric of control: Ilongots viewed as natural bandits and wild indians." In *The Reversible World: Symbolic Inversion in Art and Society*. Ed. and intro. Barbara A. Babcock. Ithaca: Cornell University Press, 1978, pp. 240–257.

Roza, Francisco Luíz da Gama. *Hygiene do Casamento*. Rio de Janeiro: Leuzinger, 1876.

Rugendas, Maurice. *Voyage pittoresque dans le Brésil*. Trans. M. de Golbery. Paris: Englemann, 1835.

Russell-Wood, A. J. R. *Fidalgos and Philanthropists, The Santa Casa da Misericórdia of Bahia, 1550–1755.* Berkeley: University of Calfornia Press, 1968.

Sampaio, Geraldo F. "Saneamento das cidades brasileiras." In *Medicina no Brasil*. Organized by Leonidio Ribeiro. Rio de Janeiro: Imprensa Nacional, 1940, pp. 190–208.

Sant'Anna, Edna Mascarenhas. "Annexo 1: As transformações ocorridas no trecho ocupado atualmente pela área central." In *A área central da cidade do Rio de Janeiro*. Brazil, Instituto Brasileiro de Geografia e Estatística, Conselho Nacional de Geografia. Rio de Janeiro: Instituto Brasileiro de Geografia e Estatística, 1967, pp. 45–47.

Santos, Francisco Agenor de Noronha. *Chorographia do Districto Federal (cidade do Rio de Janeiro)*. 3rd edn. Rio de Janeiro: Benjamin de Aguila, 1913.

———. *Meios de transporte no Rio de Janeiro. História e legislação.* 2 vols. in 1. Rio de Janeiro: Typ. do "Jornal do Commercio," Rodrigues & Cia., 1934.

Santos, Luiz Gonçalves dos (Padre Perereca). *Memórias para servir à história do reino do Brasil.* 2 vols. Reconquista do Brasil, n.s., no. 36 and 37. First published 1825. Belo Horizonte and São Paulo: Itatiaia and University of São Paulo, 1981.

Schwartz, Stuart B. *Sugar Plantations in the Formation of Brazilian Society*. Cambridge Latin American Series, 52. Cambridge University Press, 1985.

Searle, Eleanor. "Seigneurial control of women's marriage: the antecedents and function of merchet in England." *Past and Present*, no. 82 (February 1979), 3–43.

"Serviço domestico." *O Commentario*, ser. III, no. 10 (February 1906), 148–151.

O Sexo Feminino, 9 June 1889.

Shorter, Edward. *The Making of the Modern Family*. New York: Basic Books, 1975.

Silva, Fernando Nascimento. "Dados de geografia carioca." In *Rio de Janeiro em seus quatrocentos anos: formação e desenvolvimento da cidade*. Ed. Fernando Nascimento Silva. Rio de Janeiro: Distribuidora Record, 1965, pp. 29–38.

Silva, Joaquim Norberto Souza e. *Investigações sobre os recenseamentos da população geral do Imperio e de cada provincia de per si tentados desde os tempos coloniais até hoje feitas em virtude do aviso de 15 de março de 1870*. . . . Rio de Janeiro: Typ. Perseverança, 1870.

Silva, L. A. "A remoção do lixo." *Revista de Hygiene*, June 1886, 49–52.

Silva, Peçanha da. "Memoria ou observações . . . sobre a amamentação e as amas de leite," *Annaes Brasilienses de Medicina* 21 (1869), 253–256.

Silva, Rosauro Mariano da. "A luta pela água." In *Rio de Janeiro em seus quatrocentos anos: formação e desenvolvimento da cidade*. Ed. Fernando Nascimento Silva. Rio de Janeiro: Distribuidora Record, 1965, pp. 311–337.

Smith, Herbert H. *Brazil: The Amazon and the Coast*. New York: Scribner's, 1879.

Soares, Ubaldo. *O passado heróico da Casa dos Expostos*. Rio de Janeiro: Fundação Romão de Matos Duarte, 1959.

Um século no roteiro da caridade: o hospital da Misericórdia, 1852–1952. Subsídios históricos. Rio de Janeiro: "Jornal do Commercio," 1952.

Sociedade de Higiene do Brasil. *Relatorio apresentado na sessão anniversaria de 23 de junho 1893 pelo secretario geral interino Dr. Carlos Augusto de Brito e Silva*. Rio de Janeiro: Barreiros, 1893.

Souza, Francisco Belisário Soares de. *O sistema eleitoral no Império*. 2nd edn. Coleção Bernardo Pereira de Vasconcelos, Série Estudos Jurídicos, 18. First published 1872. Brasília: Senado Federal, 1979.

Souza Junior, José Modesto de. *Do regimen alimentar dos recem-nascidos* . . . Rio de Janeiro: Imprensa Gutenberg, 1895.

Stein, Stanley J. *The Brazilian Cotton Manufacture: Textile Enterprise in an Underdeveloped Area, 1850–1950*. Cambridge: Harvard University Press, 1957.

Vassouras: A Brazilian Coffee County, 1850–1900. Cambridge: Harvard University Press, 1957.

Stepan, Nancy. *Beginnings of Brazilian Science: Oswaldo Cruz, Medical Research and Policy, 1890–1920*. New York: Science History Publications, 1981.

Stone, Lawrence. *The Family, Sex and Marriage in England, 1500–1800*. London: Weidenfeld and Nicolson, 1977.

Sussman, George D. "The wet-nursing business in nineteenth-century France." *French Historical Studies* 9 (1975), 304–328.

Selling Mother's Milk: The Wet-Nursing Business in France, 1715–1914. Urbana: University of Illinois, 1982.

Sutherland, Daniel E. *Americans and Their Servants: Domestic Service in the United States from 1800 to 1920*. Baton Rouge and London: Louisiana State University Press, 1981.

Tapajós, Torquato Xavier Monteiro. . . . *Estudos de hygiene; a cidade do Rio de Janeiro; primeira parte: terras, aguas e ares; idéias finaes*. Rio de Janeiro: Imprensa Nacional, 1895.

Thompson, E. P. "Patrician Society, Plebeian Culture." *Journal of Social History* 7 (Summer 1974), 382–405.

Tollenare, Louis François de. *Notas dominicaes. Tomadas durante uma residencia em Portugal e no Brasil nos annos de 1816, 1817, e 1818.* . . . Recife: "Jornal do Recife," 1905.

Toussaint-Samson, Adele. *Une Parisienne au Brésil avec photographies originales.* Paris: Paul Ollendorff, 1883.

Trovão, José Lopes da Silva. *Discurso proferido na sessão do Senado Federal de 11 de setembro de 1895 sobre o trabalho das crianças.* Rio de Janeiro: Imprensa Nacional, 1896.

Turner, Victor. *The Forest of Symbols: Aspects of Ndembu Ritual.* Ithaca: Cornell University Press, 1967.

Val, Waldir Ribeiro do. *Geografia de Machado de Assis.* Rio de Janeiro: São José, 1977.

Vasconcellos, Carlos. "Amas de leite." *Revista de Hygiene* 1, no. 2 (June 1886), 59–63.

Vasconcellos, José Marcellino Pereira de. *Regimento dos Inspectores de Quarteirão ou Collecção dos actos e attribuições que competem a esta classe de funcionarios.* Rio de Janeiro: Typ. e Libraria de Bernardo Xavier Pinto de Souza, 1862.

Vasquez, Pedro. *Dom Pedro II e a fotografia no Brasil.* Rio de Janeiro: Fundação Roberto Marinho and Companhia Internacional de Seguros, [1986].

Vide, Sebastião Monteiro da. *Constituições primeiras do Arcebispado da Bahia. Feitas e ordenadas pelo . . . Sebastião Monteiro da Vide, 5º Arcebispo do dito Arcebispado e do Conselho de Sua Magestade: Propostas e aceitas em o synodo Diocesano que o dito Senhor celebrou em 12 de junho do anno de 1707. Impressas em Lisboa no anno 1719 e em Coimbra em 1720.* . . . São Paulo: Typ. "2 de Dezembro," 1853.

von Binzer, Ina (pseud. Ulla Von Eck?). *Alegrias e tristezas de uma educadora alemã no Brasil.* Trans. Alice Rossi and Luisita de Gama Cerqueira. São Paulo: Anhembí, 1956.

Walsh, Robert. *Notices of Brazil in 1828 and 1829.* 2 vols. London: Frederick Westley and A. H. Davis, 1830.

Werneck, Francisco Peixoto de Lacerda. *Memoria sobre a fundação de uma fazenda na provincia do Rio de Janeiro, sua administração, e épochas em que devem fazer as plantações, suas colheitas, etc., etc.* Rio de Janeiro: Laemmert, 1847.

Wheless, Joseph, trans. *The Civil Code of Brazil [1916].* St. Louis: Thomas Law Book Co., 1920.

Index